Some of These Days

Some of These Days

BLACK STARS, JAZZ AESTHETICS, AND MODERNIST CULTURE

James Donald

OXFORD
UNIVERSITY PRESS

OXFORD

UNIVERSITY PRESS

Oxford University Press is a department of the University of
Oxford. It furthers the University's objective of excellence in research,
scholarship, and education by publishing worldwide.

Oxford   New York

Auckland   Cape Town   Dar es Salaam   Hong Kong   Karachi
Kuala Lumpur   Madrid   Melbourne   Mexico City   Nairobi
New Delhi   Shanghai   Taipei   Toronto

With offices in

Argentina   Austria   Brazil   Chile   Czech Republic   France   Greece
Guatemala   Hungary   Italy   Japan   Poland   Portugal   Singapore
South Korea   Switzerland   Thailand   Turkey   Ukraine   Vietnam

Published in the United States of America by
Oxford University Press
198 Madison Avenue, New York, NY 10016

Library of Congress Cataloging-in-Publication Data
Donald, James, 1948–
Some of these days : black stars, jazz aesthetics, and modernist culture / James Donald.
pages cm
Includes bibliographical references and index.
ISBN 978-0-19-935401-6 (cloth)—ISBN 978-0-19-935402-3 (updf)—
ISBN 978-0-19-935403-0 (epub)
1. African Americans in the performing arts.   2. African Americans—Intellectual life—
20th century.   3. American literature—African American authors—History and criticism.   4. Harlem
Renaissance—Influence.   5. African Americans—Music—Influence.   6. African American theater—
History—20th century.   7. Modernism (Aesthetics)—United States—Influence.   I. Title.
PN1590.B53D66 2015
791.089'96073—dc23
2014038062

1 3 5 7 9 8 6 4 2
Printed in the United States of America
on acid-free paper

For Stephi, with love

{ CONTENTS }

Buddy Gilmore, Paris, 1926–1927 (Berenice Abbott)

Buddy Gilmore, who had worked with James Reese Europe's Society Orchestra in New York, arrived in Europe with Will Marion Cook's Southern Syncopated Orchestra in 1919 and stayed on in Paris. Berenice Abbott, who would go on to be one of the great photographers of New York, was working as an assistant to Man Ray when she took Gilmore's photograph.

Introduction

A MIGRATION OF STARS

Looking back in her memoirs, Simone de Beauvoir recalls her student days at the École Normale Supérieure in 1929, when she had recently met Jean-Paul Sartre and they were in the early days of their mutual seduction. After a day's work, they would relax by listening to jazz records. "Jazz" turns out to mean a haphazard selection of popular music: Sophie Tucker, Layton and Johnstone, Jack Hylton, the Revelers, and "Negro Spirituals." They "liked everything," pretty much indiscriminately. Their favorites included "Old Man River," "St. James Infirmary Blues," "Some of These Days," "The Man I Love," "Miss Hannah," "St. Louis Blues," "Japansy," and "Blue Skies." They did not just listen to these songs on the gramophone. Sartre sang. "Sartre had a fine voice and an extensive repertoire," reveals Beauvoir, "including *Old Man River* and all the current jazz hits."

It is an arresting image: cocky little Jean-Paul Sartre serenading Simone de Beauvoir by mimicking Paul Robeson's rendition of Jerome Kern and Oscar Hammerstein's Broadway pastiche of a Negro spiritual. There was more to this performance, however, than an eccentric piece of masculine display. At the time, the embrace of popular American culture was part of a style for living assertively in the present. Beauvoir explains how "America" had entered her life and Sartre's through the "distorting lenses" of "jazz and Hollywood films." Sartre's childhood America had been "a country of dreams," learned from dime-novel and comic-book heroes, which they now recaptured through silent Westerns, gangster talkies, the glamorous faces of stars like Greta Garbo, Marlene Dietrich, Joan Crawford, and Kay Francis, and the performances of "that luscious creature" Mae West. Historical change was thus experienced through the mediated sounds and images of a dreamworld "America," which seemed to promise an existential freedom and a subjective authenticity lacking from European culture. When these pleasures also entailed a small declaration of Oedipal independence from established

European values and conventional European narratives, "America" would often be coded black. Listening to what they took to be Negro spirituals, work songs, and blues, Beauvoir and Sartre were moved by "a voice" that "broke harshly from the very heart of darkness and rebellion" and "challenged the polite assumptions of conventional art." The songs "dwelt in our hearts, nourishing us just as certain words and cadences of our own tongue did." Through the "characteristic voice" of the "Negro," "America came to exist within us."

To pre-empt the accusation that this enthusiasm for their inner "America" was indulgent "political aestheticism," an idiosyncratic matter of taste rather than considered political commitment, Beauvoir and Sartre were careful to step back from the "miscellaneous clutter" of American culture and to condemn the political reality of the United States—a country where "capitalist oppression flourished in its most odious form" and whose racial policies allowed lynching to persist unpunished. But still the enchantment of America nagged. They sensed "something about life over there, something vast and unencumbered, which fascinated us at a deeper level, beyond all question of right or wrong." By contrast, the culture of the Soviet Union, "the scene of a social experiment which we wholeheartedly admired," failed to excite them: it "left us quite cold." The insouciance with which Beauvoir was able to quarantine their political affiliation from their cultural preferences disavowed the significance of the relationship between feeling and judgment. The conceptual geography of France, America, and the Soviet Union charted the affective infrastructure of their philosophy, as well as their politics, revealing *how they thought* and, just as importantly, *how they felt*, about such questions as freedom, being, and modernity.

In retrospect, then, Sartre's appropriation of Paul Robeson's voice can be understood as part of a pattern of cross-racial identification and "rebellion through racial ventriloquism" that was also characteristic of an emergent avant-garde literary modernism in the United States in the early decades of the twentieth century. As a writer, too, Sartre ventriloquized. In the late 1920s and early '30s, he consciously set about shedding his French stylistic inheritance—the "marmoreal phrases" of André Gide and Paul Valéry—and schooled himself in the elliptical objectivity and intensity of Ernest Hemingway's writing in his early novel *The Sun Also Rises* (1926) and in short stories like "Fifty Grand" (1927). From the start, the black American voice had a special significance in Sartre's fiction. At the end of his first novel, *La Nausée* (1938), the hero, like his creator, finds a voice that will enable him to write a new kind of book: "I don't quite know which kind—but you would have to guess, behind the printed words, behind the pages, at something which would not exist, which would be above existence." What he does know is that it will have to be "beautiful and hard as steel" and that it will "make people ashamed of their existence." This inspiration comes as he sits in a bistro, and the patronne plays a scratchy record of "Some of These Days," in which he hears, if not existence as such, then at least "sounds, vibrations in the air which unveil it." The would-be novelist daydreams about the song's creation, and about the man who wrote it:

> a clean-shaven American with thick black eyebrows, suffocating with the heat, on the twenty-first floor of a New York skyscraper. . . . He is sitting, in shirtsleeves, in front of his piano; he has a taste of smoke in his mouth, and, vaguely, a ghost of a tune in his head . . . the tune must be written down. . . . The moist hand seizes the pencil on the piano. "Some of these days, you'll miss me honey." . . . That is how it was born. It is the worn-out body of this Jew with black eyebrows which it chose to create it.

At this time, Sartre still believed in the redemptive power of art. One last time, his protagonist asks to hear "the Negress sing." "She sings. So two of them are saved: the Jew and the Negress. Saved."

A jazz historian might fret that Sartre got this all wrong. "Some of These Days" was written, not by a New York Jew, but by a black Canadian, Shelton Brooks, who migrated to Detroit. He wrote the song in the first decade of the century, and it would normally be considered more ragtime than jazz. Brooks sold "Some of These Days" to the Jewish-Ukrainian-American singer Sophie Tucker, in 1909. She recorded it in 1911 and made it her signature tune. Early in her career, in the 1890s, Tucker had performed in blackface, and she was still known as a "coon shouter." But a "Negress" she was not. From the perspective of what jazz meant for its European audiences, however, Sartre's getting the Jew and the Negro the wrong way round is beside the point. More important is how he invested meaning into what he heard and the way that, like Al Jolson's Jew blacking up in *The Jazz Singer* in order to find an American voice, his creative act was the product of mishearing and ventriloquism. Both exemplify the type of fusions, translations, and conjoinings through which newness enters the world. The creation of newness has less to do with the discovery of authenticity, it turns out, than with a generative inauthenticity, manifest in "hybridity, impurity, intermingling, the transformation that comes of new and unexpected combinations of human beings, cultures, ideas, politics, movies, songs."

Josephine Baker

In 1920s France, and in most of Europe, the iconic "Negress" who provoked more column inches about salvation, rejuvenation, regression, primitivism, and any number of other eugenic fantasies was Josephine Baker. ("The white imagination sure is something when it comes to blacks," she would later observe, world-wearily.) Born in 1906, Baker became a star when *La Revue nègre* opened in Paris in October 1925. She had grown up, deserted by her

Josephine Baker in her trademark banana skirt, Paris 1926 (Stanislaus Walery)

father and unloved by her mother, in the impoverished black neighborhood of East St. Louis, Illinois. In 1917, a white mob burned the place down in a vicious race riot and murdered many of its inhabitants. Whether she actually witnessed the events, as she would later claim, is unclear, but she certainly heard the stories. By the time she arrived in Paris, still only nineteen, Josephine had been through two husbands; she took the name "Baker" from the second, a Pullman porter. She had been farmed out as a domestic servant to wealthy white families in her childhood, earned small change by busking and dancing while living on the streets, and made it into the chorus line of the Dixie Steppers, a music and dance troupe touring the southern states. In 1921, she traveled to New York, determined to get herself hired for Noble Sissle and Eubie Blake's *Shuffle Along*, the all-black Broadway musical that made Florence Mills a star and is often credited with starting Manhattan's "vogue for Harlem." Initially rejected because she was too young, Baker became a dresser and learned the choreography. When she turned sixteen, she was given a slot in the chorus line, first in a touring company and then on Broadway, where she used her talent for comic mugging to attract notice to herself. In *The Chocolate Dandies*, their 1924 follow-up to *Shuffle Along*,

Sissle and Blake billed Josephine Baker as "the highest paid chorus girl in the world," and gave her the opportunity to appear in a glamorous scene, in addition to her usual clowning. She danced at the Plantation Club on Broadway and Fiftieth Street in Manhattan, and was again a chorus girl in *Dinah*, as well as understudy to its star, Ethel Waters. It was Waters whom Caroline Dudley, the producer of *La Revue nègre*, was hoping to hire, when she came across Josephine Baker at the Plantation.

At the turn of 1925 and 1926, the Franco-German cultural commentator Ivan Goll alerted Berliners to what they should expect when Josephine Baker arrived in their city, after her triumph in France. "The Negroes are conquering Paris," he warned. "They are conquering Berlin. They have already filled the whole continent with their howls, with their laughter. . . . All of Europe is dancing to their banjo." Although some people might be alarmed that this was "the rhythm of Sodom and Gomorrah," Goll asked why it might not equally be music "from paradise." That utopian potential explained why *La Revue nègre* was "rousing the tired public in the Théâtre des Champs-Elysées" and why "the old world calls on its failing strength to applaud them." By exposing the excessive intellectualism and spiritual lassitude of European culture, the physicality of the revue presented a "challenge to moral Europe." "Negroes dance with their senses. (White Europeans can only dance with their minds.) They dance with their legs, breasts, and bellies."

Such vitalist primitivism had become a critical commonplace in France over the first three decades of the century. To begin with, *l'art nègre* had been a coterie affair. Picasso painted *Les Demoiselles d'Avignon* in 1907, inspired by a disconcerting encounter with African sculpture in the ethnographic museum at the Palais du Trocadéro, and, a year or two before the war, Paul Guillaume opened the first gallery devoted to "Negro art," which, he believed, would act as "the fructifying seed of the spiritual twentieth century." In 1919, Guillaume staged a *Fête nègre* at the Théâtre des Champs-Élysées, featuring poetry based on legends collected in Blaise Cendrars's *Anthologie nègre* and music by Arthur Honegger, played on African instruments. Although still controversial, the postwar vogue for *l'art nègre* reemerged as a broader, more commercialized phenomenon, featuring exhibitions of objects and artworks from Alaska and Oceania, as well sub-Saharan Africa, and a range of "indigenous" literature, defined broadly enough to incorporate writing from the Harlem Renaissance and new works like the Guyanese poet René Maran's Prix Goncourt–winning 1921 novel, *Batouala*.

Jazz became part of this mélange toward the end of the war, with the arrival of "the best damn brass band in the United States Army," the band of the 15th New York Infantry Regiment, the "Harlem Hellfighters," led by James Reese Europe and featuring the dancer Bill "Bojangles" Robinson and Noble Sissle as its drum major. Afterwards, a number of black American musicians, like Louis Mitchell and Eugene Bullard, were hired by Paris music halls and cabarets, not least to keep American tourists happy. This was the moment when Jean Cocteau claimed the energy of jazz for a modernist avant-garde. At the end of 1917, just a few months after his collaboration with Picasso, Apollinaire, Diaghilev, and Ansermet on Erik Satie's ballet *Parade*, Cocteau saw the veteran (white) American dancer Harry Pilcer perform at the Casino de Paris with the French star Gaby Deslys, back in France after several successful years in the United States. To the American band's "hurricane of rhythm," the couple "danced a kind of tamed catastrophe that left them totally intoxicated and myopic." Against the backdrop of postwar exhaustion, Cocteau discerned in this frenetic vivacity the dynamism that might drive an alternative, more sensual and life-affirming modernity, even if he still used the imagery of mechanized war to describe it: "The audience gave them a standing ovation, dragged from its lethargy by this extraordinary number which is, when compared to Offenbach's extravaganzas, what a tank is to an 1870 carriage."

In his autobiography, *Manhood*, published in 1939, in the shadow of the imminent Second World War, the surrealist ethnographer Michel Leiris looked back to the period immediately after the previous war, and recalled how that exhilaration, and that aggressive newness, had attracted him and his friends to jazz. Jazz served as "a sign of allegiance, an orgiastic tribute to the colours of the moment." Through the lens of Durkheimian anthropology and the surrealism of the Collège de Sociologie, Leiris retrospectively interpreted jazz, along with "communion by dance, latent or manifest exoticism, and drinks," as a kind of magic for attaining a "sacred" possession in disenchanted modernity. The music and its ethos captured his generation's spiritual crisis and their craving for change: "a more or less conscious demoralisation born of the war, a naïve fascination with the comfort and the latest inventions of progress, a predilection for a contemporary setting whose insanity we nonetheless vaguely anticipated, an abandonment to the animal joy of experiencing the influence of a modern rhythm, an underlying aspiration to a new life in which more room would be made for the impassioned frankness we inarticulately longed for."

In 1922, the composer Darius Milhaud traveled from Paris to Harlem to hear what real jazz and blues sounded like. Seeking existential rather than musical authenticity, Leiris went in a different direction. The first encounter, through jazz, with "*Negroes*, the manifestation and the myth of black Edens," led him "to Africa and, beyond Africa, to ethnography." Inspired by his encounter with the music, he eventually became a professional anthropologist. In 1931, he served as secretary-archivist to the Dakar-Djibouti Mission, a foundational event for the discipline of anthropology in France, which led to the publication of his partly autobiographical and partly ethnographic *L'Afrique fantôme*. On his return to France, in 1933, he helped Paul Rivet to plan the *Musée de l'homme*, the ethnographic museum launched to coincide with the *Exposition Internationale des Arts et Techniques dans la Vie Moderne* in 1937.

Leiris, Milhaud, and Ivan Goll were all operating, in one way or another, with a schematic cultural geography that triangulated Europe with America and with Africa. Jazz was heard and felt as not European, even when it was made by Europeans, but rather as American (that is, as modern) and, at the same time, however speciously, because of the blackness of some of its performers, as African (as the promise of a redeemed authenticity). "This was a dance of the Egyptians, the whole of antiquity, the Orient," commented Goll, in his description of *La Revue nègre*. "One can only envy them, for this is life, sun, primeval forests, the singing of birds and the roar of a leopard, earth." Knowing his Berlin audience as well as his Paris nightlife, Goll realized that Josephine Baker would be taken up as part of the city's craze for *Amerika* and for the mass culture of movies, jazz, and sport. In the aftermath of defeat, and despite inflation and privation, Berlin aspired to be Europe's most American capital—that is, its most modern and most dynamic city. As things looked up economically, in 1925, a black American revue had been running successfully at Herman Haller's Theater am Admiralspalast, even before the arrival of *La Revue nègre: Chocolate Kiddies* featured Sam Wooding's orchestra from New York's Club Alabam, and introduced a number of songs written by the little-known young Duke Ellington. Although the composer Hans Pfitzner might regard the "jazz-fox trot flood" as "the American tanks in the spiritual assault against European culture," for radical young writers and intellectuals, jazz promised a sensual and experimental way of living in the present, as well as creating the future. "What remains of the creative force of this sterile time," wrote Alice Gerstel, a feminist psychologist, in 1922, is to be found in jazz: "the genius of the eclectic, the cocktail mix of souls, the recklessness of puppets on a string, the passion of people condemned to death."

After the primitivist clichés, Goll plays his sophisticated Berliner card, showing that he sees through the arbitrariness of the racial categories when he exposes the modern American reality behind *La Revue nègre*'s primitivist African paraphernalia. The show confronts its audience with "the strange impression of a snarling parody," as it turns out to be all about self-ironizing mockery, nothing about authenticity. "These Negroes come out of the darkest parts of New York." And yet, despite their knowing and collusive artifice, the performers do embody something creative and new: the possibility of making good the loss of primordial authenticity (Africa) through its recreation in modernity (America). That is why, even though they do not come from "the primeval forests," Josephine Baker and her fellow performers represent "a new, unspoiled race."

In the end, Goll has it both ways. He registers the reckless semiotic mixing-and-matching in *La Revue nègre*, but he still uses images of an anemic Europe and rejuvenating black blood to describe the promise of renewal.

These Negroes, he concludes, "dance with their blood, their life. . . . Its drops are slowly falling over Europe, a long-since dried-up land that can scarcely breathe. . . . The Negro question is pressing for our entire civilization. It runs like this: Do the Negroes need us? Or are we not sooner in need of them?" Although, later in life, Michel Leiris disavowed the "foolishness" of attempts "to be different by plunging—even though symbolically—into a 'primitive mentality,'" in 1929 he still shared Ivan Goll's cultural eugenics. Disdaining "tasteful" European entertainment that was devoid of "potential or actual revolt against sacred 'politeness,'" he turned instead to "Negro" art, including jazz. This appeared to have the power to break through the veneer of "politeness" and to enable moderns like him to "get closer to our primitive ancestry." For Leiris, black "blood" promised less the renewal of European culture, than personal salvation: "this music and this dancing don't stop at our skin but put down deep organic roots in us, roots whose thousand ramifications penetrate us; and though this surgery is painful, it gives us stronger blood."

Modernity

Modernity can be a curiously bloodless concept. In much social theory, it looms as a landscape of monumental yet insubstantial abstractions: *capitalist relations of production, rationalized industrialism, complex scientific and technological infrastructures, bureaucratized administration, urbanization, the public sphere, Western rationality, representative democracy*, and *secularization*. "Modernity," in this tradition, operates as a term for conceptualizing a unique, temporally bounded social formation. The grand theorizings are deployed to identify what is distinctive about the modern era, to explain the interaction between its constituent systems, and to chart the ceaseless realignment of its fields of force. Another way of telling the story of modernity, which fleshes out such models and works them through to the level of an individual experience of modernization, may be derived from the style of modernist sociology initiated by Georg Simmel. As well as the *what?*, the *when?*, and the *why?* of modernity, Simmel was interested in the subjective, *so what?* If modernity described an existing state of affairs, what was distinctive (asked Simmel) about the way that human beings experienced that state of affairs? How did they act, think, and feel differently from people who had lived under premodern social arrangements? In short, what was it like to live in what Gertrude Stein called "the complete actual present" of the modern world?

Simmel's premise, announced at the beginning of his lecture on "The Metropolis and Mental Life," published in 1903, was that "the deepest problems of modern life" are the consequence of individual's attempt to preserve the autonomy and individuality of his existence in the face of overwhelming social forces, of historical heritage, of external culture and of the technique of life."

Historical forces had "crystallized" into institutions, technologies, and bureau-
cracies, particularly in the great European cities, and they were threatening to
overwhelm the individual: "The individual has become a mere cog in an enormous organization of things and powers which tear from his hands all progress, spirituality, and value in order to transform them from their subjective
form into the form of a purely objective life." As a result, there was an "inten-
sification of emotional life." In Berlin, Paris, London, and Vienna, people were
learning to negotiate "the rapid crowding of changing images, the sharp discontinuity in the grasp of a single glance, and the unexpectedness of onrushing
impressions." "Here in buildings and educational institutions, in the wonders
and comforts of space-conquering technology, in the formations of community
life, and in the visible institutions of the state, is offered such an overwhelming
fullness of crystallized and impersonal spirit that the personality, so to speak,
cannot maintain itself under its impact." The result was a new, two-sided configuration of "personality." The blasé self was intellectualistic, calculating, and
precise, with its capacity for feeling numbed as a defense against the demands
of interacting with so many strangers and processing such frequent and intense
external stimuli. The other new dimension was creative, in the sense that the
anonymity, semiotic density, and inventiveness of the modern city opened up
previously unthinkable possibilities for fashioning a "self."

Simmel went so far as to claim that the unprecedented metropolitan "tempo
and multiplicity of economic, occupational and social life" had brought about
a realignment of "the sensory foundations of psychic life." This concern with
the preconscious and precultural frames of reference and constraint, through
which people adapt to the contingent rhythms of a modernizing world, was
developed, a generation after Simmel, by Siegfried Kracauer and Walter
Benjamin. For them, *the aesthetic* was a question of how human sense perception is organized and transformed in specific historical circumstances.
They were particularly concerned with the way that, in modernity, perva-
sive "space-conquering" technologies of communication and representation,
such as the gramophone, telephone, radio, and cinema, were disrupting and
realigning established coordinates of presence and absence, internality and
externality, familiarity and strangeness, and even space and time. At the very
least, these new communication and media technologies required, and delivered, a complex retraining of what Benjamin called "the human sensorium."
In a stronger claim, the technologies could be seen as claiming sovereignty
over and against the sensorium.

Speaking by telephone to someone miles or even continents away, for example, could produce a disconcerting experience of temporal immediacy and
spatial absence. In Marcel Proust's *The Guermantes Way*, the narrator comes
away from his first telephone conversation with his beloved grandmother
feeling that her disembodied voice is the voice of "a phantom as impalpable as
the one that would perhaps come back to visit me when my grandmother was

dead." In cinema, Benjamin saw a medium that could augment both aspects of Simmel's metropolitan personality. Defensively, it was the function of film "to train human beings in apperceptions and reactions needed to deal with a vast apparatus whose role in their lives is expanding almost daily." Creatively, however, film had "exploded" the "prison-house" of everyday modern urban life "with the dynamite of the split second, so that now we can set off calmly on journeys of adventure among its far-flung debris." Radio broadcasts across Europe—proliferating from the BBC's first transmission in 1922 to nearly 700 stations by 1927—likewise intensified the capacity for virtual mobility. They offered an imaginary cosmopolitanism, at the same time as setting in place constraining forms of domesticity and privacy. "Then a new serpent moved into his home. It hissed sweetly. It was the radio," wrote Ilya Ehrenburg in his satirical novel *The Life of the Automobile* (1929), imagining an addict to technologies of the new. At night, this early listener would no longer be found sitting at his fireplace: "no, he was whizzing through the world. His lips moved suspiciously. He was looking for waves. Here was Barcelona. . . . Here was Karlsruhe. . . . The German word 'bitte.' Bach. Spaniards. A charleston. The winner of the race at Oxford. The Royal Dutch rates. An Italian lesson: forte, morte, cannelloni. The victory of the Conservatives in Sweden. The bells of the Kremlin: The *Internationale*. Another charleston. The world moohed, bleated, meowed."

Whereas Simmel had observed how the "inner life" of the turn-of-the-century metropolis "overflows by waves" to incorporate, subjectively, "a far-flung national or international area," by the 1920s, radio and telephone were bringing external, cosmopolitan culture into the domestic sphere. In doing so, they transformed "the home" from a domestic shelter, a private and intimate space, into a node in networks of information and communication. Although this capacity for instant communication across cities and nations promised new styles of association and community, even a new universality, hearing the world "at home" often turned out, in practice, to exacerbate the experience of atomization and to instill an insidious sense of placelessness or homelessness. Virtual presence and the illusion of mobility, some feared, were achieved at the expense of a real, if narrower, closeness to things and people.

This was the strange new modernity that twentieth-century Europeans inhabited, a world in which technology simultaneously enhanced sense perception and absorbed individuals into the technology, hooking them inescapably into communication and media networks. It was populated by the ghostly presence of absent voices and animated simulacra of absent figures. It was filtered to individuals through a technologized and aestheticized public sphere. Novelists attempted to convey the visceral experience of this world. For John Cournos, in *Babel* (1922), London had "the unity of ultra-modern music, shaped out of discords, beaten but not molten into a harmony." In

The Man without Qualities (1921), Robert Musil also used imagery of dissonance and syncopation: modern Vienna was made up of "one great rhythmic beat as well as the chronic discord and mutual displacement of its contending rhythms." When the philosopher Martin Heidegger defined modernity as "The Age of the World Picture," he did not mean that people had a clear picture of the world, but rather that, for the first time, they experienced the world as spectacle, from an aesthetic distance: "the human has become the *subjectum* and the world has become a picture." These various descriptions help to explain why, in Paris, it seemed natural for Simone de Beauvoir and Jean-Paul Sartre to experience modernity as "America," as an overwhelming montage superimposed on a jazz soundtrack: "Negroes in *Hallelujah* dancing or entranced, skyscrapers towering up to heaven, prison mutinies, blast furnaces, strikes, long silk-sheathed legs, locomotives, aeroplanes, wild horses, and rodeos."

One response to modernity's inherent strangeness was to turn to apparently more grounded concepts, like "reality" or "authenticity" or "spirit," and to evoke, through them, some less alienated form of society, whether aristocratic Europe or tribal Africa. Kracauer and Benjamin saw such moves as sentimental or disingenuous. It was only *within* this strangeness, which Heidegger apprehended as "the continual never having-been-here-before," and within modernity's ontology of irony, alienation, and the uncanny, that any hope of emancipation lay. Kracauer identified the aesthetic challenge inherent in this principle, in a throwaway line in a review of an adventure movie for the

Simon de Beauvoir and Jean-Paul Sartre, the fairground
at Porte d'Orléans, Paris, June 1929

Frankfurter Zeitung, in 1923. "Genuine film drama," he remarked, "has the task of rendering ironic the phantomlike quality of our life by exaggerating its unreality and thus to point toward true reality." It was because emancipation had to work through the disorientation of modern experience, rather than work around it, that he and Benjamin were interested in the concept of *distraction*. In "The Cult of Distraction," in 1926, for example, Kracauer contends that "[i]t is not externality that poses a threat to truth." Rather, truth comes under threat "only by the naïve affirmation of cultural values that have become unreal and by the careless misuse of concepts such as personality, inwardness, tragedy, and so on." Such "lofty ideas" have lost any purchase they once had on the world, thanks to modernization. That is why "Berlin audiences act truthfully" when they shun art events that "remain caught in mere pretence," and opt instead for distraction, for "the surface glamour of the stars, films, revues, and spectacular shows." In "The Little Shopgirls Go to the Movies," a year later, he pleads that "stupid and unreal film fantasies" at least have the virtue of rendering "the *daydreams of society*, in which its actual reality comes to the fore and its otherwise repressed wishes take on form." As an historian of the present, Kracauer saw it as his task to register the "*provisional status* of all given configurations," and to highlight their transitory and transitional character.

In the 1920s and '30s, Simmel's external culture was crystallized for the citizens of Paris, Berlin, Vienna, and London in proliferating, ever-new,

Paul Robeson, Harlem 1925 (E. O. Hoppé)

ever-the-same manifestations of mass-produced, mass-mediated, and mass-consumed culture: recorded music, cinema, radio, fashion, design, advertising, photography, popular entertainment, urban architecture, and rapid travel by automobile, train, liner, and airplane. Anxious commentators denounced this modernization, and virtualization, of experience as "Americanization." More constructively, Kracauer and Benjamin perceived within this culture what has come to be called a "vernacular modernism," a concept that attempts to capture the way that mass culture, including the imagined black America conjured up through jazz, Josephine Baker, and Paul Robeson, defined a "sensory-reflexive horizon for the experience of modernization and modernity." The external culture, in other words, contained within it imaginative resources that enabled metropolitan European audiences and consumers to reflect on modernization and modernity, to react to them, and sometimes, in doing so, to make them new.

Paul Robeson

Paul Robeson's arrival in London in the 1920s did not provoke the same degree of commotion that Josephine Baker, jazz, and *l'art nègre* had stirred up in Paris and Berlin. That was, in part, because it was not until his third visit, in 1927, that he achieved real stardom, when he sang "Ol' Man River" in *Show Boat*. But the surface equanimity also resulted from the different processes of cultural gatekeeping in England, France, and Germany, and the different styles and languages the gatekeepers used to moderate the reception of black American culture.

Robeson's first visit to England was in 1922, at the age of twenty-four, to act in *Voodoo*, a plantation-set melodrama written by a New York socialite. Despite its failure at home, under the title *Taboo*, the author, Mary Hoyt Wiborg, persuaded Mrs. Patrick Campbell, a family acquaintance, to direct and star in an English tour. Robeson had sufficiently impressed "Hoytie" in New York to be hired for the trip. One story is that Robeson's part required him to whistle, which he could not do. Instead, he started to sing. "Do sing again," Mrs. Pat would whisper, all too audibly and with increasing desperation as the show foundered, "You're better than the play!" Even so, *Voodoo* did not make it to the West End.

Robeson had been born in Princeton, New Jersey, in 1898, the youngest of five children, to a pastor father who had escaped from slavery, and a school-teacher mother who, traumatically for Robeson, died in a house fire when he was six. An outstanding student, he won a scholarship to Rutgers, in 1915 still a small, racially unenlightened private college. Although only the third black student to attend, he left as star of its football team and class valedictorian. In 1920, he entered Columbia Law School, where he supported himself by coaching basketball teams, playing professional football, singing (including a stint as bass for the Harmony Kings in *Shuffle Along*), and acting (*Taboo* was his second stage appearance.) In 1921, Robeson married Eslanda Cardozo Goode, an ambitious chemistry graduate from Columbia University, always known as Essie, who decided to sacrifice a career in medicine to act as his manager and agent when, with her encouragement, he started to show more interest in becoming a performer than a lawyer.

In the three years before he returned to London, in 1925, to play the lead in Eugene O'Neill's *The Emperor Jones*, Robeson had become a significant figure in New York. He and Essie moved easily in the intellectual and artistic circles that were then circulating between Harlem and Manhattan, and fashioning distinctively American versions of modernism. He had established himself as an actor through his controversial appearances in *The Emperor Jones* and another O'Neill play, *All God's Chillun Got Wings*. He had given an historic first recital of spirituals, with his accompanist Lawrence Brown, and, although he tended to keep it quiet, he had made his first film, *Body and Soul*, for the director Oscar Micheaux. In London, the notices were again more enthusiastic about him than they were about the play, which appealed (according to Essie) only to "the intelligentsia and the society people." It was on this trip, however, that Robeson began to establish his broader appeal as a singer, when he gave his first broadcast for the BBC.

In postwar London, "America" appeared less exotic than it did in France or Germany. The shared language was an obvious factor, but so was the greater degree of economic and social integration, not least through intermarriage across the British and American power elites. Even before the war, clubs like the Embassy and hotels like the Savoy had begun to introduce elements of ragtime syncopation into their dance music. This had nothing to do with fantasies of salvation or cultural rejuvenation. The motives were commercial and musical. In London, then, it was generally not avant-garde intellectuals, like Cocteau, Milhaud, or the Dadaists, who brokered the dissemination of jazz and black America, but more often promoters, publicists, and the "society set." After the war, jazz was taken up more widely, as part of a nationwide dance craze. The Original Dixieland Jazz Band, a group of white, working-class New Orleans musicians, was brought to London in 1919, on the strength of selling over a million copies of the first jazz record, "Livery Stable Blues." They first appeared at the London Hippodrome, gave a royal command performance at Buckingham Palace, and then played to nearly six thousand people on the opening night of the new Palais de Danse in Hammersmith. This shaped the general perception of jazz in England for the next decade, as a raucous, high-energy popular music, aggressively American, but mostly played by whites and designed for dancing.

Complicating that story, however, was the visit to London, while the Original Dixieland Jazz Band was still there, of a very different type of

American jazz band. The all-black Southern Syncopated Orchestra, founded and initially led by Will Marion Cook, a classically trained musician, played in venues like the Kingsway Hall and the Philharmonic Hall, and it too was invited to give a royal command performance. Cook had achieved fame at the turn of the century as composer of *In Dahomey*, the first all-black show to play on Broadway and in London's West End, and then worked with James Reese Europe. Later, he would act as a mentor to Duke Ellington. Under his strict direction, the Southern Syncopated Orchestra offered "symphonic" jazz, played from a written score and still close to ragtime in its reliance on relatively rigid counterrhythms and fixed melodic elaborations. It was a rare but calculated indulgence when Cook allowed his virtuoso clarinetist, Sidney Bechet, to improvise on "Characteristic Blues."

The contrast between the Original Dixieland Jazz Band and the Southern Syncopated Orchestra disrupts the schemata which, on the continent, enabled Ivan Goll and Michel Leiris to link European modernity with jazz, America, Negroes, and Africa. The Original Dixieland Jazz Band denied any African American influence on their music, while Will Marion Cook's symphonic style was popularized most successfully in America, and on European tours in 1923 and 1926, by the (white) "King of Jazz," Paul Whiteman. In Europe, Whiteman's music was heard not as black, but as "the spirit of a new country, an expression of the soul of America." Whiteman, in turn, influenced British bandleaders like Jack Hylton, who disavowed the term "jazz" to describe his music, in favor of "symphonic syncopation." But then Hylton became immensely popular in Europe, especially in France, where his name had become almost synonymous with jazz by the end of the 1920s, and where he was more widely known than any black American artists, not least because their recordings were not available until the end of the decade. It was Jack Hylton, after all, to whom Simone de Beauvoir and Jean-Paul Sartre were listening in Paris in 1929.

By the time Robeson came back to London for the third time, in 1927, to appear in *Show Boat* at the Theatre Royal, the success of Florence Mills in the revue *Blackbirds of 1926* had sparked off a vogue for black America among the city's Bright Young People, and their not-so-young parents. That is why the first group to "discover" Robeson on this occasion was "the smart Mayfair set who went in search of the latest sensations and inaugurated new fashions." This recognition, according to Robeson's biographer and friend Marie Seton, set off a chain reaction: "soon the county people who came up to London for the 'season' were telling their friends to go to Drury Lane." Then, "the elderly, frowsty people who go to matinees began talking about Robeson's voice," to be followed by "the 'intelligentsia' of Bloomsbury and Chelsea, who seldom deigned to go to musical comedies." Finally, his popularity was assured when "young people from Clapham and Tooting could be heard talking about him on the top of buses and on the Underground."

This gatekeeping process revealed a London that was unevenly modernized, guardedly cosmopolitan, and racially disingenuous. Although
Robeson was now able to augment his income by singing at "smart"
parties—the Canadian newspaper magnate Lord Beaverbrook hired him
four times—the brittleness of Robeson's take-up by English "society" can
be gauged from the reactions of the novelist Evelyn Waugh, a sharp-eyed
observer from the fringes of the Bright Young People, who took a jaundiced
view of modernity and was especially sensitive to Robeson's presence in
London. It is not clear whether they ever actually held a conversation. They
first nearly met in 1925, during the West End run of *The Emperor Jones*.
Waugh's diary entry for September 15 records a drunken evening at the novelist Mary Butts's flat: "The party was given in honour of a negro who is
acting in a play called Emperor Jones but he had a fit in his dressing room
and would not come." Five years later, on May 26, 1930, they were at least
in the same room but, although Waugh now gives Robeson his name, still
not speaking: "Lunched at a women's club. Tea Olivia and Gwen. Cocktails
Sachie Sitwell. Dined Richard and Elizabeth. Small party afterwards. Paul
Robeson passed out. Went back and slept with Varda, but both of us too
drunk to enjoy ourselves."

To the extent that the animus evident in these references was personal,
the cause was "Olivia," Waugh's first and unrequited female love. Dressed
in black, her face whitened, Olivia Plunkett-Green combined a flamboyant
appetite for gin, the Charleston, and promiscuity with a self-absorbed spirituality that led her to convert to Catholicism at about the same time as Waugh.
He was self-pityingly jealous that she enthusiastically enjoyed sex with Paul
Robeson, while she refused to sleep with him. In his diary for February 1927,
he records a lunch with her and her mother, at which "Olivia could talk of
nothing except black men." His sexual insecurities appear to have been displaced into a racial hostility evident in the racist, although widespread, language of the time. That evening, he and some other friends "went later to
the Blackbirds and called on Florence Mills and other niggers and negresses
in their dressing-rooms. Then to a night club to see another nigger—Leslie
Hutchinson." Hutchinson was a handsome, bisexual West Indian pianist and
singer, who had been Cole Porter's lover in Paris, before moving to London in
1927, where he became not only a successful entertainer, but also a fashionable
object of desire. Two days later, Waugh was at a dinner hosted by a wealthy,
if shady, art dealer, Langton Douglas. "His illegitimate daughter Zena Naylor
lives with Hutchinson. . . . Olivia joined us later. We went on to a party given
by a Mrs Goossens which was entirely taken up by black people playing poker,
and white people getting drunk and cutting each other." (This seems to be
the original for the party described in *Brideshead Revisited*, at which Florence
Mills sings.) The next day, Waugh went to tea with the Douglases: "The situation of a distinguished old man's illegitimate daughter receiving in his house

her black lover and her black lover's black wife and baby might have seemed improbable in a book. However there it is."

No fantasies of redemptive primitivism here, then, just a banal fear about miscegenation as cultural and "racial" regression. Translating private pique into public caricature in *Decline and Fall* (1928), Waugh lampoons Robeson (in the figure of Sebastian "Chokey" Cholmondley) for his supposed cross-racial mimicry, and so also ridicules the gullibility of Bright Young Negrophiles.

> When I saw the cathedrals my heart just rose up and sang within me. I sure am crazy about culture. You folk think that because we're coloured we don't care about nothing except jazz. Why I'd give up all the jazz in the world for just one little stone from one of your cathedrals. . . . I've seen Oxford and Cambridge and Eton and Harrow. That's me all over. That's what I like, see? I appreciate art. There's plenty coloured people come over here and don't see nothing but a few nightclubs. I read Shakespeare. . . . *Hamlet, Macbeth, King Lear.* Ever read them? . . . My race . . . is essentially an artistic race. We have the child's love of song and the child's natural good taste. All you white folks despise the poor coloured man.

Waugh's language and prejudices were not uncommon among the London intelligentsia. In a fictionalized account of going to see Robeson in *Show Boat*, the American imagist poet H.D., reports a friend's impression that, from the distance of the dress-circle, he looked like "one of those Harvard niggers who talk English." H.D. was more alert to what Robeson embodied, however, to his formation in the Harlem Renaissance, and to their shared, although different, experiences of transatlantic migration. Originally, her group had dismissed Robeson as "a high-brow sort of over-educated negro, who was descending, out of some superior idea of fashionable race loyalty, to singing spirituals of the moment," and suspected that "his heart that afternoon had not been in the thing that he did." Nor was H.D. immune to the primitivist association between black body and nature: "across that packed house, there was ripple of delicate blue grass, there was a flight of cardinal butterflies." Nevertheless, her affective response was intense and paradoxical, as his performance reminded her of her homelessness: "Oddly and almost for the first time, in her tragically rooted London war-consciousness, [she] felt that America was her home."

For a mass British audience, for Marie Seton's "elderly, frowsty people" and the "young people from Clapham and Tooting," Robeson's popularity continued to grow during the decade that he was based in London, after bringing Essie and their newborn son over to join him in 1927. His reputation was enhanced by his critical success on stage as *Othello* in 1930, but it was his concerts around the British Isles, his frequent broadcasts on the BBC, the release of James Whale's film version of *Show Boat* in 1936, and his starring roles in six British films in the five years before he went back to the United States in 1939, that secured the breadth of his appeal. (In 1937, Robeson was voted the most popular singer on British radio and ranked tenth in the *Motion Picture Herald*'s list of popular film personalities.) It would have been through his performances that many people in these English audiences became aware of "race" for the first time. In other words, he operated as a component of vernacular modernism. In Britain, it has been observed, the figure of Paul Robeson "provided a potent means by which—for white men and women—the possibilities of the modern world came to be internally recognized, known, judged and felt."

Jazz Modernism

Neither Josephine Baker nor Paul Robeson was a jazz musician, although in her early years Baker might be described as a jazz dancer. Even so, their reception in Europe was shaped by European responses to American jazz, which meant that they functioned, like it or not, as barometers for often inchoate responses to modernity and modernization. (One historian of jazz in 1920s America has observed that "to argue about jazz was to argue about the nature of change itself.") To that extent, Baker and Robeson should be understood as part of a broader cultural movement that has been named, in retrospect, "jazz modernism."

Implicit in the idea of jazz modernism is a history of migrations and detours, the movement of ideas and influences as well as of people, between the United States and Europe and back again, as well as across racial borderlines. It condenses a number of dimensions. The first is the way that jazz, as a cultural and social phenomenon even more than as music, served as a symbol and symptom of a modernist attitude, or mentality: not just a positive attitude toward change, but a new emphasis on interiority, a new sense of the body and sexuality, and modernity experienced, viscerally, as rhythm. "The word jazz," observed Scott Fitzgerald, "is associated with a state of nervous stimulation, not unlike that of big cities behind the lines of a war." John Cournos captured this subjective dimension of jazz in *Babel*, as he describes the mental state of his hero.

> His head on the pillow, his body curled up under the sheets, his numbed brain began to thaw and release all manner of thoughts, harsh, jangling, full of contrariety, like the tunes of the band he had heard on the evening of his arrival. His mind was in a state of jazz, was jazz.

In more strictly musical terms, "jazz modernism" acknowledges that American musicians such as Duke Ellington, Louis Armstrong, and Fats Waller, all part of the same generation as Robeson and Baker, deserve recognition for developing jazz into a modernist art music, comparable within its own genre to the innovations of modernists in the visual arts, literature, cinema, or dance. "To call Armstrong, Waller, et al., 'modernists' is to appreciate their procedures as alchemists of the vernacular who have 'jazzed' the ordinary and given it new life," claimed Alfred Appel Jr., who appears to have coined the term.

A third dimension of jazz modernism, and one which is more directly relevant to the reception of Josephine Baker and Paul Robeson among European artists and intellectuals, is the recognition that certain "jazz" principles and techniques are discernible in the works of other contemporary, modernist artists. It is important to get both the timing and the aesthetic implications of this dissemination of jazz modernism right. For example, it was not until the early 1930s that the new jazz aesthetic represented by Ellington, Armstrong, and Waller achieved any sustained critical recognition, largely thanks to the enthusiasm of European intellectuals, who heard their music live for the first time when the American artists were able to undertake their first transatlantic tours. In the first half of the 1920s, when Robeson and Baker had arrived in London and Paris, an early backlash against the postwar enthusiasm for jazz described by Leiris and Cocteau was already in train among some sections of the avant-garde. In 1925, Cocteau himself issued a *rappel à l'ordre*, a "recall to order" that entailed the rejection of what he now saw as debilitating postwar hedonism, political Bolshevism and artistic anarchy, in favor of the neoclassical virtues of order, discipline, reason, and beauty.

Cocteau's revisionist, anti-jazz but pro-modernist spirit was clearly evident in an essay that the Bloomsbury art critic Clive Bell published in the *New Republic* in 1921: "Plus de Jazz" ("No More Jazz"). There, Bell rails against the "Jazz theory of art" and the stupidity of its acolytes, "on whose banner is inscribed 'No discrimination!' 'No culture!' 'Not much thought!'" In retrospect, the obituary seems shockingly premature. Bell himself reckoned that the jazz movement "bounced into the world somewhere about the year 1911," the year that Irving Berlin revived ragtime with the worldwide success of "Alexander's Ragtime Band." Bell was writing two years after the Original Dixieland Jazz Band had made their London debut in 1919, but still, it is important to remember, six years before Ellington started his residency at the Cotton Club, in 1927, and seven years before Armstrong recorded his genre-redefining "West End Blues," in 1928. The chronology apart, what is surprising about Bell's attack on jazz is that he chose to include it as the final chapter to *Since Cézanne*, the monograph he published in 1922 to champion an emerging great tradition in modern art: the painting of "Derain, Matisse, Picasso, Bonnard, Friesz, Braque, etc." Why should Bell decide to end a defense of modern painting with an attack on the modern sounds of jazz—or, rather, with an attack on the modern *phenomenon* of jazz, given that he offers no discussion or even description of jazz as music?

That silence is itself the clue. Bell was about culture wars, not music criticism. His aim was to discriminate between good modernism and bad modernism, with jazz representing the bad modernism that he deplored, and to which his good painterly modernism was supposed to provide an anti-dote. At bottom, Bell disliked jazz because it represented a "revolt against nobility and beauty." "The Jazz movement is a ripple on a wave," he scoffed, a trivial symptom of modernization that had distracted attention away from the critical value of modernism, which was "the large movement which began at the end of the nineteenth century in a reaction against realism and scien-tific paganism." The essence of jazz was its *impudence*—"impudence which finds its technical equivalent in syncopation: impudence which rags"—and the preference for instant gratification over sustained aesthetic development or intellectual depth evident in its "determination to surprise." Jazz pandered to "a typically modern craving for small profits and quick returns." Above all, the wrong people liked jazz. "Jazz is very young: like short skirts, it suits thin, girlish legs, but it has a slightly humiliating effect on grey hairs." Its fears and dislikes are "childish," and it expresses "its horror of the noble and the beautiful," not by using irony and wit, which are "the products of the cultivated intellect" and so "for the grown-ups," but "by jeers and grimaces." Childishness is then venomously racialized: "Niggers can be admired art-ists without any gifts more singular than high spirits; so why drag in the intellect?" The inventors of jazz sought out the idle, the cosmopolitan, and the unserious in the characteristic nonplaces of modernity: "in the lounges of great hotels, on transatlantic liners, in *wagons-lits*, in music-halls, and in expensive motor-cars and restaurants."

> And, of course, it was delightful for those who sat drinking their cock-tails and listening to nigger-bands to be told that, besides being the jolliest people on earth, they were the most sensitive and gifted. They, along with the children and savages whom in so many ways they resembled, were the possessors of natural, uncorrupted taste. They first had appreciated rag-time and surrendered themselves to the compelling qualities of Jazz. Their instinct might be trusted: so, no more classical concerts and music-lessons; no more getting Lycidas by heart; no more Bædeker; no more cricking one's neck in the Sistine Chapel: unless the coloured gentleman who leads the band at the Savoy has a natural leaning towards these things you may depend upon it that they are noble, pompous, and fraudulent.

For Bell, it seems, snobbery and racism were legitimate weapons in the defense of endangered cultural values: the "high seriousness, professional-ism, conscience, reverence, and vitality" that he saw in the work of his pre-ferred painters. His worry, when it came to music and literature rather than painting (where only the Italian Futurists, "with their electric-lit presenta-tion of the more obvious peculiarities of contemporary life and their taste for popular actualities," had been silly enough to attempt "a pictorial expression of Jazz"), was that good artists might be infected by jazz. In music, he admits, jazz had produced one first-rate master: Stravinsky, who, although "too big to be covered by a label," had been "influenced much by nigger rhythms and nigger methods" and had "composed ragtimes." One tier below him sat the *petits maîtres* of the jazz movement, notably *Les Six*, the group of composers, including Milhaud and Poulenc, associated in Paris with Jean Cocteau. In literature, half an hour reading Cocteau along with Blaise Cendrars would give sufficient idea of what jazz poetry could offer. In prose, James Joyce "effectually, and with a will, rags the literary instrument." Joyce adopts a principle of syncopation that "flouts traditional rhythms and sequences and grammar and logic," even if he does so with "talents which though genuine are moderate only." Although Bell was concerned that Virginia Woolf—his sister-in-law—flirts dangerously with syncopation in some of her writing, she remains among the saveable: "she is not imbued with that spirit which inspires the genuine Jazz writers, whether of verse that looks oddly like prose or of prose that raises a false hope of turning out to be verse, and conditions all that they produce." She is not, in one of Bell's favorite put-downs, *gavroche*—literally, a street urchin, but implying low-class and immature.

Bell's biggest worry was "Mr. T. S. Eliot—a poet of uncommon merit and unmistakably in the great line—whose agonizing labours seem to have been eased somewhat by the comfortable ministrations of a black and grinning muse." Eliot is accused of "playing the devil with the instrument of Shakespeare and Milton," and of using "language of an exquisite purity so far as material goes, but twisted and ragged out of easy recognition." Bell was right about Eliot to the extent that, at this stage of his career, he was not afraid to acknowledge his enjoyment of popular culture, or to work its rhythms and iconography into his poetry. In a debate at Oxford in 1914, Eliot rebuked Merton students for disavowing "how much they owed to Amurrican culcher in the drayma (including the movies) in music, in the cocktail, and in the dance." (For Bell, aesthetic discrimination was "something altogether different from telling a Manhattan from a Martini.") And Bell would hardly have been reassured by a letter in 1919, in which Eliot tried to explain his difficulties as an American outsider—a southern boy with a "nigger drawl," as he once described himself to Herbert Read—trying to make sense of England and the English. In the end, Eliot worries that "I may simply prove to be a savage."

"Thought rather than spirits is required," concluded Bell, "quality rather than colour, knowledge rather than irreticence, intellect rather than singularity, wit rather than romps, precision rather than surprise, dignity rather than impudence, and lucidity above all things: *plus de Jazz*." Knowing what the music has gone on to produce, it is easy to say that Bell got jazz wrong. But did Bell also get Eliot wrong, or had he latched onto something? Was Eliot really on the side of jazz and opposed to nobility and beauty? It hardly seems likely. So was Eliot doing something beyond Bell's wit? That is, was he experimenting with the possibility that jazz values could be transmuted into "nobility and beauty," or even considering whether nobility and beauty might *need* something that jazz had to offer, if they were to survive in the modern world? In other words, might a jazz aesthetic—as evident at this time in Eliot's poetry—actually be pressed into service for a "recall to order"?

The Waste Land certainly, even willfully, displays some of Bell's jazz vices. Bell deplored the reliance of jazz on surprise, for example; in a series of essays written while working on the poem, Eliot repeatedly stresses the aesthetic value of surprise. "The strange, the surprising, is of course essential to art," he declared in July 1921. "The craving for the fantastic, for the strange, is legitimate and perpetual; everyone with a sense of beauty has it." Bell valued "lucidity above all things" and disliked the sensual appeal of jazz to the young. *The Waste Land* is hardly "lucid." Its obscurity did not deter some young readers, however, for whom the poem's appeal lay partly in its rhythms and partly in an intuitive sense that, however classical in its references, it was viscerally in tune with other developments in modern culture. In an autobiographical essay in *Shadow and Act* (1964), for example, the novelist Ralph Ellison recalls being taught at school about the poets of the Harlem Renaissance, who failed to inspire him. "Then came *The Waste Land*." The poem "seized" his mind, and Ellison was "intrigued by its power to move me while eluding my understanding." Ellison was more interested in jazz than poetry at the time, and that was the music he felt in *The Waste Land*: "Somehow its rhythms were often closer to those of jazz than were those of the Negro poets, and even though I could not understand them, its range of allusion was as mixed and as varied as those of Louis Armstrong." On the other side of the Atlantic, the budding poet Louis MacNiece had a similar reaction when he read Eliot's poem in his final year of school, in 1926. "We had seen reviews proclaiming him a modern of the moderns and we too wanted to be 'modern,'" MacNiece recalled. Although the literary allusions and anthropological symbolism of *The Waste Land* were beyond his grasp too, like Ellison he found an alternative point of entry. "The cinema technique of quick cutting, of surprise juxtapositions, of spotting the everyday detail and making it significant, this would naturally intrigue the novelty-mad adolescent and should, like even the most experimental films, soon become easy to grasp."

What appealed to Ellison and MacNiece might have struck Clive Bell as the childish impudence of syncopation, the kind of writing that *rags the literary instrument* or *plays the devil with the instrument of Shakespeare and Milton*. Almost combatively, however, Eliot wove the syncopation of popular music into *The Waste Land*'s collage of arcane references. The most famous instance is the allusion to a 1912 song written for the Ziegfeld Follies, "That Shakespearean Rag," in which Eliot out-syncopates the syncopators by adding a syllable and making it "that Shakespeherian rag." Equally important is the placing of these lines in the section of the poem called "A Game of Chess." This chess game appears to be a mutually destructive emotional stalemate between a wheedling and resentful female voice and an emotionally cauterized, but silently screaming, interior male voice. Challenged to say what he is thinking, the lifeless male voice first responds with an honesty that is unspeakable—"I think we are in rats' alley / Where the dead men lost their bones"—and then offers bleak and perfunctory reassurance: "Nothing again nothing." Goaded further, the inner voice reinforces the deadliness of despair with the reference to *The Tempest*: "Those are pearls that were his eyes." The ragtime reference then bursts into this litany of nihilism as a desperate bid to drown out the bickering and to escape into a different psychic reality that might indeed be "so elegant, so intelligent." This is an escapism more desperate than anything imagined in Bell's caricature of the cocktail crowd at the Savoy. The rhythm of popular song also interrupts and rags the verse in "The Fire Sermon" in a pastiche that has been linked to the minstrel shows of Eliot's St. Louis childhood. The shows are evoked explicitly in "The rattle of the bones, and chuckle spread from ear to ear," but their characteristic "art of mélange" may also structure Eliot's sampling of grotesquely divergent references and quotations and their juxtaposition within the context of a nightmarish urban landscape: Spenser, Marvell, *The Tempest*, John Day's pastoral reference to hunting horns transformed into motor horns, a rude parody of the sentimental ballad *Red Wing*, Wagner's use of the Grail legend, and a line from Verlaine.

This promiscuous mixing of elite with popular culture, of authentic with inauthentic culture, and of the valuable with the meretricious, was just what Bell meant by *ragging*, although he would probably have recognized the precision of Eliot's orchestration. The difference between Bell and Eliot was not that one believed in normative cultural values while the other did not. Rather, Bell operated with a Gresham's Law view of culture, in which the circulation of bad art must always drive out the good, whereas Eliot was developing a consciously anthropological understanding of culture as a whole way of life, in which high and low necessarily coexist. Eliot was, therefore, able to see *the process of culture* as the recombination of these elements in new and distinctive patterns. This process of anthropological reinvention through recontextualization is what Eliot applauded in the way that Stravinsky's *Le Sacre du printemps* transformed "the rhythms of the steppes into the scream of the motor horn, the rattle of machinery, the grind of wheels, the beating of iron and steel, the roar of the underground railway, and the other barbaric cries of modern life." It is a process also evident, as Eliot's sometime collaborator and publisher Gilbert Seldes implied, in the poet's "use of the rhythms of jazz to contrast with the stately phrases of the past." In Eliot's art of juxtaposition and montage, to quote in a different rhythm is to transform, to make new.

What Eliot captured in *The Waste Land*'s references to popular music—and also through his invocation of communication machines like the typewriter and the gramophone—was a postwar estrangement of the senses that

Gertrude Stein with the American flag as backdrop, January 4, 1935 (Carl van Vechten)

transmuted everyday experience into a disturbing rhythm that was sometimes stultifying and sometimes febrile. This was the inner reality of modern
life, lived to the tempo of jazz. In aesthetic terms, to the extent that the startling newness of *The Waste Land* was achieved through an appropriation of
"jazz" principles or techniques, Eliot's poem can be read as a manifestation
of jazz modernism.

Modernist Migrations

Gertrude Stein's book *Useful Knowledge*, published in 1928, is made up of
thoughts about her home country from her home in France, and portraits
of friends and compatriots. One chapter, "Among Negroes," records five
American visitors to Paris in 1925: "A story of the Three of you Josephine
Baker Maud de Forest and Ida Lewelyn and Mr. and Mrs. Paul Robeson and
as they never met and as they never met. Naturally." Like *The Waste Land*,
Stein's meetings, and the supposed nonmeetings between Josephine Baker
and the Robesons, serve as a reminder of the encounter between the high

literary and artistic modernism represented by Gertrude Stein and the vernacular modernism embodied by jazz, Josephine Baker, and Paul Robeson.

Stein is astute in bringing Josephine Baker and Paul Robeson together, while yet keeping them apart. ("Naturally.") Baker and Robeson were the most successful black American stars to be based in Europe between the two twentieth-century world wars, and they were unique in that they really achieved their star status in Europe. That is what they shared, and that is why they can serve as avatars of the currency of black American culture in Europe over four decades. What differentiated them from each other was, in part, the extent to which the European Baker was very much a French phenomenon, even a Parisian one, whereas Robeson's base in London enabled him to develop an international frame of reference that embraced New York, Africa, and the Soviet Union. Although both achieved some, often ambiguous success in film roles, Baker was known primarily as a dancer and then as a music-hall performer, whereas Robeson first achieved success as a singer and stage actor. And although both brought racialized fantasies of sexuality into focus, they did so in markedly contrasting ways.

Stein's virtual juxtaposition of the two stars, and of the cultural categories that they embodied and disrupted, is important for the argument of this book. The way that Europeans (and Americans in Europe) between the wars made creative use of an imagined America, and in particular the figures of Josephine Baker and Paul Robeson, as embodiments of a fantasized black America, to work through the economic, political, social, and subjective consequences of modernization, can often be demonstrated most clearly through the interactions between avant-garde art and popular culture. Baker and Robeson provided artists and writers with the inspiration, and a license, to work through modernism's propensity for exploring cosmopolitanism, synesthesia, racial masquerade, collage, translation, and other forms of migration and imaginative border crossing. In doing so, the writers and artists played a decisive role in creating "Josephine Baker" and "Paul Robeson" as public figures, as celebrities, and as stars.

The meetings between Gertrude Stein, Baker, and Robeson also underline the overlaps and intersections between "transatlantic modernism" and the "black Atlantic." Stein and H.D. were just two of many American writers who saw in Europe the kind of freedom, cultural values, and opportunities for self-creation that they felt were smothered by American conformity and American capitalism—among the others were not only white poets, like Ezra Pound and T. S. Eliot, and novelists, including Ernest Hemingway and Scott Fitzgerald, but also black philosophers and "race leaders," like W. E. B. Du Bois and Alain Locke, the poet Langston Hughes, and the West Indian novelist Claude McKay. Some chose exile, some opted to stay and masquerade as Europeans, some discovered their Americanness in Europe, some returned to America to make a career or create a new culture. For them all, the movement back and forth across the Atlantic involved an attempt to understand "the idea of being modern and the signs and effects of modernization." Some Europeans went west, looking for the modern at its source: while Milhaud was tracking jazz to Harlem in 1922, for example, Marcel Duchamp was also in the United States, immersing himself in Hollywood movies. Most of the traffic, however, was in the other direction. Josephine Baker and Paul Robeson are significant largely because they exported the affective dimension, and the energy, of America across the Atlantic, so that Europeans needed to travel only virtually and imaginatively. They can be considered modernist, as well as modern, to the extent that they provoked in individuals and audiences new ways of experiencing the world and new ways of articulating that experience—the "freshness of transformation" that, for Wallace Stevens, was the defining feature of modernism. Their careers, their performances, and their public personae were transformative in the sense that they exemplified, or enacted, the modernist principles of restlessness, experimentation, and becoming. At the same time, through their European detours and in their difficult relationship to a home in America, Baker and Robeson lived the oscillation between belonging and dislocation that characterizes modern experience.

"The New Negro Has No Fear." Universal Negro Improvement Association
Parade, corner of 135th Street and Lenox Avenue, Harlem, 1924

New Negro

PAUL ROBESON'S FORMATION IN HARLEM

C. L. R. James, the charismatic Trinidadian polymath, described Paul Robeson as "the most marvellous human being I have ever known or seen." But, he added, his Marxism kicking in, Robeson was also "a man whose history is not to be understood unless seen in the context of the most profound historical movements of our century." James met Robeson in the early 1930s, when they were both living in London. Although Robeson had already achieved a "legendary" reputation among English audiences by that time, his status in his adopted home was paradoxical. Forty years on, in the 1970s, James reflected that Robeson had been "one of the best-known and best loved black men who ever was looked upon by British people as one of the blacks who had made it"; and yet, however much the English may have embraced him or even claimed him, in the end he remained incorrigibly American. In his last years, after he "went back home to the United States," Paul Robeson "could not have been thought of as anything else but an American citizen."

That insight into Robeson's Americanness remains true, however fractious his relationship to the United States became, and even though James appears to have forgotten that, after his return to the States, Robeson based himself in Europe for a second time, in the late 1950s and early 1960s. A more significant oversight is James's failure to mention Robeson's formation as a very particular type of American citizen in the years *before* his migration to Europe. Although British people would have recognized Robeson as being both black and American, few would have fully grasped the intellectual and psychological baggage he brought with him, as the result of his formation in the "Harlem Renaissance," or the "Negro Renaissance," as it was more commonly called at the time, in the period between the end of the First World War and the start of the Depression and the repeal of Prohibition. It may not have been what James had in mind, but this remarkable example of a black cultural politics, in an era of American national-cultural self-creation, should count as one of the "historical movements" that provides the context for understanding Robeson's career.

From this perspective, Robeson's time in Europe can be seen as a transformative interlude in an American life. Already an iconic figure in Harlem before he moved to London, Robeson embodied the modernizing values, conflicts, and anxieties of the Negro Renaissance. These were adapted and transformed as he worked through his European experience, and then dramatically put to the test on his return to the United States. This chapter tells the first part of that story. It examines the Harlem milieu of the 1920s, and it shows how Robeson experimented with a number of personae—"race man," intellectual, actor, and singer—in the process of his formation as an artist and as a public figure. In doing so, it reveals something of the American legacy that determined the trajectory of his long European detour.

Race Man

Having graduated from Rutgers, Robeson arrived in Harlem in the summer of 1919, only months after the end of the Great War, along with thousands of other migrants. Most were escaping from the harsh feudalism of the agricultural South to seek work in the industrial northeast, but many came from the Caribbean and some from Africa. Demobilized soldiers, newly returned from Europe, rubbed shoulders with ambitious young men and women seeking an education or a profession, or chasing a dream of literary fame. Just two years after the Bolshevik revolution in Russia, this was America's own explosive "Red Summer." Competition for jobs was exacerbating interracial tensions, as the demand for labor created by the war economy fell away. The Ku Klux Klan was starting to revive across the nation, still energized by continuous screenings of D. W. Griffith's *Birth of a Nation* four years after its release in 1915. Lynching was on the rise, while Congress dragged its heels on antilynching legislation being promoted by the National Association for the Advancement of Colored People (NAACP). More than two dozen race riots in major cities left scores dead and hundreds injured. At the same time, black Americans were becoming increasingly self-assertive, especially in Harlem. The demagogic oratory of Marcus Garvey was galvanizing an international movement, based on a populist hotchpotch of black nationalism, Pan-Africanism, socialism, and Booker T. Washington's ideology of self-help and self-improvement. A. Phillip Randolph and Chandler Owen were spreading the socialist word through their newspaper, the *Messenger*. In February 1919, while W. E. B. Du Bois was chairing a Pan-African Congress in Versailles, half a million people turned out to watch James Reese Europe and his band lead the returning Harlem Hellfighters, as they marched up Fifth Avenue from Lower Manhattan. When Europe turned off 110th Street onto Lenox Avenue, and the band began to play "Here Comes My Daddy Now," the crowds cheered and danced.

James Weldon Johnson—diplomat, poet, composer, author, and executive secretary of the NAACP—described Harlem in the 1920s as a "great Mecca" for "the enterprising, the ambitious and the talented of the whole Negro world." More than that, within "this city within a city, the greatest Negro city in the world," a new collective self-consciousness and a new type of society were in the making. "Harlem is more than a Negro community," claimed Johnson; "it is a large scale laboratory experiment in the race problem."

The Harlem experiment posed the question of what it meant "to be a Negro," and, more specifically, what it meant to be a metropolitan Negro in the postwar United States. The growing proportion of black Americans living in urban areas—up from less than 20 percent in 1890, to 34 percent by 1920 and nearly 44 percent by 1930—added urgency to the challenge of how they might be able to enjoy full citizenship rights, and, if they could, on what terms. In the half-century since Emancipation, conventional political and legal paths had not won them those rights. Many continued to be disenfranchised. At the same time, the broader American society was reinventing itself as a unified nation, characterized by genuinely national markets and a nationwide public sphere, and by the emergence of a self-questioning national culture that reflected widespread exasperation, fuelled by the Great War, about the viability or value of European civilization. This modernizing process created the circumstances in which the intellectuals, writers, and artists associated with the "Negro Renaissance" were able to experiment with new ways of thinking.

A key figure was the philosopher Alain Locke, whose 1925 anthology *The New Negro* became a defining document for the movement. Locke graduated magna cum laude from Harvard and then, between 1907 and 1911, studied at Oxford as the first black American Rhodes scholar. (He was rejected by five Oxford colleges because of his color, before being accepted by Hertford.) After Oxford, with the encouragement of Hugo Münsterberg, one of his Harvard professors, he moved on to the University of Berlin. He completed his doctorate at Harvard in 1918, while holding an appointment at the historically black Howard University. Dismissed from Howard in 1925, for demanding equal pay with white professors, he spent the next few years concentrating on his role as public intellectual and, in his own words, as the "philosophical mid-wife to a generation of younger Negro poets, writers, artists." (He was brought back to Howard in 1928 by its first black president.) Locke's international experience was an important determinant of the political and cultural strategy of the renaissance. He described himself as "a cultural cosmopolitan, but perforce an advocate of cultural racialism as a defensive counter-move for the American Negro." Taking its cue from nationalist movements in Ireland, India, and Czechoslovakia, the renaissance called America to account on its promises of political universality and cultural democracy, by asserting a black identity, a black history, and a black culture—the Negro, the Race—as vital components of a modern American nation. Its intellectuals took existing political categories—participation, representation, rights—and reworked them in more cultural terms. The renaissance was thus not *only* an aesthetic movement, although artistic innovation did both inspire and respond to new thinking, political activism, and institution building. Addressing the question of how it might be possible to be both "Negro" and "American" in his introductory essay to *The New Negro*, Locke insisted that the two terms need not be incompatible: "The Negro mind reaches out as yet to nothing but American wants, American ideas." For him, this meant a pragmatic experiment in creating a new "Americanism," based on "race values" and yet sharing fully in "American culture and institutions." In this context, the "racialism of the Negro" should be understood as "a constructive effort to build the obstructions in the stream of his progress into an efficient dam of social energy and power."

In the restless, transitional Harlem of 1919, Paul Robeson—a successful young man, confident in his talents, and frank about his ambition—cut a romantic figure. "Paul Robeson was a hero," wrote Eslanda Robeson, in her 1930 biography, "he fulfilled the ideal of nearly every class of Negro." Apart

*Paul Robeson in Harlem, c. 1925–1926, with an autograph inscription
to Fredi Washington: "To darling Fredi, Really my 'weakness' Much Love Paul"*

from his impressive intellectual and athletic achievements, his "simplicity and charm were captivating; everyone was glad that he was so typically Negroid in appearance, colour, and features." As "part and parcel of Harlem," Paul Robeson seemed to *embody* and *enact* the virtues of the New Negro.

> When Paul Robeson walks down Seventh Avenue he reminds one of his father walking down the main street of Somerville: it takes him hours to negotiate the ten blocks from One Hundred and Forty-Third Street to One Hundred and Thirty-Third Street; at every step of the way he is stopped by some acquaintance or friend who wants a few words with him. And always Paul has time for those few words. In 1919 Paul strolled the "Avenue," and soon became one of its landmarks; he was often to be seen on the corner of One Hundred and Thirty-Fifth or One Hundred and Thirty-Seventh Street, the centre of a group. He could talk to anyone about anything.

Even though Essie was hardly a disinterested observer, and despite his decision to become an actor and a singer rather than a lawyer, the trope of Paul Robeson as charismatic New Negro had become well established by the mid-1920s. The *New Republic* published a pen-portrait in 1926, in which Elizabeth Shepley Sergeant managed to capture the allegorical dimension of Robeson's emerging persona. "Paul Robeson is not merely an actor and a singer of Negro Spirituals but a symbol," she wrote. "A sort of sublimation of what the Negro may be in the Golden Age hangs about him, and imparts to his appearances an atmosphere of affection and delight that is seldom felt in an American audience." Robeson is presented as a star, as a glamorously desirable body that generates meanings and, in doing so, takes on a quasi-mythical aspect. "Six feet two and one half inches tall, twenty-seven years old, black as the Ace of Spades, he is a man of outstanding gifts and of noble physical strength and beauty. His figure on the slave block, in *The Emperor Jones*, is remembered like a bronze of ancient mold." Robeson was "unlike most moderns" to the extent that he "is not half a dozen men in one torn and striving body." He had a "sureness of essential being" that marked him out for an historic destiny: "Paul Robeson knows where he is bound."

This image of Robeson as both modern and yet inwardly grounded suggests why he was a *romantic* hero. In addition to being talented, beautiful, and charismatic, he appeared to embody a narrative of oppression, struggle, achievement, and a full emancipation to come, which was at the heart of a strategy of collective self-reimagining and self-assertion. This narrative was a "romance," in the sense that the genre entails a drama that plays out "the ultimate transcendence of man over the world in which he was imprisoned by the Fall," and often tells a story of the founding of a people, or collective self-identification, symbolized and inaugurated "by the hero's transcendence of the world of experience, his victory over it, and his final liberation from it." In the first half of the 1920s, Robeson, as a public figure, was, in effect, being handed a script that required him not only to exemplify the ideal characteristics of the New Negro, but also to act as a catalyst, moving the narrative forward and helping to bring into being a world in which vindicated New Negro virtues might flourish.

Part of the fascination of Paul Robeson in Harlem, at this time, lies in the way that, although he willingly took on these communal expectations, he also bridled against them. Through both that acceptance and that resentment, he acted out deep-seated differences and ambiguities within the Negro Renaissance. Robeson belonged to a generation of artists impatient with their elders' "cautious moralism and guarded idealizations," but he still felt constrained by claims on him framed in those terms. For the older generation, as Alain Locke saw it, the function of art was to "fight social battles and compensate social wrongs," and so the role of artists and intellectuals was to "be representative" and to "put the better foot forward." This is what it meant to be a "race man." Even in the 1920s, Paul Robeson didn't always want to be exemplary, and he wasn't, at least not all the time—or so some of Harlem thought. Harlem's ambivalence toward Robeson was not only about who he was, as a person. Just as much, it was about the political disputes and the intellectual doubts that informed and drove the renaissance.

Alain Locke, mid-1920s

Renaissance Man

Among the courses Alain Locke took at the University of Berlin, in 1910 and 1911, were two given by Georg Simmel: one on nineteenth-century philosophy, the other on "The problem of modern culture." By then, Locke had already articulated positions on society, culture, and value that predisposed him toward Simmel's interpretive sociology. He was certainly sympathetic to Simmel's characterization of modernity as a social formation determined by the relationship between an external world of things, or crystallized social forces, and the possibility of subjective life and individual creative development. In the same way that Simmel interpreted the significance of Germany's population shift from countryside and small towns to Berlin, Locke understood the Great Migration from the South as a qualitative, as well as a quantitative phenomenon: "a deliberate flight not only from countryside to city, but from medieval America to modern." At the same time as black Americans in the first decades of the twentieth century were being recruited to the modernity of Fordist industrial production, they were also demonstrating a desire for, or at least openness to, a subjective modernity, in which intellectuals like Locke saw the potential for progressive social change.

One thing that Locke helped to generate in the renaissance was a new conceptual understanding of *culture*, and its political significance for the creation of imagined communities. This produced two ways of thinking about black American culture. The first entailed the rediscovery or, more accurately, the creation through reimagining, of a black history, which would help to authorize a modern, American nationhood with an African thread woven inextricably through it. As Arthur Schomburg, Harlem's great archivist, put it: "The American Negro must remake his past in order to make his future." The outcome of this remaking was not only a much more positive evaluation of cultural continuities with Africa than had previously existed, but also a community-defining myth of origin that would eventually lead to a collective self-identification as "African American." Starting from this newly imagined Africa, its narrative memorialized the trauma of the Middle Passage, and established itself as American through stories and songs created in the South during the violence of slavery. This was a "diasporic" conception of culture, distilled into a story that could articulate a sense of shared racial ancestry and destiny, and so nurture "race consciousness" and "race pride." The alternative, more "ethnographic" way of thinking looked less to the past than to a new culture in the making, here and now, and shared Alain Locke's positive evaluation of black urbanization. This ethnographic perspective saw a specifically African American culture (or possibly subculture) being generated through the interaction, even when negative or conflictual, between Harlem's "cultural racialism" and the "vogue" in white Manhattan for Harlem art, Harlem culture, and Harlem nightlife. The "mongrelization" of Manhattan paralleled the negrophilia flourishing in postwar Paris, Berlin, and London. Although white interest in black music, art, and literature might seem a positive development, it was often, with some justice, denounced as transient, prurient, and patronizing. Harlem's cabaret culture, it was feared, threatened to dilute the uniquely Negro quality of the renaissance. The anxiety was that the vogue might pollute the political integrity of the movement, through the commercialization and vulgarization of black culture for white audiences, and also that it might undermine its moral authority through its overt and (though this was less openly spoken) heterodox sexuality. Scorning this angst, the poet Langston Hughes took a polemically ethnographic view of the emerging culture. It was, he insisted, the commercial success of *Shuffle Along* on Broadway that "gave a scintillating send-off to that Negro vogue in Manhattan" and created the space for the intellectual and political manifestations of "Manhattan's black Renaissance." *Shuffle Along* "gave just the proper push—a pre-Charleston kick—to that Negro vogue of the 20's, that spread to books, African sculpture, music and dancing."

Both the diasporic and the ethnographic narratives of an emergent African American culture shared their pragmatism, their pluralism, and their modernism. The *pragmatism* of the renaissance, deriving from the philosophies of William James and John Dewey, was encapsulated in the principle that America's modern "identity" would be *created* through experience and experiment, rather than discovered or recovered, even if the newly minted identity would routinely be portrayed as the retrieval of a folk history and ethnic traditions. Its *pluralism*, heavily influenced by the relativizing anthropology of Franz Boas, was inherent in its redefinition of "race" in terms of cultural difference and reciprocity, rather than natural hierarchies, and in its attempts to articulate African inheritance as one defining component of an emerging modern America, interacting with others. The *modernism* of the Negro Renaissance lay, above all, in the emphasis on the constitutive role of art and culture in this broader movement of American national self-invention, or self-reinvention. In 1928, Locke reflected that it had been "a fortunate thing" that the radicalism of "Negro art" had coincided with trends in "American art at large in search of its national soul." The Renaissance emphasis on "folk music and poetry as an artistic heritage" found its equivalent in the avant-garde struggle against "conventionality" and "Puritanism." Both movements believed in "re-rooting art in the soil of everyday and emotion," and this convergence gave "the Negro artist" every reason "to be more of a modernist than, on the average, he yet is, but with each younger artistic generation the alignment with modernism becomes closer."

On the ground, in Harlem's "experiment in the race problem," the dissemination of new ideas was mediated through two competing journals, *The Crisis* and *Opportunity*. *The Crisis* had been launched in 1910 as a mouthpiece for the NAACP, although with Du Bois as editor it was always clear that the journal would be just as much as a vehicle for his own beliefs and priorities. Its implicit readership was his putative "talented tenth," a black social and intellectual elite that the journal was designed to nurture into being. *The Crisis* accepted the NAACP's axiomatic equation between the "emancipation of the Negro race in America and the emancipation of America itself," but with Du Bois's additional gloss that whatever was most essentially American in American culture would have had an African American origin. *Opportunity* started publication only in 1923. Sponsored by the National Urban League, which focused on social-welfare and reform activities more than civil rights, it was edited by the sociologist Charles Spurgeon Johnson, who, at thirty, was twenty-five years younger than Du Bois. The novelist Zora Neale Hurston called Johnson "the root of the so-called Negro Renaissance."

Although literary writing had not been part of the original vision for *The Crisis*, Du Bois soon began to publish contributions that, in his somewhat Victorian view, attempted a truthful, but respectful, portrayal of black American life and history. With the appointment of the novelist Jessie Fauset as literary editor in 1919, *The Crisis* gave greater prominence to the rising stars of the Harlem Renaissance: the Caribbean Marxist Claude McKay first appeared in 1919, Langston Hughes's first poem, "The Negro Speaks of Rivers," in 1921, and Jean Toomer's "Song of the Sun," in 1922. Even so, Du Bois was never wholly at ease with the prominence given to art in the renaissance, if it threatened to detract from the politics. In 1921, defending Eugene O'Neill's controversial play *The Emperor Jones* against charges that it reproduced offensive stereotypes, he had urged black Americans not to "shrink at the portrayal of the truth about ourselves," and insisted that equating art with propaganda "is wrong and in the end it is harmful." By 1926, however, with his cultural authority under challenge by Alain Locke and Charles Johnson, Du Bois was testily reasserting the primacy of politics over art. "All art is propaganda and ever must be, despite the wailing of the purists. I do not give a damn for any art that is not used for propaganda."

Although Du Bois liked to rail against its supposed advocacy of "art for art's sake," *Opportunity*'s cultural policy in fact reflected less aestheticism than Charles Johnson's sociological training at the University of Chicago, under the mentorship of Robert Park. Park had always insisted on the detailed, empirical, and unsentimental observation of people and groups, in their social and cultural settings, and Johnson applied the same principle to literature. "The beginning of the twentieth century has been marked in America by a conscious movement 'back to the concrete'," he explained. This modernist realism delivered "the new fascination of watching the strangeness and beauty of familiar things," and represented "America in revolt against the stiff conventionalism of borrowed patterns." Its fresh way of seeing compelled a new generation of Negro writers and artists to reject the sanitized ideals of their elders and to discover "a new beauty in their own lives, ideals, and feelings."

To the newness of American culture, they contributed the "liberated energy" of their poetry, with its "new and beautiful life conceptions." "Investing negro life with a new charm and dignity, and power," modern black writing promised to reveal the full range of black American experiences in, and on, their own terms. "No life for them is without beauty, no beginning too low."

The differences between *The Crisis* and *Opportunity* came to a head, explosively, with the publication of Carl Van Vechten's novel *Nigger Heaven*, in 1926. A wealthy critic, collector, photographer, and man-about-town, Van Vechten liked to act as gatekeeper between the renaissance and Manhattan and as tour guide to Harlem for his white friends. ("Like Van Vechten, start inspectin'," exhorted Fats Waller's collaborator Andy Razaf in his 1930 song "Go Harlem.") Zora Neale Hurston considered him Manhattan's number one "Negrotarian"—a white humanitarian, with a genuine interest in the New Negro movement. The *Herald Tribune* picked up on Essie Robeson calling him "godfather," and profiled him as "the beneficent godfather of all sophisticated Harlem." The Marxist Mike Gold, in contrast, denounced Van Vechten as "the worst friend the Negro has ever had": "a white literary bum," pruriently obsessed by "gin, jazz and sex," who had "created a brood of Negro literary bums." Undeniably a dilettante, Van Vechten was also—for good or ill—a friend and patron to many figures in the Harlem Renaissance, including Paul and Essie Robeson.

Van Vechten's novel depicted Harlem as a social microcosm, uniquely black yet unequivocally American, and attempted to avoid what Van Vechten saw as the twin dangers of racial stereotyping and "uplift" sermonizing. Whatever the novel's literary merits and shortcomings, the title alone was guaranteed to start a row, and the aura of sex and drugs and wailing Harlem jazz helped to make the book sell in the tens of thousands. "Negroes did not read it to get mad," recalled Langston Hughes, another Van Vechten protégé. "They got mad as soon as they heard of it." Robeson, however, was enthusiastic. "Nigger Heaven amazing in its absolute understanding and deep sympathy," he telegraphed Van Vechten. "Thanks for such a book. Anxious to talk to you about it." In his review for *Opportunity*, James Weldon Johnson took a sanguine view of his friend's portrayal of Harlem in all its aspects, from its self-regarding bourgeois salons to its underbelly of jazz clubs, sensuality, cruelty, and crime: "It is all life. It is all reality." Alain Locke regarded it as "a studied but brilliant novel of manners" in the modernist style.

Du Bois loathed the book—"a blow in the face," he called it in his review in the December 1926 issue of *The Crisis*. The date is significant, as by this time Jessie Fauset had resigned as literary editor. Without her moderating influence, Du Bois was starting to turn on younger writers whom he had once championed, and his attacks on the Harlem Renaissance were becoming more strident. The appearance of the novel seemed to confirm his worst fears about "white 'decadence' in art concerning the Negro." Here was proof that white publishers really were putting out books highlighting the "sordid" aspects of negro life, pandering to white readers all too happy to read "about filth and crime and misfortune" among black Americans. Unable to convey any intellectual or psychological depth in its Harlem characters, thundered Du Bois, Van Vechten just slops about in "the surface mud." Van Vechten saw life as "just one damned orgy after another, with hate, hurt, gin and sadism." His novel was "an affront to the hospitality of black folk and to the intelligence of the white."

The Van Vechten scandal and the broader debate about the political function of art and culture in the Negro Renaissance bring into focus some of Paul Robeson's ethical dilemmas, at this stage of his career. Although part of Van Vechten's bohemian social set, and a contributor to *Opportunity*, he still felt accountable to an often socially conservative Harlem community, which, as Langston Hughes despaired, wanted white audiences to see "only good Negroes, clean and cultured and not-funny Negroes, beautiful and nice and upper class." Robeson could not afford Hughes's disdain for "the smug Negro middle class," nor his indifference to the claims of "uplift." Robeson had to manage the demand that he embody black authenticity and exemplify New Negro aspirations, and yet he could establish a sustainable career only by attracting white audiences. Playing to both sets of expectations at the same time inevitably exacerbated the experience of that "double consciousness," which Du Bois had diagnosed twenty years before: that is, the black American's "sense of always looking at one's self through the eyes of others" and the sense of "twoness," of being, at the same time, "an American, a Negro; two souls, two thoughts, two unreconciled strivings; two warring ideals in one dark body." Hence Robeson's public performance as "Paul Robeson." "As soon as another person came into the room," observed Gertrude Stein, with piercing sarcasm, "he became definitely a negro."

Actor

Nowhere were the competing claims of a responsibility to Harlem and the creative opportunities opened up by his engagement with Manhattan modernism more clearly evident than in Robeson's decisions about the parts he should accept as an actor. In *Here I Stand*, the autobiography-cum-apologia he published in the 1950s, he acknowledged that, early in his career, most "Negro performers" had taken the view that "the content and form of a play or film scenario was of little or no importance." It was the opportunity to perform at all that mattered, and "for a Negro actor to be offered a *starring* role—well, that was a rare stroke of fortune indeed!" He conceded, however, that he later "came to understand that the Negro artist could not view the matter simply in terms of his individual interests, and that he had a responsibility to his people who rightfully resented the traditional stereotyped portrayals of Negroes on stage and screen." Two controversial roles, both in 1924, illustrate the conundrum: one in O'Neill's *The Emperor Jones*, the other his long-ignored appearance in Oscar Micheaux's film *Body and Soul*.

The Provincetown Players first staged *The Emperor Jones* on November 3, 1920, at their Greenwich Village theatre. The part of Brutus Jones, the Pullman car porter who becomes the dictator of "an island in the West Indies as yet not self-determined by white marines," was played not by Robeson, but by Charles Gilpin, a seasoned actor who, although hired while running an elevator at Macy's department store, had twenty years experience in fairground song-and-dance acts and minstrel shows, as well as in "straight" roles with companies like the Harlem-based Lafayette Players. The Provincetown Players were trying to create a radical modern American drama that combined, really for the first time, progressive social and political attitudes with formal innovation in dramaturgy. *The Emperor Jones* met both criteria, not only as the first serious American drama to feature a black protagonist, but also as an experiment in expressionist effects. The production placed unprecedented demands on its leading actor. Gilpin had to sustain a single, increasingly delirious monologue over six scenes, lasting something over an hour, as Jones flees through a jungle from his rebellious subjects and unravels, mentally and spiritually, in the face of the demons representing America's history of racial oppression as

Charles Gilpin as the Emperor Jones (Jesse Tarbox Beales)

well as his own moral corruption. At the same time as he confronts his "form-less fears," Jones is stripped bare physically, tearing off his clothes to reveal a male body, whose blackness was highlighted by setting it against a blank white cyclorama, as throbbing tom-toms underscored his regression.

Gilpin's performance was widely acclaimed, but his relationship with O'Neill was never easy. Although the playwright admired Gilpin's talent, they fell out over the play's language. Whereas O'Neill felt that he was captur-ing the music and the integrity of black American vernacular speech, Gilpin took exception to the script's relentless repetition of the word "nigger." When he began to slip in alternatives like "Negro" and "colored man," an enraged O'Neill threatened to "beat the hell" out of him. In 1923, O'Neill complained to his friend Mike Gold that he had "stood for more from him than from all the white actors I've ever known—simply because he was colored!" Gilpin "lived under the assumption that no one could be found to play his part and took advantage accordingly." That, along with his alleged drunkenness, is why O'Neill decided not to risk starring Gilpin in the 1925 London production. Instead, he "corralled another Negro," who was prepared to stick to the letter of the script—Paul Robeson, "a young fellow with considerable experience, wonderful presence & voice, full of ambition and a damn fine man personally

Paul Robeson in The Emperor Jones, *London, 1925 (Sasha)*

with real brains—not a 'ham.'" In the event, unexpectedly, Robeson got to play Brutus Jones in New York before London, when the Provincetown Players revived the play for a week's run in May 1924, as a stopgap, while they sat out attempts to ban O'Neill's new play about an interracial marriage, *All God's Chillun Got Wings*, in which Robeson was supposed to debut.

Despite their critical success, Robeson's appearances in *The Emperor Jones* and, even more, in *All God's Chillun Got Wings*, in which he kissed the hand of the white actress Mary Blair, provoked a mixed, and often hostile, reaction in Harlem. The plays' language apart, the main objection was that O'Neill perpetuated the "doubtful formula of hereditary cultural reversion"; that is, the canard that even the modern black man wears rationality, sophistication, and civilization merely as a mask, which will slip, given the slightest provocation, to reveal his innate irrationality and primitivism. "I am still being damned all over the place for playing in *All God's Chillun*," Robeson complained in *Opportunity*, and countered by rebuking his critics for their "petty prejudices" and by objecting that they "know little of the theater and have no right to judge a playwright of O'Neill's talents." Robeson's positive case for *The Emperor Jones* was that Brutus is a kind of Everyman, whose "exultant tragedy" is "the disintegration of a human soul." Warped by racial suffering, Jones in the forest "re-lives all the sins of his past—experiencing all the woes and wrongs of his people—throwing off one by one the layers of civilization until he returns to the primitive soil from which he (racially) came." Despite the character's moral corruption, Robeson sees Jones as heroic to the extent that he confronts his demons: "here was a man who in the midst of all his trouble fought to the end."

As with other primitivist fantasies in 1920s modernism, *The Emperor Jones* can be read as a projection of the social anxieties and tensions of modernity onto the black body. While acknowledging that such displacement can occlude the history of sustained violence and brutality against actual black male bodies, looking at the *process* of projection suggests what those anxieties and tensions might have been. Doubtless O'Neill was externalizing his own inner demons, although less onto the character of Brutus Jones than onto his narrative. The play's trope of a "real" self beneath the façade of civilized modern man—a self that is primordial, obscene, and monstrously without form, a self that demands too much and gives too little—is narrativized as the horror of being inescapably haunted by both biographical traumas and historical forces. O'Neill's own "formless fears," it has been argued, may have included his emotional entrapment by a dysfunctional and self-destructive family, as well as a sense of social marginality as a result of his own ethnically ambiguous status as Irish-American. ("I created the role of the Emperor," taunted Charles Gilpin. "That Irishman, he just wrote the play.") The flight, regression, and destruction of Jones in the jungle thus render the melancholic and corrosive sense of never-quite-belonging that characterizes modern subjectivity. In this context, Brutus Jones's blackness is semiotically arbitrary but culturally overdetermined. It activates a relay of misreading, mimicry, and projection that freights the narrative with inordinate imaginary significance, but that is rendered uncanny in performance as the physical reality of the black actor playing "Brutus Jones" interrupts the purely imaginary nature of the fantasy. To put that another way, the nature of the projection onto "Brutus Jones" would have been different from the projection onto either Charles Gilpin or Paul Robeson playing Brutus Jones. It matters *which* black male body acts as the point of cathexis for the projection. When he played Brutus Jones in 1920, Charles Gilpin was already over forty, and his body showed it. Robeson was twenty years younger, and his athletic physique must have, at least, confused the play's evocation of an oppressed underclass with its "noble physical strength and beauty" and its connotations of classical statuary. Robeson may not have changed the lines, but his physical presence would unavoidably have added an epic dimension to the tragedy invested in the traumatized body of Brutus Jones.

The dissonance between the tragic role of Brutus Jones, or Jim Harris in *All God's Chillun*, and the romantic destiny projected onto him by his Harlem contemporaries, may help to explain a recurrent ambivalence in Robeson's

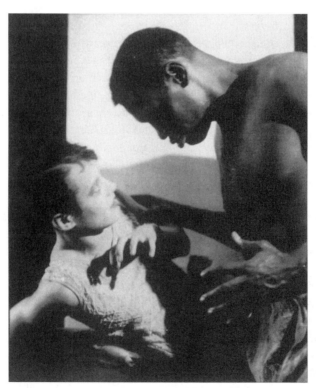

Paul Robeson and Fredi Washington in Black Boy, *1926 (Edward Steichen)*

reception. Intuiting this, critics would often draw a distinction between the offensive role and the exemplary actor. Robeson appears to have been allowed no such indulgence, however, in his first starring role on screen, in Oscar Micheaux's *Body and Soul*, shot in 1924 and released in 1925. Micheaux was no Harlem intellectual, but a low-budget filmmaker, who had cut his teeth during the flurry of independent black production in reaction against Griffith's *Birth of a Nation*, and who continued to treat cinema as a kind of demotic public sphere. Essie Robeson brokered the deal immediately after Paul's critically successful, but financially unprofitable, run with the Provincetown Players. In hiring him for *Body and Soul*, Micheaux may have hoped to cash in on Robeson's popularity in the black community. Apart from that, he also found in Robseon his latest controversial topic.

The narrative of *Body and Soul* is incoherent, not just because of Micheaux's characteristic use of multiple dream constructions and flashbacks, but also because of its implausible central premise. Two identical brothers, both played by Robeson, are living in the same Georgia town. One is an ambitious and hardworking young inventor, a Washingtonian New Negro, while the other embodies the consolidation of two African American folk characters, the trickster and the preacher. The Reverend Isiaah T. Jenkins is a charismatic ex-convict and hustler, masquerading as a pastor, who ruthlessly dominates and exploits his congregation. What holds *Body and Soul* together, it has been argued in a controversial reading by the cinema historian Charles Musser, is the way that Micheaux deploys these various manifestations of black masculinity to challenge the racial ideology he perceived in three contemporary white-authored plays about "Negro life"—all of which happened to star Paul Robeson. The most significant was *Roseanne*, a melodrama by Nan Begby Stephens, which supplied the outlines, and many of the details, of *Body and Soul*'s narrative about a venal pastor, a devout washerwoman, and her abused daughter. The other two were *The Emperor Jones* and *All God's Chillun Got Wings*. From *The Emperor Jones*, Micheaux borrowed the trope of an escaped convict, who manipulates a naïve black community by claiming supernatural powers, until they rise up and turn on him. *All God's Chillun* appears to have prompted him to portray the "good brother," Sylvester, as a black man ambitious to succeed in a white world, in pointed contrast to O'Neill's depiction of the neurotic, psychologically paralyzed Jim Harris, whose hopes of passing his bar exams are systematically undermined by his hysterical, and increasingly deranged, white wife.

Apart from his bewildering play with splitting, doubling, masquerade, and parody, the new narrative element Micheaux brought to this synthesis was its conclusion. *Roseanne* ends with the redemption of the pastor, as the washerwoman forgives him, and *Emperor Jones* with the hero's death. In *Body and Soul*, Rev. Jenkins repays the washerwoman for allowing him to escape by killing her son, who is one of his pursuers. At this point, she finally wakes up, to reveal that the whole baffling, de-formed narrative has been a dream: a nightmare about betrayal by her pastor. The scandalous insinuation of this denouement, in the revisionist reading, was that, not unlike the trickster-minister, Paul Robeson, Harlem's much admired New Negro, may also have provided false leadership for his community. That indictment, rather than the fantastic complexities and non sequiturs of the plot, delivers the real coherence and thrust of *Body and Soul*.

If that is right, the puzzle is what Robeson might have done to antagonize Micheaux. His most likely offence was his willingness to take on ideologically repellent roles, in plays like those by O'Neill and Begby, and so, by the way, his contribution to the decline of the less compliant, and more racially conscious, Charles Gilpin. (Apart from *Emperor Jones*, Gilpin had quit the lead role in *Roseanne*, again to be replaced by Robeson, only three months before shooting started on *Body and Soul*.) Micheaux may also have reacted against the sanctimonious rhetoric Robeson sometimes used to justify himself. Overall, then, the director perhaps felt that his star needed cutting down to size because he was naïve, egotistical, and sometimes less than frank, and because, in the attempt to rationalize his roles, Robeson appeared to obfuscate the racial ideologies they perpetuated.

Whether or not this was how *Body and Soul* was intended, and whether or not its charges were justified, the film had little impact. Few in its audience

Paul Robeson in Body and Soul, *1925*

would have seen the O'Neill and Begby plays, and Micheaux's coding of his critique was so arcane and allusive that none of *Body and Soul*'s reviewers even mentioned its source white plays. Harlem's intellectuals would probably have given the film a miss. (Cinema does not rate a mention in *The New Negro*.) Robeson himself, however, may have got the point. Although he kept quiet about the film, even later in life, it could be that Micheaux and, especially, Gilpin were among those he had in mind when he acknowledged that "the Negro artist" had "a responsibility to his people who rightfully resented the traditional stereotyped portrayals of Negroes on stage and screen."

Concert Singer

Even more than his performance in *The Emperor Jones*, the event that foreshadowed Paul Robeson's future career was his first public recital of spirituals, with Lawrence Brown as his accompanist. The two men had first met in 1922, in London, while Brown was living there and Robeson was rehearsing for *Voodoo*. Brown was an accomplished pianist and musicologist, who had established himself as accompanist to the classical tenor Roland Hayes. Robeson's musical abilities were already known. Du Bois had spotted the Rutgers undergraduate as a talented "baritone soloist" in 1918, and, the following year, Robeson sang at a memorial service for the bandleader James Reese Europe, who had been killed by a deranged musician. At their first meeting, Robeson and Brown talked about the spirituals and, when Brown published arrangements of five "Negro spirituals" for solo singer with piano and cello accompaniment in 1923, he remembered their conversation, and sent a copy to Robeson.

Returning to New York for his father's funeral two years later, Brown bumped into Robeson, who took him along to an evening in Greenwich Village with James Light, Robeson's director in the two O'Neill plays. During a conversation about the variety of emotion to be found in spirituals, Robeson suggested that they perform "Swing Low, Sweet Chariot" and "Every Time I Feel the Spirit." When Brown joined in as second voice, Light told them that they should give a concert together. A semipublic performance followed, at one of Van Vechten's parties. "Carl was amazed and just begged for more and more songs," enthused Essie in her diary. He and his wife, the actress Fania Marinoff, "just raved about Paul's voice and Larry's rhythm. Larry is really fine. Carl is so interested he is almost jumping up and down." Van Vechten put some money into the public concert, to be given three weeks later on April 19, 1925. The Provincetown Players offered the use of their MacDougal Street theater in Greenwich Village and also helped out with administration and staging. Van Vechten and the NAACP's Walter White used their address books to drum up an audience, and the *New York World*'s drama critic, Heywood Broun, promoted the show in his column.

The concert Paul Robeson and Larry Brown were planning built on what Brown had achieved with Roland Hayes. Although his reputation was based on performances of the European song repertoire, in recent years Hayes had begun to include Negro spirituals in his recitals. "It pleased me to believe that I was restoring the music of my race to the serious atmosphere of its origins," Hayes recalled, "and helping to redeem it for the national culture." This sense of recovering the racial specificity of "Negro" music in the service of an inclusive American culture chimed with Alain Locke's views about the need to fuse black cultural particularity with cosmopolitan aesthetic universals. In celebrating Hayes's return to the United States after his long stay in Europe, in the December 1923 *Opportunity*, Locke praised the way that he had presented spirituals to European audiences, along with classical songs. Even if it had not yet have evinced "an admission of equal value—that could not be expected," the juxtaposition of the two genres at least raised the prestige of the spirituals.

What was new, and courageous, about Robeson's recital was that no solo artist had previously devoted a program exclusively to Negro songs. For Hayes, it remained a principle not to do so: "I will never sing spirituals without classics, or classics without spirituals, for properly interpreted they are classics." The risk in Robeson and Brown's experiment was that their approach might not be accepted as a "proper interpretation." The timing, however, was propitious. The Harlem vogue had produced a thirst for "the real thing," for "authentic" black culture. As a result, the small theater was packed out. Some disappointed customers snuck into the wings to listen. Scores more were turned away. The predominantly white crowd was, noted Essie, "very high class."

Hiding their nerves, Robeson and Brown entered, dressed discreetly in tuxedos. Brown sat at the keyboard. Robeson stood facing him, resting one hand on the piano, and signaled he was ready. "I have never seen a more civilized, a more finished artistic gesture than his nod to his accompanist, the signal to begin his song," wrote Elizabeth Shepley Sergeant in her *New Republic* profile. "The gesture is the final seal of Paul Robeson's personal ease in the world." The recital lasted for about three-quarters of an hour. An opening set of four spirituals, arranged by Harry T. Burleigh, was followed by four secular songs: Burleigh's humorous "Scandalize My Name," Avery Robinson's arrangement of "Water Boy," and two love lyrics by Paul Laurence Dunbar in settings by J. Rosamond Johnson (James Weldon Johnson's brother) and Will Marion Cook. The second half consisted of eight spirituals, all arranged by Brown. The enthusiastic audience demanded five encores, three additional songs, and repeated curtain calls. The next day's press reviews were flattering. One critic described the concert as "the first appearance of this folk wealth to be made without defence or apology."

In the following months, a "vogue" for spirituals prompted a debate about the function of concepts like *authenticity, modernity, folk,* and *art* in shaping the narratives of the Negro Renaissance. In November 1925, an *Opportunity* editorial identified two schools of thought. One believed that "the songs should be preserved in all their native simplicity"; the other that "the original tunes should be used as the basis for the limitless development of a new music which would, of course, preserve the distinguishing characteristics of the original." Thus authenticity was posed against artistry, and people lined up to support either the supposedly "natural" baritone of Paul Robeson or the trained, Europeanized tenor of Roland Hayes.

In *The Book of American Negro Spirituals*, published by J. Rosamond Johnson and James Weldon Johnson, the latter was carefully even-handed. Through his "supreme artistry," Hayes was taking the spirituals "high above the earth"; he "sheds over them shimmering silver of moonlight and flashes of the sun's gold." In contrast, it is through "sheer simplicity, without any conscious attempt at artistic effort," that Robeson "achieves substantially the same effect." For Johnson, it was less important whether Hayes or Robeson was more *authentic*, than that they were both manifestly *sincere*: "they both feel the Spirituals deeply." The poet Carl Sandburg, an occasional contributor to the *Crisis*, was less diplomatic. Hayes "imitates white culture and uses methods from the white man's conservatories of music" and, as a result, his delivery of spirituals attracts praise for its educated musical technique. Robeson singing spirituals, on the other hand, is "the real thing" and Sandburg's reaction is that he "kept of the best of himself" and had "not allowed the schools to take it away from him."

Van Vechten, of course, championed his protégé Robeson. In a program note for a later concert, he contrasted the authenticity of Robeson and Brown's "evangelical, true Negro rendering" against the "sanctimonious, lugubrious" delivery of spirituals and "the pseudo-refinement of the typical concert singer." Their aim was "to restore, as far as they are able, the spirit of the original primitive interpretation to these Spirituals." Once again, the "authentic" was being conflated with the "primitive," and then contrasted against a white Western culture that had become overrefined and inauthentic. James Weldon Johnson also believed that the spirituals "cannot be properly appreciated or understood unless they are clothed in their primitive dignity" and praised Robeson's "devoted adherence to the primitive traditions." At the same time, again like the Johnson brothers, Van Vechten was well aware that, in performance, the primitivism of "these simple, spontaneous outpourings from the heart of an oppressed race" had to be, if not manufactured, then, at least, artfully recreated. "Under primitive conditions," he noted, the spirituals had always been "sung in harmony by a chorus, one voice leading with a verse to which the chorus responds." Robeson and Brown modernized this tradition, for their concert performances, by having Robeson undertake the solo parts, "while Lawrence Brown sang the choral responses, the piano filling in the harmonies." A major part of Brown's contribution to the partnership lay in his ability to rework the songs, not only to fit Robeson's voice, but also to give their performances "natural" and "authentic."

"I'm afraid we shall never agree on the subject of the Spirituals," Van Vechten wrote to Alain Locke in October 1925. In his *New Negro* article on "The Negro Spirituals," Locke had accepted Van Vechten's criticism that some "Negro composers," like Burleigh, may have been "too much influenced by formal European idioms and mannerisms in setting these songs," but he resisted any forced choice between Robeson's "robust and dramatic style" and Hayes's "subdued, ecstatic and spiritually refined versions," on the grounds that the folk tradition embraces both. His preference for Hayes was clear, however. The spirituals were "caught in the transitional stage between a folk form and an art form." Preserving their folk authenticity was essential, but Locke did not accept that this should mean confining them to "'simple versions' and musically primitive molds." Looking to the future, Locke foresaw that "an inevitable art development awaits" the spirituals, just as "in the past it has awaited all other great folk music." In Hayes's delivery, Locke heard the creative tension between folk authenticity and modern artistry. Hayes had a "voice of artistic paradoxes," a voice "refined but unaffected, cultivated but still simple." He had retained the "primitive race gift," but transformed it through a formal musical development that was both "critical and sophisticated."

For Robeson, the partnership with Brown offered an opportunity for rehabilitation after the wounding criticism of his appearances in O'Neill's plays. The "deep racial quality" in his delivery of the spirituals was widely acknowledged, and Paul Robeson was once again being hailed as "the embodiment of the aspirations of the New Negro." Achieving the status of Hayes, but with broader popular appeal, not only made obvious career sense, it also suggested how Robeson might be recognized as an engaged and responsible artist. When Robeson sang spirituals, he presented "the distinctive gift the Negro has made to America," yet he did so in a style that was "in keeping with the aspirations of the modern Negro." He had found a voice that combined the folkloric legacy of the Negro diaspora, with the ethnographic modernity of the renaissance.

There was a third, dissenting view on all this, pointedly expressed by two women writers. In her contribution to Nancy Cunard's *Negro*, Zora Neale Hurston, an anthropologist as well as a novelist, deplored the appearance of "neo-spirituals." Without naming names, she seems to have had both Roland Hayes and Paul Robeson in her sights—Essie certainly, and resentfully, thought so—when she complained that concert singers might "put on their tuxedos, bow prettily to their audience, get the pitch and burst into magnificent song," but what they sang was "not *Negro* song." However much Robeson may have aspired to an authentic delivery, the spirituals as recreated by Brown and others lacked ethnographic authenticity: "All good work and beautiful—but *not* the spirituals." Gertrude Stein was even more succinct.

Zora Neale Hurston, 1935 (Carl Van Vechten)

As Robeson fashioned a persona for the times, she warned her friend not to overinvest in the spirituals. "Gertrude Stein did not like hearing him sing spirituals," records *The Autobiography of Alice B. Toklas*. "They do not belong to you any more than anything else, so why claim them, she said. He did not answer."

We Younger Artists

When Alain Locke predicted that a future "art development" of the spirituals was "inevitable," he was wrong. The reworking of the spirituals by the renaissance composers, and the performances of Roland Hayes and Paul Robeson, turned out to be their high point and, pretty much, their end point. Locke's overoptimism reveals a blind spot in renaissance thinking: the way that an emphasis on *folk* roots, as the basis for a future art, tended to entail a disdain for modern black *vernacular* culture. This alternative culture found its most eloquent advocate in Langston Hughes, whose ecumenical vision embraced the vernacular alongside the avant-garde. In his famous 1926 polemic "The

Negro Artist and the Racial Mountain," Hughes proclaimed that his generation of writers, artists, and performers was creating an aesthetic that was "truly racial" ("like the singing of Robeson"), and yet also distinctively American and modern. Indifferent to anxieties about the purity or authenticity of its cultural lineage, their bricolage mixed invented traditions of an African origin with imagined narratives of black experience in the South and, not least, with contemporary commercial culture.

> Let the blare of Negro jazz bands and the bellowing voice of Bessie Smith singing Blues penetrate the closed ears of the colored near-intellectuals until they listen and perhaps understand. Let Paul Robeson singing "Water Boy," and Rudolph Fisher writing about the streets of Harlem, and Jean Toomer holding the heart of Georgia in his hands, and Aaron Douglas drawing strange black fantasies cause the smug Negro middle class to turn from their white, respectable, ordinary books and papers and catch a glimmer of their own beauty. We younger artists who create now intend to express our individual dark-skinned selves without fear or shame. If white people are pleased we are glad. If they are not, it doesn't matter. We know we are beautiful. And ugly too. The tom-tom cries and the tom-tom laughs.

Jazz was at the heart of Hughes's modernism. As "one of the inherent expressions of Negro life in America," it expressed both the primordial—"the

Langston Hughes, 1932 (Carl Van Vechten)

eternal tom-tom beating in the Negro soul"—and the new: "the tom-tom of revolt against weariness in a white world, a world of subway trains, and work, work, work; the tom-tom of joy and laughter and pain swallowed in a smile." Given this creative potential, Hughes teased, why worry if one audience's myth of origins is read by another audience as exotica? "We know we are beautiful."

For Paul Robeson, however, jazz was a worry. Although Hughes saw Robeson as a fellow member of the jazz generation, and although Essie's diary in the mid-1920s records happy visits to Harlem nightspots, Robeson's public utterances about jazz were hostile. Unlike the spirituals, the folk origins of jazz had been warped by its commercial exploitation. Jazz "reflects Broadway, not the Negro. It exploits a Negro technique, but it isn't Negro." The music may retain "something of the Negro sense of rhythm, but only some." Because jazz "is no longer the honest and sincere folk-song in character," it can claim "no spiritual significance." It will have no "serious effect on real music."

In *The New Negro*, J. A. Rogers tried to redeem jazz by adopting a typical renaissance critical strategy. On the one hand, Rogers extrapolated whatever elements in jazz, ragtime, and blues could be attributed to a folk heritage and folk values, and welcomed the way even a commercial form like jazz (as then understood) was perpetuating them. On the other hand, he looked forward to the potential future development of the music, both artistically and socially. To balance jazz's acknowledged links to a shady nightlife culture, its appropriation by a white-dominated entertainment industry, and the need to expunge its artistic "vulgarities and crudities," Rogers invoked a familiar rhetoric of cultural eugenics—this time, the conductor, Leopold Stokowski, enthusing that jazz would "have the same revivifying effect as the injection of new, and in the larger sense, vulgar blood into dying aristocracy." Rogers then made a link to an analogous social function for jazz in "the daily lives of people." As a "leveller," jazz "makes for democracy." Its "popular mission" would be to put "more reality in life" by "taking some of the needless artificiality out." Jazz could encourage spontaneity and communal participation, and so it made the expression of "joy" possible. Given this capacity, Rogers concluded that the wise response was not to protest against jazz, but instead to "try to lift and divert it into nobler channels."

This "nobler" jazz would, in Rogers's view, build on the disciplined, "symphonic" music of orchestras "like those of Will Marion Cook, Paul Whiteman, Sissle and Blake, Sam Stewart, Fletcher Henderson, Vincent Lopez, and the Clef Club Units." They did not yet display the soon-to-emerge jazz ideals of spontaneity, individual brilliance, and improvisation, but rather the New Negro virtues of musical sophistication, polished self-presentation, and exemplary competence. The interesting transitional figure among the various black and white bandleaders cited by

Rogers, and also a revealing point of comparison with Paul Robeson, is Fletcher Henderson, who was recognized as the leading figure among the middle-class black musicians bringing a new professionalism to the business of popular music in Harlem.

Henderson and Robeson were born within four months of each other, they were both college graduates, and they arrived in Harlem within a year of each other, both planning further study at Columbia—a Masters in chemistry, in Henderson's case—before deciding to switch careers. The two men's paths crossed from time to time. Early in 1923, for example, "F. Henderson, Paramount Recording Wizard" featured as pianist in a new Clef Club Orchestra formed by Will Marion Cook, with which Robeson appeared as a guest singer at least once. Growing up in Georgia, Henderson had been immersed in European concert music, with the result that, when he arrived in Harlem, he was no jazz musician. Instead, he started as an apprentice in a changing industry. For the first time, "mechanical royalties," based on the sale of records, were becoming more important as a source of revenue than sheet music sales, and the success of Mamie Smith's "Crazy Blues" in 1920 had led to a boom in "race records." Henderson soon graduated from being a song plugger and arranger to accompanying some of the leading women blues singers of the time, including Bessie Smith. He was also appointed musical director of the new Black Swan label, which was originally intended to specialize in "uplifting" music, but which actually succeeded by releasing the blues of Alberta Hunter, Trixie Smith, and Ethel Waters. Ethel Waters saw that her music "isn't his kind at all," when Henderson spent seven months on the road with her, but it was through this range of experience that Henderson was transforming himself into a certain kind of jazz musician. By 1923, as well as being the most widely recorded accompanist in New York, Henderson was gathering the nucleus of a regular band around him. His musicians had to meet two criteria: they should be able to play jazz, but, above all, they had to be able to read music. His was the first black band to make its name through recording. Although it only began to play "live" at Club Alabam in January 1924, between spring 1923 and October 1924, when Louis Armstrong joined, the band released nearly one hundred sides. Henderson was also quick to seize the opportunities opened up by radio: his orchestra began regular broadcasts from the Roseland Ballroom in 1924.

By 1925, when Paul Robeson and Larry Brown developed a concert style that, they believed, could reanimate the "authentic" folk tradition of the spirituals in a modern presentation, Fletcher Henderson had learned an assortment of musical idioms and he was contributing to the creation of a new music. In his music, jazz or not, Henderson absorbed and reworked elements of the classical tradition, blues and ragtime, as well as contemporary urban popular music. Following in the footsteps of Will Marion Cook and

James Reese Europe, he had recalibrated his respectable, but restricted, musical formation to fit Harlem's cosmopolitan and liberated ethos. This journey involved less a search for folk roots or racial authenticity, than Henderson's self-reinvention as a modern American musician. His emerging style epitomized the principle of jazz celebrated by *Opportunity* in 1925. "The Negroes," claimed the journal, not only expressed the spirit of "modern American life" through jazz, but they had also discovered, in jazz, "the key to the interpretation of the American spirit."

In later years, after the jazz wars of the 1940s, a normative history of the music set in place a teleology of black expressivity that saw nothing but inauthenticity and compromise in Henderson's achievements during the 1920s. Even his foresight in hiring Louis Armstrong was turned against him, as Armstrong, and the great improvisers who followed him, were claimed in retrospect to have foreshadowed *real* jazz (improvisatory and often noncommercial) as opposed to *false* jazz (formal and unashamedly commercial). It is true that Armstrong, rather than Henderson, embodied the most compelling future forms of jazz, although it was only in 1927 and 1928 that he began to record the "hot jazz" subsequently used by critics to redefine the criteria for both authenticity and value. Despite his influence on Duke Ellington's style and the swing bands of the 1930s more broadly, Henderson's was not the main road followed by jazz. In the mid-1920s, however, in the Harlem of the renaissance, his music was accepted as original, American, black, and modern.

If Fletcher Henderson's orchestra is sometimes heard, with the condescension of historical judgment, as being not "authentic" enough, then it is reasonable to ask what Paul Robeson did next in pursuing his own negotiation of the demands for authenticity and the need for a career, after *Emperor Jones* and the spirituals. The answer, of course, is that he took on his third defining role of the 1920s, as the shiftless stevedore Joe, singing "Ol' Man River" in *Show Boat*, first on Drury Lane, then on Broadway, and finally in Hollywood. Robeson complained that jazz "reflects Broadway, not the Negro." However often it was (and is) called a spiritual, "Ol' Man River" is Broadway through and through, authentic pastiche if it is authentic anything. J. A. Rogers, by now European correspondent for the *Amsterdam News*, reported black reactions to the opening of *Show Boat* in London in 1928. He heard "many harsh things" being said about Robeson "for lending his talent and popularity toward making it a success." "If anyone were to call him a 'nigger', he'd be the first to get offended," protested one interviewee, "and there he is singing 'nigger, nigger' before all those white people."

Both Paul Robeson and Fletcher Henderson had tried to achieve the difficult balance between commercial success and professional integrity, while creating a musical style that was uniquely black, and yet also modern and American. And just as Henderson was overtaken by the more radical innovations of Louis Armstrong, so Robeson's reclamation of the spirituals was eventually displaced by a rejuvenated style of popular religious music apparently untouched by the aspirations and anxieties of the renaissance. This new gospel music represented a move away from the allegory of the spirituals, or the formality of the hymnal, toward a more sensual Christian blues, which seemed to capture the intensely personal nature of black American spirituality. The difference can be heard in a song like "Precious Lord," written in 1932 by Thomas A. Dorsey, who, as the hokum blues singer and pianist Georgia Tom, had made successful records in the 1920s with the guitarist Tampa Red. (The bawdy "Tight Like That" sold over a million copies.) Dorsey had also built a reputation to rival Henderson's as an accompanist to blues singers like Ma Rainey. Drawing on that background, he introduced a feeling of "gut-bucket heartache" (Langston Hughes again) into religious music, using jazz-inflected rhythms, direct language, and a more intimate address that gave his songs an urgent, and almost erotic, charge. Decades later, in the 1960s and 1970s, Dorsey's music was part of the soundtrack to the Civil Rights movement, and it also spawned the Gospel tradition of Mahalia Jackson, Sam Cooke, and Aretha Franklin, which eventually crossed over and was resecularized in the 1950s and 1960s as an assertively African American soul music. Like bop and its successors, Dorsey's legacy thus helped to displace the myths of diaspora, in favor of an ethnographic, or "ethnic," understanding of race and African American self-expression.

After the event, Langston Hughes reflected wryly that most Harlemites "hadn't heard of the Negro Renaissance. And if they had, it hadn't raised their wages any." Not so for Paul Robeson, even leaving his future earning power to one side. (His success in *Show Boat* gave him long-term financial security.) By the time he moved to Europe, Robeson had been formed within a certain American modernism. Or, it might be more accurate to say, he had internalized, without yet resolving, the fluid relationship between three variants of modernism in 1920s New York: first, Alain Locke's strategic blending of cosmopolitanism with "cultural racialism"; second, the free-thinking, anti-Victorian bohemianism of Carl Van Vechten and Eugene O'Neill in Greenwich Village; and, third, the vernacular modernism that emerged as Langston Hughes's "younger generation" of black artists remixed avant-garde with popular culture. As a result, Robeson arrived in London as an accomplished performer with a developed sense of racial pride and a not wholly formed commitment to progressive and libertarian ideas, used to being lionized socially, sensitive to insult or condescension, and tractable when it came to balancing artistic and ethical principles against the needs of his career. The story of Paul Robeson's later life would largely be determined by the interaction between this formation and the contending rhythms of European modernity that he encountered in the 1930s.

Auguste Perret, Théâtre des Champs-Élysées, Paris, 1911–1912

Between the Jungle and the Skyscraper

JOSEPHINE BAKER IN PARIS AND BERLIN

In 1925, the American writer Janet Flanner had just started her long-term residency as Paris correspondent for the *New Yorker*. One of her early letters reported the arrival of Josephine Baker and *La Revue nègre*. "Paris has never drawn a colour line," Flanner told her readers. "It likes blondes, brunettes, or Bakers, more now than ever." Looking back fifty years later, in her memoirs, Flanner accused herself of writing "like a dullard." In an attempt to convey the layers of memory, myth, and historical significance that had been generated by the *danse sauvage* that closed the *Revue*, she rewrote the record. Baker made her entry, as Flanner now told the story, almost naked, "being carried upside down and doing the split on the shoulder of a black giant." After a pause, he "swung her in a slow cartwheel to the stage floor, where she stood like his magnificent discarded burden, in an instant of complete silence. She was an unforgettable female ebony statue." In that moment, Josephine Baker's "magnificent dark body" appeared as "a new model that to the French proved for the first time that black was beautiful." Compared with that first visceral impression on the astonished audience, "whatever happened next was unimportant."

The argument here is that, contrary to what Janet Flanner says, "what happened next" in Josephine Baker's Paris debut *was* important, in the sense that, as well as being a performance, the *danse sauvage* was an *event*: a scandalous moment when something new was created through a relay of cultural misreading, parody, *bricolage*, and masquerade. To explain why it took the form it did, or to account for the passionate reactions it provoked by appealing, as Flanner did, to the anachronistic 1970s slogan "black is beautiful" is inadequate. Terms from the time are needed. In Harlem, Alain Locke had overlain a "cultural racialism" onto philosophical cosmopolitanism, in order to win recognition for the "American Negro." In Paris, a comparable mishmash between the cosmopolitan and a version of "the racial" was designed to achieve recognition for *La Revue nègre*, the *danse sauvage* and the star persona of "Josephine Baker." The Parisian experiment was less philosophically considered and politically strategic than aesthetically improvised and culturally opportunistic. Even so, the dance that emerged was both a modern phenomenon and a modernist performance.

La Revue nègre

The premiere of *La Revue nègre*, on October 2, 1925, lasted about three-quarters of an hour and made up the second half of an evening's entertainment at the Théâtre des Champs-Élysées on the avenue Montaigne in Paris. Before the event, the audience's expectations had been aroused by a striking publicity poster, designed by the artist Paul Colin (see Plate 3). The image made use of dramatic variations in the size of the type, deployed just three colors—red, black, and white—and depicted three figures. The iconography alluded to the styles on display at the city's current *Exposition internationale des arts décoratifs et industriels modernes*, which gave a name to Art Deco, and it also shows the influence of caricatures of Harlem figures in *Vanity Fair*, drawn by Miguel Covarrubias, *La Revue nègre*'s young Mexican designer. An iconic "Josephine Baker" figure, with hip cocked, arms akimbo, and hair slicked down is the smallest of the three figures, set off-center as the apex of a triangle of figures. The other two, larger and more to the fore, are a moon-faced man in a tuxedo, which fails to do justice to the show's handsome bandleader Claude Hopkins, if it is supposed to be him, and the revue's choreographer and tap dancer, Louis Douglas, in a bowler hat. Red is used to accentuate their Negroid lips, and they are given wide black-and-white eyes. Although such features were often used to make black subjects look bewildered and bestial, here the effect is to make the entertainers appear alert and spirited. Despite the gross stereotypes, the message that comes across is that "energetic, rhythmic, boldly new entertainers have arrived." A marketing strategy was set in place to reinforce Colin's poster and to ensure that *La Revue nègre* would be a media event. Just four days after the troupe's arrival, and a week before the premiere, a select audience of celebrities and journalists was invited to a midnight preview of two scenes from the show, followed by a lavish champagne supper party. Among the guests were the music-hall star Mistinguett and negrophile artists and intellectuals, including Fernand Léger, Paul Guillaume, and Kees Van Dongen. Josephine Baker, now dressed in a gown by Paul Poiret, made her entry on the arm of Paul Colin. The campaign was a success, to the extent that the opening night audience included Gertrude Stein, Francis Picabia, Blaise Cendrars, Robert Desnos, Man Ray, and Jean Cocteau—who returned six times, not least because his lover, the bantamweight boxing champion Panama Al Brown, had joined the company as a tap dancer.

The "Mississippi Steam Boat Race" scene from La Revue nègre, *Paris, 1925*

The seven sketches in *La Revue nègre*, set against Miguel Covarrubias's colorful backdrops, were designed to show off the talents of the two dozen members of the company and, supposedly, to reflect aspects of black American life. The music was composed by the New Orleans musician and songwriter Spencer Williams and played by a seven-piece Charleston Jazz Band led by Hopkins, a young Howard University graduate. Of the featured performers, Sidney Bechet played an extended clarinet solo in "The Peanut Vendor," Louis Douglas demonstrated his rubber-legged tap in "Les Pieds qui parlent," and Maud de Forest sang the blues in "Louisiana Camp Meeting." As for Josephine Baker, in the opening "Mississippi Steam Boat Race" sketch, in blackface and Topsy costume, she sang "Yes Sir, That's My Baby," crossing her eyes and twisting her body into bizarre shapes, then danced the Charleston and sang "I Want to Yodel" in the "New York Skyscraper" sketch, and mimed a fight with Maud de Forest as two brides expecting to marry Louis Douglas in "Louisiana Camp Meeting," before reappearing for the *danse sauvage* in the final "Charleston Cabaret". This delirious representation of black America for that Parisian audience, at that moment and in that theater, was designed to create something that was challenging and progressive, as well as profitable. If *La Revue nègre* was incoherent in focus, tone, and style, that is because it embodied the conflicting understandings of "America" and, especially, of "blackness" by its two producers, Caroline Dudley Reagan and Rolf de Maré.

Caroline Dudley Reagan was a young heiress in a shaky marriage to the American commercial attaché in Paris. Her father, a wealthy liberal Chicago physician, had often invited black guests to dinner when she was a child; Caroline liked to claim that she had grown up "on Booker T. Washington's knee." Dr. Dudley also took Caroline to vaudeville shows on State Street, where she heard ragtime and the beginnings of jazz, and saw the work of black American dancers and comedians. With time on her hands as an embassy wife, wanting to make her own mark in the world, and encouraged by Carl Van Vechten, Caroline Dudley traveled from France to Harlem to recruit performers for "a show of authentic Negro vaudeville" that would celebrate "their independence and their savagery, and also that glorious sensual exuberance that certain critics call indecency." Rolf de Maré was a wealthy Swedish enthusiast for the visual arts, dance, and ethnography. He had invested early in the work of Picasso, Braque, and Léger, and he had accumulated a substantial collection of ethnographic artifacts during his travels around the world. He developed his interest in dance in the late 1910s, and established the Ballets Suédois in 1920 as a vehicle for his lover, the dancer Jean Börlin. At the same time, de Maré discreetly bought the lease of the Théâtre des Champs-Élysées to provide the company with a home.

In the five years of its existence, the Ballets Suédois was at least as experimental as its major rival, Diaghilev's Ballets Russes, but the company also developed a distinctive interest in popular culture, *l'art nègre*, and America. One of its 1922 productions was *Skating Rink*, choreographed by Börlin with music by Arthur Honegger and designs by Fernand Léger, which was based on a poem by the Italian Futurist Riciotto Canudo, that in turn derived from Charlie Chaplin's 1916 film *The Rink*. *La Création du monde*, in 1923, was their attempt at a *ballet nègre*, again with choreography by Börlin and designs by Léger, but this time based on African creation myths collected by Blaise Cendrars and with Milhaud's jazz-influenced score. (The other half of that bill was Cole Porter's *Over the Quota*, about the predicament of a Swedish immigrant to the United States.) *Relâche*, in 1924, was the company's last and most controversial ballet. Conceived by the Dadaist Francis Picabia, with music by Erik Satie, it incorporated a screening of René Clair's experimental film *Entr'acte*, in which Picabia and Satie appeared with Marcel Duchamp and Man Ray. De Maré disbanded the Ballets Suédois at the beginning of 1925, when the company was close to bankruptcy and Börlin, suffering from nervous exhaustion, had decamped. At a time when the franc was collapsing and the Paris entertainment industry was having to rely on the dollars of American tourists, de Maré had to decide what to do with the remaining year of the Théâtre des Champs-Élysées lease. He announced that he would be changing its name to the Opéra Music-Hall des Champs-Élysées and presenting work that would combine the popular appeal of music hall with the quality of opera. By April, the stage had been converted to that of a *théâtre music-hall*, and in September Caroline Dudley's troupe arrived from New York.

Years later, in the last of her several autobiographies, Josephine Baker still recalled the sting of de Maré's appalled reaction to the first run-through. "We had thought our show was marvellous and Monsieur Rolf's verdict— 'Catastrophic'—struck us like a thunderclap." Even if Caroline Dudley's image of "real" Negro vaudeville was based on her memories of Chicago, it had also been influenced by Broadway shows like *Shuffle Along* and *Runnin' Wild*, as had the performers, who had learned to adapt to white audience expectations, while working in those shows and in the clubs of New York. For de Maré, schooled in European modernism and alert to his contemporaries' voyeuristic interest in black performances and black bodies, Caroline Dudley's package made too many concessions, or the wrong type of concession. There was too much tap, the chorus-line was too mechanical, and Maud de Forest's blues were too lugubrious. There was too much toned-down Broadway, not enough Ballets Suédois radicalism. *La Revue nègre* just wasn't sexy enough, primitive enough, or *black* enough for the audience de Maré was after.

De Maré and his artistic director, André Daven, therefore set about changing the tone of the show, even though they had less than two weeks for

Josephine Baker and Joe Alex perform the danse sauvage

rehearsals. De Maré "was an able and agreeable taskmaster," recalled Baker, "and we did what he wanted although it meant working night and day." To add a more populist touch, Daven turned to his friend Jacques Charles, a producer at the Moulin Rouge. Although Charles claimed that it was he who revamped the show, plucking an unknown Baker from the chorus and making her a star, his role was probably always secondary to that of de Maré. There was, in any case, no dispute that Josephine Baker, rather than Maud de Forest, should be the star. Adding the *danse sauvage* to the final scene does seem to have been Charles's idea, however, and he hired Joe Alex, a Martinician dancer already working in Paris, to partner Baker. The new pas de deux was supposed to make the show more "African," by recreating the eroticism and exoticism of *La Création du monde* or Paul Guillaume's 1919 *Fête nègre*. At the rehearsals, de Maré and Daven asked Baker if she could perform an African dance. "Driven by dark forces I didn't recognise, I improvised, crazed by the music, the overheated theatre filled to the bursting point, the scorching eye of the spotlights," wrote Baker, again burnishing history to fit the myth. "Each time I leaped I seemed to touch the sky and when I regained earth it seemed to be mine alone." Rather than conjuring up anything truly atavistic, Baker's "dark forces" in reality represented a negotiation between de Maré's mediated vision of Africa and her own cultural and technical formation as a dancer in the black American entertainment industry.

Growing up in East St. Louis, and then touring with the Dixie Steppers, Josephine Baker would have learned dances like the Mess Around, the Itch, and Trucking, and, while in the *Shuffle Along* chorus, she performed contemporary black dances like the Shimmy, the Buck-and-Wing, and the Texas Tommy, as well as the Charleston and the Black Bottom. On Broadway, Baker started to carve out her own niche. Against all the rules of an ensemble dancer, she stood out, as a *Dance Magazine* critic observed, by "letting her knees fold under her, eccentric wise" and then, at the climax of the show's hit song, "I'm Just Wild about Harry," she crossed her eyes. Although there may have been "nothing very beautiful about a cross-eyed coloured girl," nevertheless "it was the folding knees and the cross-eyes that helped bring back the choruses for those unforgettable encores." Sissle and Blake indulged this scene-stealing, to a degree, because they recognized her talent and the force of her personality. Noble Sissle, especially, explained how to construct and pace an act, instead of relying on spontaneity and mugging. Although, when faced with an audience, Baker would often revert to attention-seeking, she did develop a degree of self-discipline. "She began to realize," Sissle reflected, "that a finished artist always knew what to do next and could weave a pattern of tricks and effects into an interesting sequence." Her clowning, however ingratiating and embarrassing, had, in any case, served its purpose. It got her noticed in New York. In *The Chocolate Dandies*, the 1924 follow-up to *Shuffle Along*, Sissle and Blake continued to make use of Baker's reputation, casting her as the blackface ragamuffin Topsy Anna, wearing bright cotton smocks and clown shoes. In the final scene, however, they had her reappear as a femme fatale, in an elegant white satin gown with a slit up the left leg, vamping the featured comedians Lew Payton and Johnny Hudgins. At this time, Ethel Waters identified Baker's transitional status: still a chorus girl, but a chorus girl permitted to perform a specialty turn in each show. "Josephine was a mugger with a great comic sense, and she had a beautiful form," judged Waters. "She could dance and she could clown joy into you."

These, then, were the hard-won abilities Josephine Baker brought to her improvisation for Rolf de Maré: athletic dancing, nerveless clowning, knowing how to work an American audience. She was driven, not by some throwback to Africa, but by her will to succeed and a ruthless desire to please her audience. Her formal moves were probably close to those she had learned on the streets of St. Louis or in the chorus lines of New York, but if "Monsieur Rolf" wanted African primitivism, then African primitivism was what he would get. However fantastic the conceptions of "authenticity," and however confused the signals between impresario and dancer, the occasion actually drew from Baker an expressively fresh style of dance.

In his work with Baker, Rolf de Maré would have been conscious of the need to tailor the *danse sauvage* to fit the space and the ambience in which it would be performed. The Théâtre des Champs-Élysées was located some way away from the main entertainment centers of Paris, and that distance signified its niche in the life of the city. It had always offered an alternative to both commercial show business and the stiff official culture of the Paris Opera. The theater was built in 1913, to a comparatively austere initial design by the Belgian Art Nouveau architect Henry van de Velde, which was adapted and completed by Auguste Perret. From the start, its purpose was to present modern music, dance, and opera for a sophisticated audience—one contemporary described the Théâtre as "a sacred asylum where dilettantes concocted a kind of modernism." This reputation was secured, within months of its opening, when the premiere of Nijinsky's production of Stravinsky's *Le Sacre du printemps*, on May 29, 1913, provoked a near riot—to be followed by another, ten years later, when the "bad boy of American music," George Antheil, played his new work *Mechanisms*, as a prelude to a Ballets Suédois performance. (This fracas was filmed by Marcel l'Herbier and included in *L'Inhumaine*, in 1924.) The theater had also started to present jazz concerts as the Great War was ending. In August 1918, James Reese Europe's Harlem Hellfighters performed for allied officers, before sailing back to New York, and the following year Will Marion Cook and his Southern Syncopated Orchestra appeared, after their English tour and their royal command performance. This unconventional theater's *genius loci* was the American dancer Isadora Duncan, whose body provided the model for all the bas-reliefs on the façade, by Émile-Antoine Bourdelle, depicting Apollo and the Muses, and whose image appeared in the interior murals and frescoes by Maurice Denis. In his memoirs, Paul Colin commented that, when the *Revue nègre* performers arrived, the figures in these frescoes "seemed to stiffen at the sight of this black tumult": "Celestial harpists reacted in visible horror to the clattering sound of tap shoes."

The ghostly presence of Isadora Duncan in the fabric of the Théâtre des Champs-Élysées brings into focus some of the significant issues about Josephine Baker's performance there: dance, nature, the female body, and decorum. Both Duncan and Baker danced almost naked and, as Janet Flanner recorded, what electrified the audience for *La Revue nègre* was, above all, Baker's "magnificent dark body." To see Baker's unclothed body was to contradict, spectacularly, many European myths about black female anatomy. It was not just her color that startled them, but the fact that here was a different *type* of female body: "a new model" that was recognizably modern and whose beauty lay in its athleticism and its energy rather than in voluptuousness or any play of concealment and display. Although the press may have chosen to treat Isadora Duncan's nudity as a scandalous act of exposure, her audiences had, for the most part, accepted that performing with minimal clothing was an aesthetic decision about the costume most appropriate to her dance. Duncan and Baker both enacted a "back to nature" fantasy for at least some

Josephine Baker on the roof of the Théâtre des Champs-Élysées, 1925

spectators. Whereas Duncan embodied Greek purity and a classical ideal of unspoiled humanity, however, Baker represented African primitivism allied to modern energy. Both chains of association gestured toward something lost, but potentially recoverable in the present through the ritual of their dance. If Duncan's celebration of the body signified a rejection of industrial culture in favor of nature, the sight of Baker's body in motion—like the sound of jazz—was recognized as a product of machine-age modernity, but at the same time as something elemental or natural or primitive that might redeem the abstraction and rationality of the age. Baker's nudity did not suggest a nakedness beyond or outside culture. It was a distinctive costume, chosen to condense many of the complicated cultural and social meanings projected onto her.

Reactions to *La Revue nègre* and to Josephine Baker invariably revealed presuppositions about race, sexuality, the body, nudity, modernity, and much else, although some contemporaries also paid attention to the show's stylistic innovations. Conservatives were predictably alarmed about the dangers of regression to lubricity, savagery, and bestiality: the Academician Robert de Flers condemned this "lamentable transatlantic exhibitionism which makes us revert to the ape in less time than it took us to descend from it." Supporters, like the dance critic Fernand Divoire, saw Baker as the bearer of a "savage rejuvenation" that might revive French culture. More thoughtful, because more focused on her performance than her eugenic significance, was the émigré Russian ballet writer André Levinson. He grasped the dynamic of call and response between dance and music, and he understood how Baker "led the spellbound drummer and the fascinated saxophonist in the harsh rhythm of the 'blues.' . . . The music is born from the dance." In the *danse sauvage*, he responded first to its mimetic allusions. Some of Baker's poses—"back arched, haunches protruding, arms entwined and uplifted in a phallic symbol"— recalled "the finest examples of negro sculpture." "The plastic sense of a race of sculptors came to life and the frenzy of the African Eros swept over the audience," he observed, invoking familiar cultural references to make sense of her. "It was no longer a grotesque dancing girl that stood before them, but the black Venus that haunted Baudelaire." However, Levinson also recognized that Baker's dance had the power to transcend this framework and to create a moment of pure expressivity: "The dancer's personality had transcended the character of her dance" ("Sa personnalité dépasse le genre").

Another ballet critic of the time, Arnold Haskell, compared Baker unfavorably to Florence Mills, who, he felt, had been "always true to herself, proud of the true Negro origins of her art." Baker, by contrast, had been "totally Parisianised" and "always seems to me to be playing up to what the public wants the negress to be." Again, Baker's self-authoring (and so modern) performance was judged to be less ethical, or less "real," than some supposed primordial identity. The disdain toward Josephine Baker evinced by some of the Americans who saw *La Revue nègre* in Paris, including several of the jazz musicians around Paris, often combined this emphasis on being true to the race with a concern about the cultural implications of the show. Their worry was not whether it threatened to contaminate or dilute European culture, but that it failed to live up to the aspirations of the Negro renaissance on the other side of the Atlantic. Essie Robeson wrote confidentially to Carl Van Vechten that she thought the show "rotten," and despaired at Josephine's "ridiculous, vulgar, and totally uncalled for wiggling." Will Marion Cook, the composer and leader of the Southern Syncopated Orchestra, had advised Caroline Dudley about possible recruits for *La Revue nègre*, until they fell out. Louis Douglas was his son-in-law and his daughter was one of the dancers, and so Cook was positive about the quality of the performers. He was damning about the production, however, dismissing it as the latest in a series of "rank and weak imitations of sordid, unfunny white plays." "With Europe begging us for a Negro novelty, first Arthur Lyons took that awful *Chocolate Kiddies* to Berlin—and now this Paris abortion," he protested. "The prostituting of Negro talent by encouraging imitation of all that is weak, low, and vicious must stop. Let Broadway wallow in its own filth!" Cook accused Caroline Dudley of betraying genuine black culture because she knew nothing about it: "From now on let's have the real thing." In terms of a vernacular modernism, however, in Paris as in Harlem, the question was whether "the real thing" was to be discovered by tracing it back to a racially pure source, or whether it was to be created through the kind of experimental and mongrelized bricolage undertaken by Josephine Baker and Rolf de Maré.

La Folie du Jour

In December 1925, less than three months after their Paris opening, the *Revue nègre* performers took the train from Paris to Berlin. Josephine Baker immediately fell in love with the place. "The city had a jewel-like sparkle, especially at night, that didn't exist in Paris. The vast cafés reminded me of ocean liners powered by the rhythms of their orchestras. There was music everywhere." On New Year's Eve, an invitation-only performance launched a run at the Nelson Theatre. Fashionable German audiences, like those in Paris, were beguiled by Baker's combination of supposed African primitivism and manifest American modernism. "In her the wildness of her forefathers, who were transplanted from the Congo Basin to the Mississippi, is preserved most authentically," raved a reviewer for the *Berliner Tageblatt*; "she breathes life, the power of nature, a wantonness that can hardly be contained." More pragmatic in his response, and with an eye to how the characteristics and talents of American "Negroes" might be exploited aesthetically, was the theater director, Max Reinhardt. He had already seen *Shuffle Along* in New York, where, although he had admired the mobility and control of the dancers, he had been impressed above all by the expressive body language of the comedians. In this physicality he saw a potential resource for European theater. "The expressive control of the whole body, the spontaneity of motion, the rhythm, the bright emotional colour: these are your treasures—no, not yours alone—these are American treasures," he told Baker, as he tried to persuade her to take up a "serious" career on the stage. "With such control of the body, such pantomime, I believe I could portray emotion as it has never been portrayed." Reinhardt introduced Baker to his friend, the wealthy aesthete Count Harry Kessler. Equally captivated, Kessler tried to unscramble the mixed signals he was receiving from *La Revue nègre*: "They are somehow between the jungle and the skyscraper. The same is true of her music, jazz, in its colour and rhythm. It is ultraprimitive and ultramodern. Their tension generates their forceful style." Kessler had collaborated with Diaghilev before the war, and now he compared the power of these American performers to the impact of the Ballets Russes. Both "Negroes" and "Russians" showed how overintellectualized and tame German culture had become: "without inner tension and therefore without style, like a limp bow string."

Despite Reinhardt's offer of a contract in Berlin, Baker eventually decided to return to Paris and honor her commitment to star in the Folies-Bergère revue for 1926, *La Folie du Jour*. This was the engagement that established her as a star with broad appeal, rather than a fashionable avant-garde enthusiasm, and it was here that she first wore the skirt of bananas that was to become her

Josephine Baker as Fatou, from the Folies-Bergère programme for La Folie du Jour, *1926*

trademark (plate 4). Her new routines shifted her image away from the fantasized America-Africa of *La Revue nègre* to a more explicitly French colonial backdrop. At the Folies-Bergère on opening night to write up *La Folie du Jour* for *Vanity Fair* was the poet e. e. cummings. He tried to capture the essence of Baker's performance in the famous Fatou sketch, in which a "native girl" materializes before a dreaming French explorer asleep by a river in the jungle. "She enters through a dense electric twilight, walking backwards on hands and feet, legs and arms stiff, down a huge jungle tree," begins cummings, but words soon begin to fail him as he attempts to capture the essence of what she is. Just as Harry Kessler found that Baker eluded the available categories of explanation—she was *ultra*-primitive and *ultra*-modern—so cummings was reduced to defining her by saying what she is not: "a creature neither infrahuman nor superhuman but somehow both: a mysterious unkillable Something, equally nonprimitive and uncivilized, or beyond time in the sense that emotion is beyond arithmetic." Rather than lingering on the question of what this unkillable Something that resists representation might be, cummings instead disavows the incoherence of his response and shifts his focus onto Baker's new Parisian incarnation. He had already seen her on Broadway, doing her antithetical turn in the chorus line of *The Chocolate Dandies*. Then, she had been a "tall, vital, incomparably fluid nightmare which crossed its eyes and warped its limbs in a purely unearthly manner," scandalously subverting the anonymity and order of the ensemble. Now, implausibly, through the mechanics of revues, which "use everything trivial or plural to intensify what is *singular and fundamental*," Josephine Baker had been transformed into the most beautiful star of the Paris stage. "In the case of the Folies-Bergère, the revue is a use of ideas, smells, colours, Irving Berlin, nudes, tactility, collapsible stairs, three dimensions and fireworks to intensify Mlle. Josephine Baker."

Covering the event for *Vogue* was Nancy Cunard, the rebel shipping heiress, poet, and anti-racist activist, who also recognized that what was singular and fundamental in the show was the personality of its star. *La Folie du Jour* "might very easily be called rotten," reported Cunard, "but can be sat through, even to twelve-thirty, because of the perfect delight one gets from Josephine Baker. She makes all the nudity and glitter of the rest (even the so well-drilled Tiller Girls) curiously insipid by comparison." Now that she had escaped from the line once and for all, Baker could be more relaxed with the members of the chorus. The young women in that Tiller troupe in Paris remembered her as being unusually friendly for a top-of-the-bill performer. Although she was about the same age as them—they would have been in their late teens or early twenties—and she had been a star for only a few months, they recognized that they were "worlds apart as women and as performers." Trained to "sink their personalities into the line," one of them recalled, these Tiller girls were "filled with admiration for her highly individual personality."

Nancy Cunard, 1926 (Man Ray)

Mass Ornament

However "insipid" Nancy Cunard found them in Paris, a year later the Tiller Girls became the subject of one of Siegfried Kracauer's most important Weimar essays. At the time, he was editing the arts and culture section of the left-liberal *Frankfurter Zeitung*, and using his position on the newspaper to develop a style of cultural criticism that, mixing Simmel with Freud, analyzed an epoch's "inconspicuous surface-level expressions," which "by virtue of their unconscious nature," open up "unmediated access to the fundamental substance of the state of things." In the case of "The Mass Ornament," Kracauer looked at the popularity of the dance troupes, along with a fashion for elaborately choreographed mass gymnastic displays. There was nothing especially novel in writing about the Tiller Girls as a "surface-level" symptom of modern mass culture. A cartoon the previous year had shown them rolling off Henry Ford's mass-production line, and a leading theater critic, Herbert Ihering, had already made a connection between the rhythm of the revue form—and especially its dancing girls—and "the needs of the modern metropolis": "the audience reacts to movement, to tempo. . . . The rhythm, the lightness, the exactness are electrifying." It was the athleticism and precision of the Girls that were the key to their modernity, not the display of sexuality: "Beauty on stage, not through its nakedness, but through motion."

In "The Mass Ornament," Kracauer symptomatically assumed that, because the Tiller Girls were modern, they must be "products of American distraction factories." They were, in fact, the brainchild of John Tiller, a turn-of-the-century Lancashire cotton broker, who hired young women from towns like Manchester and Blackpool and trained them in a style of formation dancing that owed more to military drills and displays than to classical ballet. By the 1910s, Tiller was dispatching his girls on order to cities around the world. One troupe, renamed the Empire Girls for the occasion, performed in the Ziegfeld Follies on Broadway, where they were seen by the Berlin impresario Herman Haller, who hired them to come to Germany to perform in his 1924 revue *Noch und Noch* (*More and more*). Haller's main rival, Eric Charell, responded by setting up his own troupe, which he named the John-Tiller-Girls. Other imitators soon appeared, including the Hoffmann Girls and the Jackson Girls. In exasperation, Haller adopted the slogan "*Oft kopiert—nie erreicht!*" for *his* Tiller Girls: "Often copied—never equaled!"

Where all these girls actually came from was less important than the way that, in their performances, they seemed to embody or enact or perform the

Tiller Girls, 1920s

modernity of *Amerika*—or, more precisely, the Americanization of modern life. They had become an assembly of body parts, interchangeable components in an automaton that was also a new kind of commodity. They formed human chains with arms around each other's waists, and synchronized their high kicks precisely. Their line moved up and down staircases, broke apart, regrouped, and shifted from one pattern to another. As they went through Taylorized routines of aggregation and ornamental display, the individual sexuality of each female body was neutralized. This body culture had become cut off from any organic connection to nature, and the female bodies had been transmuted into raw material: "The human figure enlisted in the mass ornament has begun the *exodus* from lush organic splendor and the constitution of individuality toward the realm of anonymity to which it relinquishes itself when it stands in truth and when the knowledge radiating from the basis of man dissolves the contours of visible natural form." As the mass ornament had hollowed out traditional forms of community and personality, its significance could be deciphered only through socially and historically specific analysis: "the remaining unconnected parts are composed according to laws that are not those of nature but laws given by a knowledge of truth, which, as always, is a function of its time." Kracauer the cultural detective therefore turned his attention to the way that the mass urban audience responded to these spectacles. He identified in that response the modern predisposition to distraction, or *Zerstreuung*—that is, an aesthetic of "pure externality" based on a "fragmented sequence of splendid sense impressions"—which then enabled the true structure of modern reality to reveal itself.

Through this historically contingent truth, the choreography of the Tiller Girls made visible the rhythm of a labor process, in which the individuality of the worker has become subordinated to the logic of the machine and the production line. (Fritz Lang's *Metropolis* had appeared in 1926; Charlie Chaplin's *Modern Times* would follow ten years later.) Modernization and the instrumental reason of capitalism had reduced embodied subjectivity to abstraction and fragmentation. In "The Mass Ornament," the logic of the Tiller Girls' routine *reflects* that of "the entire contemporary situation" and their legs *correspond to* the hands in the factory. Four years later, in his essay "Girls and Crisis," Kracauer looked back on the way he had explained the Tiller Girls. "Like an image become flesh," he had believed that the Tiller Girls *embodied* "the *functioning* of a flourishing economy." "They were not merely American products but a demonstration at the same time of the vastness of American production." As the dancers formed themselves into "an undulating snake, they delivered a radiant illustration of the virtues of the conveyor belt; when they stepped to a rapid beat, it sounded like 'business, business'; when they raised their legs with mathematical precision over their heads, they joyfully affirmed the progress of rationalisation; and when they continually repeated the same manoeuvre, never breaking ranks, one had the vision of an unbroken chain of automobiles gliding out of the factory into the world and the feeling that there was no end to prosperity."

Although Josephine Baker and the Tiller Girls may have appeared on the same bill from time to time, and both were interpreted as symptoms of modernity, they were nonetheless "worlds apart," not only in terms of recognition and status, but also in their dance styles. The Tiller Girls were de-individualized, controlled, and mechanical, whereas Josephine Baker was unique, idiosyncratic, and natural. In that contrast, there is an echo of Simmel's divided modern self, with one style drilled into mechanical conformity, the other exploiting opportunities for self-creation to the point of eccentricity or self-caricature. If the Tiller Girls provided an analogue of industrial production and capitalist rationality, Josephine Baker represented an avant-garde invention, even though one increasingly recuperated for the entertainment industry. Both the Tiller Girls and Josephine Baker might also be considered as *brands*. In the former, the human element—the "Girls"—was infinitely substitutable: impresarios bought recognition of the "Tiller" name, the reliability of the product, and the consistency of the service. When the name "Josephine Baker" was licensed for use on dolls, clothes, perfumes, and, most successfully of all, Bakerfix hair gel, what was being sold was her uniqueness and her integrity—in short, the commodified "personality" of Josephine Baker. And, of course, in European eyes, both the Tillers and Josephine Baker embodied *American* modernity: Fordism and mass society on the one hand, enterprise and individualism on the other.

Travels

By 1928, Josephine Baker had already started to move away from her *sauvage* incarnation. She had appointed Pepito Abatino her manager, and they claimed to have married. Although Baker's friend Bricktop, the nightclub owner, dubbed him "the no-account count," Abatino proved to be an inspired entrepreneur and a loyal, long-suffering companion. Two years after the success of *La Revue nègre*, Abatino realized that the clock was ticking against Baker in Paris, that she needed to remove herself from the scene for a while, and that she should come back with a new persona and a new act. They embarked on a two-year, twenty-five-country tour. In Vienna, Baker was caught up in a "Negerskandal" ("nigger scandal"), as the theatrical establishment, the Catholic Church, the Nazis, and other political parties tried to prevent not only her appearance, but also the staging of Ernst Krenek's "jazz opera," *Jonny Spielt Auf!* at the Opera House. When they reached Berlin, it appears that Baker may have considered putting down roots there. She bought a house in the Grunewald and opened a club on Behrenstrasse, where she performed in her own *Bitte Einsteigen (Joséphine)* revue, as well as starring at the Theater des Westerns. In just three years, however, the cultural mood and the political climate had changed. This visit coincided with the appearance of Bruno Frank's *Politische Novelle*, a novel featuring a Baker-based black dancer, who embodies the threat to Germany posed by the convergence of the primitive, the foreign, and the feminine. The perception of primitivism and female sexuality as contaminations was now stronger than any hope that they might act as rejuvenating, life-enhancing forces. Baker's shows were panned as kitsch, and she quickly moved on. The Jazz Age values she represented were now widely seen as self-indulgent, decadent, and dangerous.

The combination of economic depression after the stock market crash in 1929 and political events in Germany also prompted Siegfried Kracauer to rethink his views on the Tiller Girls and their imitators. In his study of office workers, published as *The Salaried Masses* in 1930, he shifted from the nuanced phenomenological analysis of the Weimar essays toward an ideological critique that saw mass culture as an instrument of class rule and collective repression. When sales clerks and stenographers resorted to the "pleasure barracks" of the pleasure industry, he came to believe, that signified an ideological homelessness and an existential despair born of "a life which only in a restricted sense can be called a life." In 1931, a performance by the Alfred Jackson Girls at the Scala in Berlin had him looking back on his earlier enthusiasm for the Tiller Girls. "I clearly recall seeing such troupes in the season of their fame," he wrote in "Girls and Crisis" in 1931, but any hint of utopianism had now disappeared.

> One market crash after the other has rocked the economy, and the crisis has long since given the lie to one's faith in never-ending prosperity. One no longer believes them, the rosy Jackson Girls! They continue to attend just as meticulously to their abstract trade, but the happy dreams they are supposed to inspire have been revealed for years now as foolish illusions. And though they still swing their legs as energetically as before, they come, a phantom, from yesterday dead and gone. Their smiles are those of a mask; their confidence a leftover from better days; their precision a mockery of the difficulties in which the very powers they call to mind now find themselves. Though they may continue to snake and wave as if nothing had happened—the crisis to which so many factories have fallen victim has also silently liquidated this machinery of girls.

When Josephine Baker returned to Paris for the 1930–1931 season, she took another step into the mainstream of the French entertainment industry. Now a recognized *vedette*, or star, she had top billing in the Casino de Paris revue *Paris qui Remue*, singing French songs and dancing on pointe in choreography by Georges Balanchine. In doing so, she alienated some of her avant-garde fans. The surrealist poet Philippe Soupault thought she had "covered herself in ridicule" by trying to imitate Mistinguett, but this was just

symptomatic of an industry-wide problem, the "disfiguration" of black dancers to suit Parisian prejudices. "The famous producers of Paris and London
impose limits on what they term savagery and obtain in this way that organ-
ised savagery which is enough to make one vomit." Unabashed by such objections, Abatino had Baker star in two films, *Zouzou* (1934) and *Princesse Tam
Tam* (1935), before undertaking perhaps their most ambitious move: a return
to New York to star alongside Fanny Brice in the Ziegfeld Follies of 1936.

Baker rehearsed intensively, working on her voice and receiving more dance
training from Balanchine. "In Paris rehearsing is a pleasure," commented
Baker. "In New York it is a matter of discipline." The director, John Murray
Anderson, decided to present her as a sophisticated Parisian singer, rather
than as a dancer. "You are from Paris," he told her. "It's stupid to let you sing
Harlem songs." Even though she had achieved success through a European
fantasy of America, in America, she was now being told to be European. When
the show opened in New York, the response was cool, but it was outright hostile toward Baker. "Miss Baker has refined her art until there is nothing left in
it," complained Brooks Atkinson in the *New York Times*, comparing her unfavorably to Fanny Brice and, pointedly, to the tap-dancing Nicholas Brothers,
who "restore your faith in dusky revelry." A vicious review in *Time* magazine
had very little to say about her performance; it went straight for the woman.
"Josephine Baker is a St. Louis washerwoman's daughter who stepped out of a
Negro burlesque show into a life of adulation and luxury in Paris in the boom-
ing 1920s," it said, concentrating its polemic on European gullibility and on
putting an uppity black woman in her place. "In sex appeal to jaded Europeans
of the jazz-loving type, a Negro wench always has a head start. The particular tawny hue of tall and stringy Josephine Baker's bare skin stirred French
pulses." Baker's color, skin, and body provoke the classic response of the racist: Look, a Negro! "She was just a slightly buck-toothed young Negro woman
whose figure might be matched in any night-club show, and whose dancing
and singing might be topped practically anywhere outside of Paris."

Baker blamed Abatino for the American debacle, and he returned to Paris
before her. What he thought was hepatitis turned out to be cancer and he died
in the autumn of 1936, before she arrived back in Europe. Without Abatino,
her career stalled. No longer used to setbacks on this scale, she retreated to
familiar ground. Back in Europe, she signed to star in the Folies-Bergère revue
for 1936, *En Super Folies*, even though it was a step down from the Casino de
Paris. The novelist Colette, who had herself performed in the music hall and
knew the discipline and pain involved, wrote a preview. In contrast to the
Time review, she focuses, lovingly but unblinkingly, on the body of Josephine
Baker, the dancer.

> The hard work of the company rehearsals seem to have made her slimmer,
> without stripping the flesh from her delicate bone structure; her oval knees,

her ankles flower from the clear, beautiful, even-textured brown skin with which Paris is besotted. The years, and coaching, have perfected an elongated and discreet bone-structure and retained the admirable convexity of her thighs. Joséphine's shoulder-blades are unobtrusive, her shoulders light, she has the belly of a young girl and a high-placed navel. Naked except for three gilt flowers, pursued by her four assailants, she assumes the serious unsmiling look of a sleepwalker, which ennobles a daring music-hall number. Her huge eyes, outlined in black and blue, gaze forth, her cheeks are flushed, the moist and dazzling sweetness of her teeth shows between dark and violet lips—her face shows no response to the quadruple embrace under which her pliant body seems to melt. Paris is going to see, on the stage of the Folies, how Joséphine Baker, in the nude, shows all other nude dancers the meaning of modesty.

For Colette, Baker's personality has become her costume, even more than her skin: hence the "modesty" of her performance. This perspective demonstrates an aesthetic engagement with dance, which operates not through cultural prejudices or even through Kracauer's keen eye and critical intellect, but through what has been described as "a kind of muscular sympathy, a projective identification with the bodies of dancers." As George Balanchine put it, one has to focus on "this dancer who is now this moment under your eyes." This is what de Maré had done in working with Josephine Baker to create a modernist dance that combined fantasies of America and Africa for a European audience, and what Kracauer perceived in the vernacular modernism of Berlin audiences, as they engaged with the rhythms of modern life through the routines of the Tiller Girls. In their different ways, Josephine Baker and the Tiller Girls danced modernity into being.

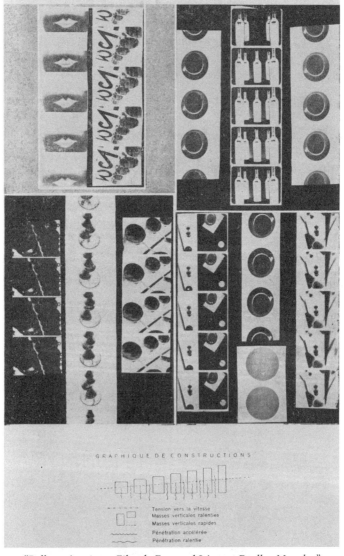

"Ballet mécanique: *Film de Fernand Léger et Dudley Murphy*,"
L'Esprit nouveau 28 (1925)

Ballet mécanique

JAZZ AESTHETICS AND MODERNIST FILM

In histories of avant-garde cinema, Dudley Murphy appears as the bohemian young Californian who collaborated with the painter Fernand Léger to make *Ballet mécanique*, one of the key experimental films of the 1920s. In histories of African American cinema, Dudley Murphy features primarily as the director of Paul Robeson's first sound film, *The Emperor Jones*, in 1933. Both accounts tell only part of the story. To make sense of Dudley Murphy's journey from *Ballet mécanique* in Paris to *The Emperor Jones* in New York, it helps to look once again at the creative interaction between black American culture and the European avant-garde in the 1920s and 1930s. Like Josephine Baker's dance for Rolf de Maré, Murphy's early career is another iteration of "jazz modernism."

The Emperor Jones

Hardly a conventional Hollywood movie, *The Emperor Jones* is the closest thing to an "art film" to be found even on the margins of the American mainstream cinema of its time. However controversial it had been in the 1920s, *The Emperor Jones* as a play had accrued considerable cultural prestige, and that prompted the independent producer Samuel Goldwyn to make an offer to buy the screen rights. O'Neill turned him down. He was appalled that Goldwyn wanted to cast the white baritone and MGM actor Lawrence Tibbett as Brutus Jones. (Blacked up, Tibbett had played the role in Louis Gruenberg's opera of *The Emperor Jones* for the New York Metropolitan in January 1933.)

Enter, at this point, two inexperienced but ambitious young producers, John Krimsky and Gifford Cochran. In 1932, they had made more money than they immediately knew what to do with as US distributors of Leontine Sagan's all-female *Mädchen in Uniform*. Now they wanted to make an equally confronting American film. Dudley Murphy, whose career at the time was suffering from a scandal involving a socialite mistress found dead in his apartment, made the introductions to O'Neill. Enticed by their promise to cast Paul Robeson in the title role, and assailed by debts, O'Neill sold Krimsky and Cochran the rights to *The Emperor Jones* for $30,000.

Even though Robeson had not yet appeared in a commercial movie, Krimsky and Cochran calculated that he was an internationally bankable star. Robeson was initially reluctant to leave Europe, but the offer of a salary of $15,000 for six weeks' work in the United States, with travel expenses, won him over. He also insisted on a guarantee that he would not be required to work south of the Mason-Dixon line, which scotched plans for location shooting in the swamplands of South Carolina. Instead, elaborate jungle sets had to be built in the Astoria Studios in New York City, which Paramount was happy to hire out cheaply, given the downturn in film production.

Krimsky and Cochran brought together a disparate, multitalented team to work on *The Emperor Jones*. DuBose Heyward, author of the 1925 dialect novel *Porgy*—the source for *Porgy and Bess*—wrote the screen adaptation. William De Mille, Cecil B.'s brother, took on a nebulous function, which included coaching Robeson for his delivery of Jones's long monologue in the jungle. The cinematographer was Ernest Haller, early in his career; later credits would include *Gone with the Wind* (1939), *Mildred Pierce* (1945), and *Rebel without a Cause* (1955). Art direction was by Herman Rosse, a European-trained designer who had won an Oscar for his first Hollywood feature, MGM's Paul Whiteman vehicle, *King of Jazz* (1930), and then worked on Universal's horror cycle, notably *Frankenstein* in 1931. (Dudley Murphy would have known him from his own time at Universal that year when, uncredited, he wrote much of the dialogue for Tod Browning's *Dracula*.) J. Rosamond Johnson, James Weldon Johnson's brother, oversaw the film's sound design. He translated its narrative logic—a sequence of episodic tableaux recording Brutus Jones's rise from Pullman porter to island emperor, and then his tragic fall into madness and death—into a quasi-anthropological musical arc. African rhythms, over the image of a circular tom-tom that fills the screen during the opening credits, give way first to the Gullah music of South Carolina, and then to the sophistication of Harlem jazz, before finally reverting to the voodoo tom-tom—a rhythm calibrated (as in O'Neill's original conception) to replicate the beat of the human heart. Even though production was slowed down by interference from the Hays Office, shooting was completed in thirty-eight days, on a modest budget of $280,000. When it was released in September 1933, only a couple of months later, *The Emperor Jones* was predictably controversial, especially among black American audiences. In the end, although it almost broke even, Eugene O'Neill's judgment of the film probably represents the consensus view: "a compromise neither artistic nor commercial."

On the set of Black and Tan, *New York, 1929*

Some of the story behind Dudley Murphy's collaboration with Robeson is frozen in an intriguing photograph taken at RCA's Gramercy Studio in New York in 1929, four years before *The Emperor Jones* and just a few weeks after the Wall Street Crash. It is a production still for *Black and Tan*, a twenty-minute film featuring the music of Duke Ellington and directed by Murphy.

To start with its most disconcerting element, the female figure dumped unceremoniously on the floor of mirrored glass—a reference to the Cotton Club—is Fredi Washington, one of the great beauties of the Harlem Renaissance and often held up as the ideal New Negro woman. She had toured in the chorus line of *Shuffle Along* with Josephine Baker, to whom she remained a lifelong friend, and in 1926 she established herself as an actor when she appeared in the play *Black Boy* with Robeson, with whom she started an affair that was to last, sporadically, for over twenty years. In *Black and Tan*, she plays a dancer who sacrifices her life to protect Ellington's career. She again worked alongside Robeson and Murphy on *The Emperor Jones*, playing the prostitute, Undine. (Many of her scenes with Robeson had to be re-shot as the Hays Office decided that she was too light-skinned and feared that audiences might infer a sexual relationship between Robeson and a white woman.

In the retakes, Washington was required to apply layers of darker make-up: to black up, in effect.) Soon after completing *The Emperor Jones*, she married Duke Ellington's trombonist, Lawrence Brown. Her only real mainstream success came when she starred in John Stahl's *Imitation of Life* in 1934, and even this proved double-edged, as her portrayal of a black woman "passing" led to her being typecast as "the tragic mulatto." Her movie career petered out and she increasingly devoted herself to writing and to civil rights causes, including the creation of the Negro Actors Guild.

The three men in the foreground, posed in stiff mimicry of the three Graces, appear jarringly oblivious to Fredi Washington's presence. Duke Ellington, dapper as ever, stands in the center, shaking hands with the tweed-suited figure on the right of the photograph, a stranger to the set, judging by the fact that he is holding hat and gloves in his left hand. This is Carl Van Vechten, who may have been more than a casual visitor. Some people say that he had a hand in scripting the scenario for *Black and Tan*, and also for *St. Louis Blues*, a similar film that Murphy had made a few months earlier, featuring Bessie Smith in her only screen role. Even if that overstates his involvement, in his role as Harlem's cross-racial broker Van Vechten would have relished the opportunity to help get the films made.

Rather than returning Van Vechten's gaze, Ellington's head is averted, looking over his right shoulder, as if he is reacting to a noise on the set or, more likely, although his head is tilted down rather than up, listening to what was being said by the gangling figure behind him. This is Dudley Murphy, who had become part of Van Vechten's Negrotarian set on his return from Europe in the mid-1920s, and who, at the time the photograph was taken, was establishing a reputation in the industry as a man with a knack for working well with black performers. One story is that, apart from any lobbying Van Vechten may have done, Murphy had persuaded RKO to let him make *St. Louis Blues* and *Black and Tan* by bragging about his Harlem connections and his conquests among Harlem women. That reputation may still have carried some weight with Krimsky and Cochran, four years later.

This much can be inferred from the photograph. However, the longer back-story of how Murphy came to direct *The Emperor Jones* involves not just his Harlem credentials, but also the way that he discovered jazz through European modernism and, above all, his prescient fascination with the choreographic potential of the movie camera. Born to artists in Boston in 1897, Murphy had moved to Southern California in 1915 with his mother and sister when his parents divorced. He dropped out of his engineering studies to become an aviator and fly bombing missions from England during the endgame of the Great War. Returning to Los Angeles, he spent a year as a Hollywood art director and camera apprentice, while also writing about film for the *Los Angeles Evening Express*. In 1920, he made his first films: three experimental dance shorts, very much in the Isadora Duncan mode, synchronized to music by composers like Debussy. The best known is *The Song of the Cypress*, featuring his first wife, Chase Herendeen. While still working on his "visual symphonies" and sound-image synchronization, Murphy spent August 1921 researching lenses and camera technology at the physics department of Dartmouth College. In 1922, he made his most ambitious film to date. *Danse Macabre*, set to the music of Saint-Saëns, marked a departure from Californian imagism in favor of a more expressionist style, including graphic and animated effects.

Having developed this "calling card" portfolio of films, and accompanied by his second wife, the young dancer Katherine Hawley, Murphy headed to Europe. When he returned to the United States a couple of years later, he picked up his vagrant career on the margins of the American industry. He developed a treatment for *Skyscraper*, for example, a film designed to celebrate the fantastic speed and rhythm of this jazz age in New York, even though he did not get to direct it. The two jazz shorts and *The Emperor Jones* probably represented the high points of his American career, but his best-known achievement remains, unquestionably, *Ballet mécanique*.

Ballet mécanique

One of the surprising things about Murphy as a young American traveling to Europe in 1923 is that, despite his novel ideas about cinema as a choreographic medium capable of combining music, dance, and movement, jazz was not part of his baggage. It was only while in Europe that he learned to embrace jazz and, in *Ballet mécanique*, developed for film the type of jazz aesthetic that T. S. Eliot had toyed with in *The Waste Land*.

Ballet mécanique—planned, shot, and edited in Paris over a number of months in 1923 and 1924 and first screened at the Internationale Ausstellung für Theatertechnik in Vienna on September 24, 1924—might be considered the definitive avant-garde film of those years. It was one of the first attempts to create a truly abstract cinema, although whether that abstraction is best described as cubist, dadaist, vorticist, or purist remains a matter of debate. The film has remained controversial in other ways too, most notably with regard to the question of who should be regarded as its true begetter, or, more pertinently, begetters. The systematic repression over several decades of Murphy's contribution has now largely been made good, but what role was played by three other large American egos—those of Ezra Pound, the surrealist artist and photographer Man Ray, and the controversial composer George Antheil—remains an intriguing, if in the end irresolvable, enigma. In terms of understanding the interaction between black American culture and European modernism in the 1920s, however, the significance of *Ballet mécanique* lies in the extent to which it can usefully be regarded as a *jazz film*, in the sense that it embodies jazz modernism's alchemy of the vernacular: its power to "jazz" the ordinary and give it new life.

Ezra Pound, who had edited *The Waste Land* to create the version that was published by the jazz enthusiast Gilbert Seldes in *The Dial* in 1922, helped to broker the social connections that led to the production of *Ballet mécanique*, and probably had a hand in its production as well. When Dudley Murphy arrived in Paris, he called on Pound, with whom the Murphy family had earlier shared a holiday in Italy. "Dudley Murphy," wrote Pound in a letter to his father, "whom I met in Venice in 1908, he being then eleven; turned up a few days ago. His dad is a painter, he is trying to make cinema into art. ETC." Pound had developed an interest in the "vortographic" experiments of the photographer Alvin Langdon Coburn, and he was therefore interested in the lenses (or lens covers) that Murphy had developed at Dartmouth, which produced a similar kaleidoscopic fragmentation of the image. There is some evidence that the two of them did at least some production and editing work on the film, with Pound in January 1924 again reporting to his father: "Also work on vorticism film—experiment interesting—but probably Murphy hasn't brains enough to finish the job in my absence or without pushing." Murphy's recollection in later years—and no one's account of these events wholly tallies

Ezra Pound, vortograph, 1917 (Alvin Langdon Coburn)

with anyone else's—emphasizes less collaboration than the way that Pound set in motion the chain of events that led to *Ballet mécanique*: "One day, when I was visiting Ezra Pound and talking about my work, he told me that a friend of his, Ferdinand Leger, wanted to make a movie. Also George Anteil, the young protégé of Stravinsky would like to make a movie. So he brought the three of us together and we decided to make one."

This version does not acknowledge that Murphy had already met Man Ray, possibly on July 6, 1923 at the Dadaists' "Evening of the Bearded Heart." Along with music by Milhaud, Satie, and Stravinsky, poems from Apollinaire, Cocteau, and Soupault, and a play by Tristan Tzara, several experimental films were screened, including Man Ray's *Le Retour à la raison*. Whatever he was doing with Pound and Léger, Murphy seems to have suggested a collaboration with Ray and they started to build up an archive of footage. Out in the city, they filmed shop windows, traffic, and an amusement park. They shot various still-life arrangements, a parrot, Murphy himself, Katherine Murphy sniffing flowers while sitting prettily on a swing, and extreme close-ups of the mouth and eyes of Man Ray's girlfriend, Kiki de Montparnasse, in flat white mime make-up. They also planned to intercut pornographic footage of the two couples between shots of pistons and other machine parts pumping up and down. Soon, predictably, the money ran out. At Ezra Pound's prompting, Léger was approached to support the project, and possibly also the American heiress Natalie Barney, who hosted a salon in Paris and volunteered to underwrite what Léger called "a musical synchronized adaptation" by George Antheil—at this time probably more a protégé of Pound's than of his former mentor, Stravinsky.

In his autobiography, Antheil claims that he alone had initiated the whole project. His story is that, in October 1923, following the *succès de scandale* of an earlier, riot-interrupted concert, he announced in the press that he was working on a new composition to be called *Ballet mécanique* and that he was looking for "a motion-picture accompaniment to this piece." Supposedly egged on by Pound, Murphy accepted the challenge, on the condition that he would collaborate with Léger. In the end, working independently and not from any prints, Antheil did produce a score for synchronized player-pianos, sirens, motor-horns, electric bells, airplane propellers, and assorted other mechanical objects and musical instruments, which he described as "a dream of niggers, skyscrapers and glittering polished surfaces." This dissonant, noise-based music was well adapted to leading Léger and Murphy's mechanical dance. There were just two problems: the score was not completed until 1925 or 1926, and it was twice as long as the film. Apart from that, Antheil would claim, Léger "said it was beyond his expectations and that it was as right as right can be." Even if that is true, Antheil's intransigence in refusing to adapt the score to an existing print meant that, for many years, *Ballet mécanique* the film and *Ballet mécanique* the composition led separate lives.

George Antheil, 1924 (Man Ray)

Whoever did what, with whom, and in what order, there is no doubt that Léger was becoming more and more interested in film by 1923. In 1922, although contributing nothing himself beyond a poster design, he had followed the production process of Abel Gance's film *La Roue* (*The Wheel*), through the participation of his friend Blaise Cendrars, and he wrote enthusiastically about aspects of the film. It was neither the drama nor the emotion that interested him but, rather, what he perceived as "a new plastic contribution," in which a "mechanical element" is crucial: "This new element is presented to us through an infinite variety of methods, from every aspect: close-ups, fixed or moving mechanical fragments, projected at a heightened speed that approaches the state of simultaneity and that crushes and eliminates the human object, reduces its interest, pulverizes it."

This emphasis on the plastic, the mechanical, and the kinetic, and on the new ways of seeing made possible by the close-up and by montage, was no doubt, in part, a projection of Léger's thinking about his own art. It was during his war experience that he "discovered the beauty of the fragment" and "sensed a new reality in the detail of a machine, in the common object." As a result, he had reinvented his style, developing a new vocabulary of form, color, and rhythm intended to capture the dynamic movement and intensity of the modern metropolis. Having been "criticized severely" for tackling "the mechanical element as a plastic possibility," he insisted in 1923 that: "The mechanical element *is only a means and not an end.* I consider it simply plastic 'raw material,' like the elements of a landscape or a still life." What interested him, even if spectators found it challenging, was the creation of "an intensive organized state," in which "the weight of masses, the relationship of lines, [and] the balance of colors" are subjected to "absolute orchestration and order" and to "the law of plastic contrasts." His new approach was to "group contrary values together; flat surfaces opposed to modeled surfaces; volumetric figures opposed to the flat façades of houses; molded volumes of plumes of smoke opposed to active surfaces of architecture; pure, flat tones opposed to gray, modulated tones or the reverse."

The modern world, as Léger saw it, was a geometric world, characterized by "*frequent contrasts*." He cited everyday examples: "the advertising billboard—sharp, permanent, immediate, violent—that cuts across the tender and harmonious landscape" or a "contemporary fashionable party," where "the men's severe, crisp black clothes" contrast with "the prettier and more delicately colored dresses of the women." His surprising and disconcerting juxtapositions were in tune with this "epoch of contrasts": "So I am consistent with my own time." In this context, the power of film, and especially the power of the close-up, lay in its technical capacity to direct the spectator's attention to the plastic form and dynamic of the modern world—or, simply, the power of "*making images seen.*" The consequence of the "cinematic revolution" was thus "*to make us see everything that has been merely noticed.*" Having observed the planning and shooting of *La Roue*, and having seen how Cendrars constructed a montage sequence to convey the power of a locomotive through rapid cuts, syncopated visual rhythms, and violently contrasting machine imagery, Léger declared that he "wanted to make a film at any cost."

Léger's explicit aim was to achieve a *machine aesthetic* in film. Hence his selection of objects in *Ballet mécanique*: industrial machines and machine-made objects carefully patterned in the artist's characteristic assemblages, or in such extreme close-up that they become unrecognizable. Léger wanted to provoke spectators not just into seeing them anew, but into seeing them as *beautiful*. By that, Léger did not intend any old fuzzy aestheticism. Like his fellow purists Le Corbusier and Amédée Ozenfant, he aspired to create a classical and yet uniquely modern "Beauty." In trying to define the essence of that machine-age Beauty, Léger suggested why there are so many saucepan lids, whisks, flan dishes, and other kitchen utensils dancing around in *Ballet mécanique*: "The Beautiful is everywhere: perhaps more in the arrangement of your saucepans in the white walls of your kitchen than in your eighteenth-century living room or in the official museums."

What appealed to Léger about cinema as a vehicle for a machine aesthetic were the possibilities of "the mechanical element" becoming the leading

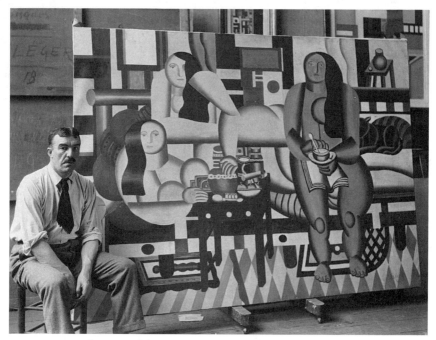

Fernand Léger with his painting of three women, 1926 (Therese Bonney)

character, of composing visual fragments into an artistic whole (montage), and of introducing a temporal dimension (a *modern rhythm*) into his art. In 1923, he designed a futuristic laboratory as the setting for the climactic scene in Marcel L'Herbier's film *L'Inhumaine*, but it was only in *Ballet mécanique* that he found the opportunity to create a film that demonstrated the mathematical principles of order, discipline, and, especially, rhythm that he saw as being intrinsic to the times, but that were also indicators of the emerging *rappel à l'ordre*.

> The particular interest of the film is centered upon the importance which we give to the "fixed image," to its arithmetical, automatic projection, slowed down or accelerated—additional, likeness.
> No scenario—Reactions of rhythmic images, that is all.
> Two coefficients of interest upon which the film is constructed:
> The variation of the speeds of projection:
> The rhythm of those speeds.

Dudley Murphy's aesthetic ambitions were less developed theoretically and less explicitly articulated than Léger's. More intuitive and hedonistic than his collaborator, he wanted to expand the boundaries of film as a medium for the creation and representation of dance. One of Murphy's dominant memories was of getting hold of the mannequin legs to be used in the stop-motion

Charleston sequence: "In bringing the legs to the studio, I drove through Paris in an open cab, with a leg over each shoulder, screaming. Even the Frenchmen were startled by this." With Pound, Murphy seems to have been happy to make a vorticist film, and with Man Ray to produce a dadaist celebration of machines and machinery—"I insisted on my Dada approach if we were to work together, to which he readily agreed." When Man Ray decamped, Léger recalls how he and Murphy would discuss his more classical and disciplined ideas, before they set out into Paris to photograph things that stimulated his imagination. "The premise on which we decided to make the film," according to Léger, at least, "was based on a belief that surprise of image and rhythm would make a pure film without drawing on any of the other arts, such as writing, acting, painting." This is not to assume that Murphy was a naïve technician, at the beck and call of egotistical artists. He was himself an artist who could learn, pragmatically rather than theoretically, from each of his collaborators, but he was also a filmmaker who had something to teach them. Just as Murphy acquired, from Léger, a more considered cinematic grammar for his future dance experiments, so Léger learned, from his collaboration on *Ballet mécanique*, a new understanding of the meaning and associations of objects and new ideas about how to work their kinetic plastic juxtaposition into his future paintings.

The competing stories about the provenance of *Ballet mécanique* make it tempting to suggest that there was something jazz-like about its production. At least five idiosyncratic voices were articulating dissonant styles and yet, somehow, they managed to "hear" enough of what the others were doing to be able to respond, interact, and, in the end, produce a single dynamic film art work. This is no more than an analogy; it is not where the film's jazz aesthetic lies. Even so, it does suggest a way of looking at *Ballet mécanique* that is more alert to its improvised polyphony than those critical views which want to tie the film down to embodying one school or another, or belonging to only one author or another. The provocative dadaist voice of Man Ray ("All the films I made were improvisations") is there in some of the imagery and in the film's eroticism; Pound's residual vorticism can be seen in the kaleidoscopic fragmentation of the image; Léger's "more theoretical" purism shapes the film's structure, as well as the look of many of the parts; and, in the end, it is Murphy's cinematic choreography that holds the whole thing together—preferably to Antheil's machine-music accompaniment.

Seen like this, the opening minutes of the film appear not just as an exercise in abstract cinematic rhythm, but as more argumentative and more culturally engaged than is often supposed. Before the title credit we see Charlot, Léger's Charlie Chaplin marionette, of which more later. *Ballet mécanique* starts, then, with the mechanical choreography of stop-frame animation, which combines a time-based cubist design with the implication that this film stands in some sort of relation to the energy of popular

The opening sequence of Ballet mécanique

cinema. After the title, the images appear to be Murphy's and Ray's, even if the logic of their montage may largely be Léger's. We see Katherine Murphy, smiling coyly and fluttering her eyelashes as her garden swing sets up the underlying metronomic rhythm for the sequence, before the scene is interrupted (in accordance with Léger's graph of the film's construction) by a rapid montage of objects: a straw boater hat, numerals, colored circles and triangles (Léger's nod to the abstract cinema of Richter, Fischinger, Eggeling, and Ruttmann, perhaps), bottles, Kiki's mouth demonstrating the rhythmic mechanics of a smile, the boater again, Kiki's mouth again, spinning circular objects that could be umbrellas or just painted discs, a vertiginously gyrating pendulum.

Then the first rhythm is restored, by a return to Katherine on her swing, but this time projected upside down. Is this inversion nothing more than a formal device? The visual pun of "the world turned upside down" was hardly new or subtle. Look, it says: this is the romantic ethos of the type of modern dance exemplified by Isadora Duncan—feminine, Arcadian, natural—that our film will overturn. In this revolution, what is the new aesthetic on offer? Next we see, reflected in a swinging Christmas-tree ball, whose arc and rhythm replicate exactly those of the inverted swing, a movie camera and two men, Murphy operating the camera and Léger in the foreground directing. So: out with the female body in a pastoral setting, in with the mechanical eye of the camera, in with the cameramen who create new ways of seeing, and in with a new vision of modern woman, made up, hair waxed and reduced (like Charlot) to a montage of parts.

At this point, Murphy's kaleidoscopic prism over the camera lens is brought into action, creating a vorticist choreography of objects or part objects—often, so far as they can be made out, saucepan lids, flan dishes, jelly molds and other utensils photographed from disorienting angles or distances. This is Léger making us see, and see the plastic beauty of, "*everything that has been merely noticed,*" whether that be these objects or the abstract shapes or the extreme close-ups of Kiki's mouth and eyes, with which they are interchangeable. Then, as the end point of this prelude, Dudley Murphy himself emerges from the jumble of objects, like Botticelli's Venus rising from the surf.

This way of seeing the film locates it in its cultural moment. And it is with this historical contextualization that jazz legitimately comes into the analysis. It was the prevailing jazz ethos of 1923 Paris, which the makers of *Ballet mécanique* rendered in the film's mechanical imagery, plastic contrasts, and rhythm. To define that ethos, it is worth citing again the account of jazz given by Michel Leiris in *Manhood*:

> In the period of great license that followed the hostilities, jazz was a sign of allegiance, an orgiastic tribute to the colours of the moment. It functioned magically, and its means of influence can be compared to a kind of possession. It was the element that gave these celebrations their true meaning, with communion by dance, latent or manifest exoticism, and drinks, the most effective means of bridging the gap that separates individuals from each other at any kind of gathering. Swept along by violent bursts of tropical energy, jazz still had enough of a "dying civilization" about it, of humanity blindly submitting to The Machine, to express quite completely the state of mind of at least some of that generation: a more or less conscious demoralisation born of the war, a naïve fascination with the comfort and the latest inventions of progress, a predilection for a contemporary setting whose insanity we nonetheless vaguely anticipated, an abandonment to the animal joy of experiencing the influence of a modern rhythm, an

underlying aspiration to a new life in which more room would be made for the impassioned frankness we inarticulately longed for. In jazz, too, came the first appearance of *Negroes*, the manifestation and the myth of black Edens which were to lead me to Africa and, beyond Africa, to ethnography.

Leiris's signs of the times make it possible to see how, in *Ballet mécanique*, jazz context was transmuted into film art. For Léger, no doubt more than his American collaborators, one motivation for his radical change of style and his attempt to create an art adequate to the times was the "demoralisation born of the war." Murphy was the only one of the American collaborators on the film to have seen active service, but, for him, the experience had been exhilarating rather than traumatic. In their individual ways, however, each of the Americans would have shared Leiris's ethical ambivalence about that "contemporary setting," whose insanity they "vaguely anticipated," or, in a word, modernity.

Certainly, Léger at this time showed a fascination, whether naïve or not, with "the latest inventions of progress"—including cinema—even if it stopped just short of "blindly submitting to The Machine." In *Ballet mécanique*'s contrasts between two representations of "the modern woman," and in the copulatory rhythms and erotic symbolism of its machines and objects, there is, at

Self-portrait, c. 1921, Man Ray

least, a gesture toward "the impassioned frankness" about sexual matters that Leiris wistfully invoked. This catalog reveals a degree of thematic congruence between ethos and film, but without yet identifying how jazz functioned as a transformative aesthetic. The nature of jazz's alchemical power may be inferred from something *not* visible in the film: that is, Leiris's "Negroes."

L'Art nègre

At the same time as they were working on *Ballet mécanique*, most of its creators were also contributing, in one way or other, to the contemporary French vogue for *l'art nègre*. Although his 1926 photographs of Nancy Cunard bedecked in African ornaments and of Kiki de Montparnasse with an African mask are notorious examples, Man Ray did have a degree of self-knowledge about his relationship to black art. A year or two before *Ballet mécanique*, he had shot a slyly ironic portrait of himself. He poses as a stylized jazz drummer, with sticks at the ready and regulation shadows projected onto the wall. There are no drums, however, just a small cymbal attached to what looks, on the wall, very like a grand piano, but which on closer inspection turns out to be an ordinary gramophone. Any jazz in this image is mechanically reproduced, and Man Ray declares himself to be a white consumer, rather than a black producer, of the music; or perhaps his point was that, in the very act of appropriating the music as an expatriate white Jewish American dadaist, he might actually be reworking it according to his own cosmopolitan lights, and so doing something a little bit alchemical, or transformative.

Most explicit about the impact of *l'art nègre* on the ethos of the time when *Ballet mécanique* was being made was George Antheil. "Since Wagner, music has had two giant blood infusions," he wrote, in his contribution to Nancy Cunard's *Negro* anthology (1934): "first the Slavic, and, in recent times, the Negroid." In postwar Paris, "Negro music" helped to relieve "a bankrupt spirituality; to have continued within Slavic mysticism would have induced us all, in 1918, to commit suicide."

> Negro music made us to remember at least that we still had bodies which had not been exploded by shrapnel and that the cool 4 o'clock morning sunshine still coming over the hot veldt of yesterday was this morning very, very sweet. We needed at this time the licorice smell of Africa and of camel dung . . . the roar of the lion to remind us that life had been going on a long while and would probably go on a while longer. Weak, miserable, and anaemic, we needed the stalwart shoulders of a younger race to hold the cart awhile till we had gotten the wheel back on. But first acquaintance with this charming and beautiful creature, the Negro, made us love him at first sight; we could not resist him.

Here Leiris's "demoralisation born of the war" is hyped into Antheil's "bankrupt spirituality," Leiris's "bursts of tropical energy" and "animal joy" find their parallel in Antheil's realization "at least that we still had bodies," and, above all, Leiris's response to "Negroes" as "the manifestation and the myth of black Edens" is given a eugenicist twist in Antheil's vision of "this charming and beautiful creature, the Negro," whose historic role would be to reinvigorate a white race rendered "weak, miserable, and anaemic." One difference is that, whereas Leiris knew very well that he was listening to African *American* jazz, Antheil, whether naïvely or disingenuously, reproduces the primitivist conflation of jazz with Africa. Despite all his rhapsodizing over the veldt and the camel dung, however, Antheil also thought of jazz in terms of a machine aesthetic. The music represents "an incredible musical machinery." "One can scarcely believe," he exclaims, "that one has not to do with a civilized race, *masters of steel, mathematics, and engineering*, in hearing these choruses from the Congo."

At the same time as he started work on *Ballet mécanique*, Léger was designing the costumes, sets, and curtain for *La Création du monde*. In creating the look and sound of this ballet, both he and Milhaud tempered a primitivist aesthetic with the principles of the *rappel à l'ordre*, aiming for a "purified" Africanism. Léger's set and costume designs may have presented an anthropologically dubious pastiche of images from the "deepest jungle," filled with "savage idols" and "wild beasts," but he insisted that they were based on "African sculpture from the classical period" and that their purpose was

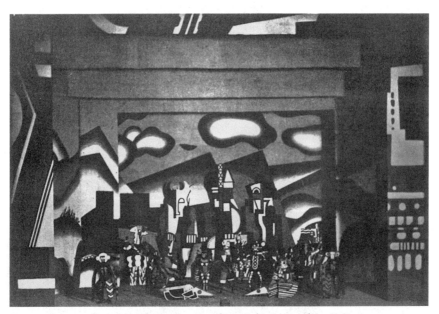

Decor and costumes for La Creation du monde, *Fernand Legér, Paris, 1923*

to turn dancers into a "mechanism like everything else." In a similar vein, Milhaud compared the jazz bands he admired to well-oiled machines, and stressed that he used "the jazz style to convey a purely classical feeling."

The inference from the fact that Man Ray, Antheil, and Léger were all caught up in *l'art nègre* is that they would have experienced what Leiris called "the influence of a modern rhythm" through jazz and specifically as Negro jazz. This is the symptomatic condensation: a modern rhythm was at the same time the rhythm of the machine and the rhythm of "Negro music." The claim that *Ballet mécanique* embodies a jazz aesthetic rests on the extent to which its vernacular imagery of everyday life and ordinary objects is rhythmically "jazzed," and so given new life. In this reading, *Ballet mécanique* is not purely abstract, although abstraction is a necessary first step in the jazzing process: it renders the world down to geometric and tonal images, which can then be put into a syncopated rhythmic relationship to each other. In 1923, Léger referred to the way that a painting "organized, orchestrated, like a musical score, has geometric necessities exactly the same as those of every objective human creation (commercial or industrial achievement)." In film, those "geometric necessities" are orchestrated temporally and everything becomes rhythm, although rhythm rooted in a still recognizable cultural vernacular. The film, in other words, demands not only a sensory response that might be described as abstract, but also a more poetic reading that picks up on cultural clues and references.

Jazzing

An example of the predominance of the purely sensory impact of rhythm can be found in the sequence of the washerwoman climbing the steps. Both Murphy and Léger laid claim to it, and the shades of difference between their accounts are revealing. "I saw an old washerwoman climbing a flight of stone stairs," recalled Murphy. "When she reached the top, she was tired and made a futile gesture." Although he saw the sequence primarily as an exercise in montage, he also recognized a certain metaphoric significance: "The scene in itself was banal, but by printing it 20 times and connecting the end of the scene with the beginning of her climb, it expressed the futility of life because she never got there. This scene in the editing followed a very intricate piece of shiny machinery, somehow correlated in movement to that of hers." For Léger, by contrast, the sequence had nothing to do with the futility of life. It was a mathematical experiment that took to the extreme the sensory effect of rhythm and repetition on the body. "Reactions of rhythmic images, that is all": that was the principle around which the film was constructed. "We persist up to the point when the eye and spirit of the spectator will no longer accept. We drain out of it every bit of value as a spectacle up to the moment when it becomes insupportable." Léger therefore saw the sequence in more purely theoretical terms than Murphy: "I wanted to *amaze* the audience first, then make them uneasy, and then push the adventure to the point of exasperation. In order to 'time' it properly, I got together a group of workers and people in the neighborhood, and I studied the effect that was *produced* on them. In eight hours I learned what I wanted to know. *Nearly all of them reacted at about the same time.*"

An example of jazzing the semantic vernacular, so that it becomes almost pure rhythm, is the treatment of the spoof headline "On a volé un collier de perles de 5 millions" (Pearl necklace worth 5 million stolen). Léger regarded modern advertising, and especially billboards, as part of the "enormous stage set of life" that provided his plastic raw material. But they were also both symbols and expressions of contemporary urban life, part of the overload of information that produced its defining sensations of temporal discontinuity and spatial disorientation. Léger's original work notes suggest that he had planned to reproduce this modern sense of unease by incorporating and interpreting some of the "plastic and theatrical values" through which commerce intruded into public space, most notably billboards ("publicity images like Bébé Cadum") and the press ("the projection of a whole page of newspaper advertising.") Such ideas may have been inspired by the American artist Gerald Murphy's set design for the Ballets Suédois production of Cole Porter's *Within the Quota*. The huge backdrop showed the front page of an American tabloid, with headlines like "UNKNOWN BANKER BUYS ATLANTIC," "Ex-Wife's Heart-Balm Love Tangle," and "RUM RAID LIQUOR BAN." Behind this lay a long-standing cubist fascination with the graphic power of typography, evident not only in a painting like Léger's own *The City* (1919), but also in Picasso's *Guitar, Sheet Music, and Glass* (1912), where the chopped-short newspaper masthead LE JOU connotes not only "Journal" but also *jouer*, to play. In the end, Léger scaled back his ambitions for *Ballet mécanique* to a single decontextualized headline. It is already unanchored from its story, but Léger and Murphy take it apart, break it into fragments, reverse its letters and numerals and stretch them out spatially and temporally. Zeros flash, singly or in groups, then alternate on screen with fragments of the message. Both words and numerals take on a dynamic force that overwhelms any referential meaning. They too become grist to the rhythmic mill. They are jazzed.

In a third example of the film's jazz-like alchemy of the vernacular, the plastic raw material is so freighted with cultural significance that it cannot be drained of value, even though it unquestionably contributes to the rhythm of the film. The raw material, in this case, is the image of Charlie Chaplin, the Cubist Charlot marionette. Léger had adored Chaplin's films, and been inspired by them, ever since Apollinaire had introduced him to them during the war. In 1920, he had provided four illustrations for Ivan Goll's book *Die Chapliniad: Eine Kinodichtung*, and in 1922, he designed the sets and costumes

Decor and costumes for Within the Quota, *Gerald Murphy, 1923*

for Jean Börlin's Chaplin-inspired ballet *Skating Rink*. Between these two projects, Léger had begun to develop quite an elaborate scenario for an animated film, *Charlot Cubiste*, and it is material from this uncompleted project that he imported into *Ballet mécanique*. What Léger most admired about Chaplin, as a film clown, was his ability to affect and manipulate his audiences. The presence of Charlot at the beginning of *Ballet mécanique* may, therefore, be a statement of Léger's faith in the power of cinema in general, and of this film in particular, to control audience response.

"Overwhelmed by the enormous stage set of life," Léger had asked himself, "what can the artist who aspires to conquer his public do?" Opening with the Charlot figure suggests that one technique for conquering the public, in this film, will be a certain cinematic rhythm, insofar as Chaplin was widely taken to embody cinematic rhythm. In a 1926 interview, for instance, Murphy would insist that "the secret of Chaplin's success lies in his consummate knowledge of and feeling for tempo." In the first issue of *The Criterion* in 1922–1923, another fan, T. S. Eliot, had observed that Chaplin's "egregious" merit lay in the fact that he had "escaped in his own way from the realism of the cinema" and had thus "invented a *rhythm*."

On both occasions that the Charlot figure appears in *Ballet mécanique*, he is juxtaposed against Katherine Hawley Murphy. And, on both occasions, it is the contrast between Charlot's jerky stop-frame choreography and bodily disintegration, and the metronymic regularity and balletic elegance of Katherine's human movements that is most striking. At one level, this may be experienced as one of Léger's rhythmic plastic contrasts. At the semantic level, however, the opening contrast needs to be linked to the close-ups of Kiki's mouth, which follow Katherine on the swing, and then to the juxtaposition of the swing image inverted against the reflected image of Léger and Murphy.

The sequence of contrasts thus runs in this order: (1) articulated/disarticulated male marionette figure (Charlot), (2) integrated female human figure (Katherine), (3) disaggregated female figure (Kiki), (4) inverted integrated female figure (Katherine), (5) reflected and distorted male figures (Léger and Murphy). From this, it may be inferred that the presentation of Katherine as female, classical, and integrated is contrasted against Kiki as female, modern, and disintegrated, and that the disintegrated and reconstituted Charlot may represent a rhythm that is masculine, modern, and urban. The framing of Katherine, before by Charlot and after by Léger and Murphy, also indicates a degree of erotic aggression that becomes more overt in the second iteration of the Charlot/Katherine juxtaposition. On this occasion, it follows another sequence designed to test the limits of the spectator's exasperation: almost half a minute of rapid, split-second intercutting between a round boater and an unmistakably phallic shoe. That visual assault is then relieved by a cut to Katherine, in the garden. The rhythm slows, but then the frenetic Charlot marionette reappears and disassembles, or disintegrates, in reaction to the image of the woman and shoots off-screen left, leaving only his head to tip his hat to the audience. Here Charlot embodies (or disembodies) not just a rhythm of urban modernity but the daemonic energy of modern male sexuality. This, too, was part of jazzing.

Ballet mécanique should be taken primarily on its own terms, as the presentation of a *ballet* that is genuinely and ingeniously *mechanical*. This mechanical dance conjured up through the machinery of cinema takes a number of forms. The "mechanical element" takes a leading role, as the beauty of all those machine-objects is revealed when they are set in rhythmic motion. The film explores both the mechanics and the aesthetics of the human body as it moves, and the kinetics of the mechanically fragmented image. And it is also an experiment in technologically mediated, or technologically created, forms of choreography, both through montage and through animation.

The film does not appear to have been a self-conscious attempt to articulate a jazz aesthetic, in the programmatic sense that Léger wanted it to demonstrate a machine aesthetic. Nevertheless, its principles of construction are informed by a chain of cultural associations that linked together, however arbitrarily, machine, modernity, rhythm, jazz, and negritude. There is evidence that both Léger and Murphy were aware of this jazz dimension of

Ballet mécanique: *Katherine Murphy and Charlot*

the film, as each came up with his own solution to the nonappearance of Antheil's score. When *Ballet mécanique* was first screened at the London Film Society on March 14, 1926, the program notes contained a revealing semi-apology: "Mr. George Antheil was engaged in the composition of music for this picture but, according to Mr. Léger, his music is not likely to be suitably ready for some time and a jazz accompaniment suggested by Mr. Léger will accordingly be played instead." Later that year, when Dudley Murphy presented his print of the film at the Film Arts Guild in New York, he quite independently came up with a comparable but distinctly American response: "I got a Negro drummer from Harlem, who played on drums, tin washpans and washboards, and who would watch the film as he played interpretations in his own far-out manner, to the images which excited him on screen." After the event, and despite their different perspectives and claims on *Ballet mécanique*, both Léger and Murphy at least *heard* it as a jazz film.

The differences between Léger and Murphy remain one of the pleasures of *Ballet mécanique*. The film combines an energetic impudence that rags with a new kind of neoclassical discipline that orders, without ever coming down decisively on one side or the other. "The romantic pushes to the left—an excess of subjectivity (a warm state)," observed Léger in 1923. "His opposite pushes toward the right—an excess of objectivity (a cold state)." If Dudley Murphy and Man Ray veered toward this version of the left, here Léger knew himself to be (if only in this sense) a man of the right, predisposed to objectivity above all. The experience of working on *Ballet mécanique*, says Léger, taught him to consider the event of objectivity as a very new contemporary value.

Encore de Jazz

If there was a jazz aesthetic that informed works like *The Waste Land* in 1922 and *Ballet mécanique* in 1923, it turned out to be, for the most part, a passing phenomenon. The arrival of *La Revue nègre* in Paris and Berlin in 1925 may well have marked the beginning of the end of the 1920s jazz phenomenon in Europe, as well as the beginning of its popular dissemination. Many of the artists and intellectuals who had flirted with jazz as a rhythm and as a cultural phenomenon that could help to convey what it felt like to live in that disconcerting, modernizing, unhappy, and exhilarating time, soon turned their back on the music. Comparing Gertrude Stein's style to saxophones and the Charleston in a review, T. S. Eliot warned that if her kind of jazz-influenced writing were the way of the future, then the future is "of the barbarians" and that "this is the future in which we ought not to be interested." (After that, jazz and popular music became a private pleasure for Eliot.) In France, Darius Milhaud felt that jazz had done whatever good it was going to do by way of rejuvenating war-battered Western traditions, and decided that it was time to sign up to the *rappel à l'ordre*. "But already the influence of jazz has passed like a beneficial storm after which one again finds a clearer sky and more stable weather," he wrote. "Little by little the renascent classicism replaces the broken gasps of syncopation." In his *Negro* article, even if with an overly melodramatic flourish, George Antheil called this concerted "reaction" for what it was: "the musical world of Europe" becoming "alarmed at its racial problem." "Every time a white composer was caught consorting with Negro music," he observed, "he was promptly run off and musically lynched; after a vigorous year of campaigning Europe sat back and told itself that Negro music was no more."

When Dudley Murphy returned to his maverick film career in America, he was either unaware of such recantations or unfazed by them. He retained from his European sojourn an appreciation of jazz as part of his personal vision for cinema: that is, cinema as a medium that could combine music and dance under the sign of a machine aesthetic. Post-Europe, this jazz aesthetic surfaced only from time to time in Murphy's films but, when it did, those moments usually constituted his best work.

For all the archival significance of Bessie Smith's presence, for example, the most arresting sequence in *St. Louis Blues* features Jimmy the Pimp (Jimmy Mordecai), a dead ringer for the character of the Scarlet Creeper in Van Vechten's *Nigger Heaven*. Jimmy's louche charisma is celebrated in an astonishing dance that allows Murphy to show what he had learned in making *Ballet mécanique*. As James P. Johnson's band swings into an up-tempo number in a crowded speakeasy, and as a prelude to Jimmy's entrance, the waiters break into a dance that involves them spinning their round metal trays on their fingers. Jimmy glides around the room greeting acquaintances. As he eases into his dance, recalling the mechanics of Kiki's face, the washerwoman endlessly repeating her climb up the steps or Charlot's daemonic energy in the earlier film, Jimmy's body becomes machine as his arms flail in circles and his legs drive like pistons around the comparatively still axis of his torso.

Jimmy Mordechai as Jimmy the Pimp, St. Louis Blues, *1929*

Black and Tan, *1929*

In *Black and Tan*, too, it is neither the heavy-handed Amos 'n' Andy–style humor around the repossession of Duke Ellington's piano in the first section that is most compelling, nor even the final, chiaroscuro scene in which, in an exceptionally moving performance, Fredi Washington's self-sacrificing dancer lies on her death-bed, surrounded by musicians and a choir performing "Black and Tan." Rather, it is the central sequence in the film's triptych, in which Murphy's machine aesthetic surfaces once again as Ellington's band performs in the mocked-up Cotton Club. A troupe of male dancers, the Five Hot Shots, enters in tight formation from screen left. Disavowing individuality, the five bodies combine to create a dancing machine: a human train that offers a visual correlative to the sounds of Ellington's streamlined locomotion. This dancing-machine is first duplicated by its reflection in the mirrored floor of the club. Then, motivated as Fredi Washington's hallucinatory point of view, it is multiplied into kaleidoscope fragments by the same beveled prisms that Murphy had used on *Ballet mécanique*. A camera-created dance is thus overlaid onto the already machine-like choreography of the dancers. This is very far from the primitivist fantasy of Josephine Baker's *danse sauvage*, although that is evoked in the costumes of the Cotton Club dancing girls and in Fredi Washington's frenetic, fatal dance. What Murphy was responding to, and seeking to develop further, was the geometrical discipline and mechanical precision of the Hot Shots' black dance: a style of jazz dancing, attuned to the camera, that articulated his sense of a machine aesthetic.

Given this history, one inevitable question has to be asked about the film version of *The Emperor Jones* in 1933. Whatever happened to Dudley Murphy's jazz aesthetic? The answer, which points to the conundrum of the film, is that Murphy's predilection for dance appears to have run into the monumentality

Paul Robeson in Dudley Murphy's movie of The Emperor Jones, *1933 (Edward Steichen)*

of Paul Robeson, without achieving any satisfactory synthesis between the two. Whereas the stylistic (or ideological) differences between Murphy and Léger had resulted in an irresistible creative tension in *Ballet mécanique*, the mismatch between Murphy and Robeson produced something closer to an impasse. DuBose Heyward's rewriting of O'Neill's play pulled the film toward a conventional narrative structure, but character-driven narrative drive was not what Murphy was interested in or good at, and so that middle ground was not an option. Had he read it, Murphy would doubtless have been stung by the review in *Close Up* by his fellow experimentalist Herman G. Weinberg, who compares *The Emperor Jones* with King Vidor's all-black *Hallelujah!* (1929). Having criticized Murphy's film for being too imitative of O'Neill's play without being equally "taut, tightly woven, nervous and foreboding," Weinberg comments that "*Hallelujah* was ten times better cinema than *The Emperor Jones*. It had rhythm and swing, cadence shunted into cadence and the whole remained a unity in the mind of the director from its inception." Despite Murphy's persistent commitment to adventurous choreography, Weinberg accuses this film of lacking cinematic rhythm: "*The Emperor Jones* as a film has the rhythm of the drum beats but *Hallelujah* was rhythm personified. It had what René Clair calls 'inner rhythm'—it MOVES!"

Lack of movement and rhythm is the last thing to be expected from a Dudley Murphy film, and it may be the result of Paul Robeson's dominating presence. For all his extraordinary charisma, contemporary collaborators and admirers did acknowledge his technical limitations as an actor. He could sometimes be ungainly in his physical movements, he had a tendency to declaim, and his switches in vocal register and emotional tone could be over-abrupt. These weaknesses slowed down the film's momentum and Murphy, it seems, was unable to animate his star. (It is impossible not to wonder whether a very different director, Sergei Eisenstein, might have been able to turn Robeson's statuesque embodiment of heroism to better effect, if their plans to make a film about Toussaint L'Ouverture had ever come to fruition.)

Even in *The Emperor Jones*, Murphy's rhythmic touch and his choreographic machine aesthetic do surface briefly at least once, in a sequence he set in a Harlem jazz club. The camera follows a waiter's hand, again spinning a circular tray, as he moves among the tables toward a line of chorus girls and a precocious tail-coated kid—a very young Harold Nicholas, later of Nicholas Brothers fame—who breaks into a tap routine that is a smoother, more restrained version of Jimmy Mordecai's dance in *St. Louis Blues*. Some narrative business follows between Jones, his closest friend Jeff (Frank Wilson), who arrives with the recently dumped Undine (Fredi Washington), and Undine's replacement. This leads to a violent parody of dance, as the two women get into a catfight on the dance floor. A cut reveals Jones collecting his hat from the club's cloakroom, which happens to be lined with an unusually large number of round straw boaters—another nod back, perhaps, to the

The Emperor Jones, *1933*

many circles in *Ballet mécanique*. "I travels light," Jones tells the hat-check girl. There is a cut to a montage sequence over train wheels, showing the path of his travels around the country. Here Murphy puts the motif of spinning wheels fleetingly to narrative purpose. In doing so, he may have been looking back to the montage that Léger had admired in *La Roue*, but he was also paying homage to the locomotive rhythms that were now being incorporated into the music of big band jazz and swing.

In sequences like this, Murphy was staying true to the idea of a jazz-machine aesthetic that continued as a minority discourse in debates, as often as not in Europe, about the cultural significance of jazz. One intellectual who did not recant his belief in jazz was a professor at the Conservatoire Rameau in Paris, Albert Jeanneret—the brother, as it happens, of Charles-Édouard Jeanneret, or Le Corbusier. Albert published an article on "Le Nègre et le jazz" in *La Revue musicale* in 1927, which restated the case that jazz, far from being a music opposed to a new classical order, should be welcomed as a contribution to bringing that classicism into being. Describing the creators of good jazz as "masters of steel, mathematics, and engineering"—the exact words used by Antheil for his *Negro* article seven years later—Jeanneret approached jazz less as a cultural phenomenon than in formal musical terms. From this perspective, jazz signified "the restoration of a principle of economy." "The negro brings to European music an imperative recall to rhythm," argued Jeanneret, but not without being influenced in return. America has taught "the negro" mathematical structure and "the value of meter." Put African rhythm and European mathematics together, proclaimed Jeanneret, and the outcome will be a more muscular and more rational modern music. "One can say then that an intellectualized way of thinking, conditioned by the methods of a productive mathematics and based on physicality and instinct will orient our musical creation towards a new sentiment of order and economy." Although this classical or objectivist reading was initially less influential than romantic and expressivist responses, it paved the way for a later modernist recuperation of jazz in the post-bop era.

Whether it had represented a conscious strategy or an intuitive response to the times, the jazz aesthetic of the early 1920s had been one aspect of broader artistic attempts to give sensory and rhythmical expression to industrial modernization, urban life, and a more inclusive and anthropological conception of culture. Even if it turned out to have put down only shallow cultural roots in European art, jazz modernism has had enduring consequences for the connotations and international appeal of black American culture and especially of black American music.

In cinema, jazz modernism lingered on fitfully, in the later American films of Dudley Murphy and in some styles of film musical and film dance. After *The Emperor Jones*, Murphy continued to experiment and look for new opportunities and styles. He directed a few, mostly undistinguished features in Hollywood and in Mexico. He pioneered "soundies"—early forerunners of music videos—in the mid-1940s. He spent time with William Faulkner fruitlessly exploring the possibility of adapting *Absalom! Absalom!* for the screen. In the 1950s, although retired, Murphy still hoped to make his mark on Hollywood. He even tried to persuade Cecil B. DeMille that his old prismatic lenses might solve the problem of how to part the Red Sea in *The Ten Commandments* (1956).

However unfulfilled it turned out to be—he ended up running a classy restaurant and motel in Malibu designed by Richard Neutra, and he made money buying and selling land—Murphy's thwarted film career does act as a reminder of a dimension of cinema that is often underplayed. Cinema as a medium is defined neither by images, nor by photography nor by narrative, even though the mainstream industry thrives by telling and selling character-driven stories. Rather, what defines cinema is *movement*, the organization of movement over time, and so *rhythm*, and so *choreography*. Reconsidered from this point of view, Murphy's obsession with using cinema to make objects dance—whether they be California girls, kitchen utensils, or black male bodies—may turn out to have been less eccentric than it appears at first sight. Whatever his limitations as a filmmaker, he did at least understand that cinema is a choreography-machine. He spotted an affinity between jazz and cinema in terms of their modernism, as well as their modernity. What jazz and cinema had in common was that both were improvisatory. Both remade the world by inventing new ways of dancing.

Josephine Baker performs the Charleston, Paris, 1926 (Stanislaus Walery)

Jazz in Stone and Steel

JOSEPHINE BAKER AND MODERN ARCHITECTURE

The Viennese architect Adolf Loos liked to dance. He also had a long-standing interest in dance as a cultural phenomenon. In 1926, for example, he not only gave a lecture, in Berlin, on the cultural implications of the Charleston and the Blackbottom, he was also taught how to Charleston, in Paris, by Josephine Baker. Loos and Baker became friends and, two years later, he designed a house for her. Apparently, she had not been aware that Loos was a famous architect when she began to complain about her current architect's work on some renovations. He offered to build "the best house in the world for her." Although he did come up with plans and a model, the house was never built, not least because Baker left Paris in 1928 for her two-year-long tour of Europe and South America.

In the second year of that tour, sailing to Buenos Aires on the *Giulio Cesare*, Baker met another architect, Charles-Édouard Jeanneret—Le Corbusier. He was going to give a series of lectures, and to advise on a number of projects around Brazil and Uruguay. It turned out to be a transformative experience for him. South America taught him a deeper and more intense understanding of how region, topography, climate, and folk culture impinge on urban planning, and he developed more radical views on the need for wholesale demolition and rebuilding, after visiting the slums of Rio de Janeiro and Buenos Aires. During the tour, Le Corbusier saw Baker in "a stupid variety show" in São Paulo, where she sang "Baby," apparently with "such an intense and dramatic sensibility" that he was "moved to tears." Her performance strengthened his belief that there was an affinity between contemporary black American music and his vision of a new architecture, which would be truly modern, because both were energized by a redemptive primitivism. At some point, Baker and Le Corbusier became lovers. As they sailed back to Europe, this time on the *Lutétia*, Baker would sing to him in his cabin, accompanying herself on her ukulele—songs like Florence Mills's "I'm a Little Black Bird Looking for a Blue Bird"—and he drew sketch after sketch of her. With her manager and supposed husband Pepito Abatino sidelined, Le Corbusier and Baker decided to go together to a fancy-dress ball for first-class passengers. He designed their costumes. Blacked up, with a waistband of feathers, Le Corbusier went as Josephine Baker. She accompanied him, dressed as a clown, in whiteface, with her eyes ringed in black to mimic his trademark spectacles. "She glides over the roughness of life," Le Corbusier wrote in his journal, "She has a good little heart."

Le Corbusier did not design a house for Baker, but he did sketch out a dance scenario for her. Although the dance went unperformed, just as Loos's house remained unbuilt, the two embryonic projects show how these leading twentieth-century architects folded ideas and assumptions about modernity, primitivism, exoticism, and female sexuality into their designs for her, and on her. In doing so, the two men revealed more than they may have intended about their idiosyncratic, yet historically symptomatic, styles of thought, feeling, perception, and desire. Their meetings also provide two more examples of Josephine Baker's catalyzing role in specific conjunctions of modernism.

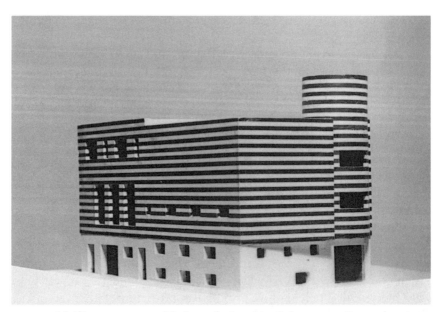

Adolf Loos, maquette of the house for Josephine Baker, avenue Bugeaud,
16th arrondissement, Paris, 1927

The Loos-Baker house

The house Adolf Loos designed for Josephine Baker was a compact, box-like oblong, with a flat roof and a turret in one corner, and a façade finished in black and white marble stripes. The house had few windows, in an irregular pattern. There was a functional reason for this: the house included a large interior swimming pool. Although Baker's lover, Marcel Ballot, had already had a marble pool expensively built into the apartment he maintained for her on the Champs-Élysées, Loos's pool was to be more than just a place to swim. He planned a spectacular reception area overlooking it, on the top floor of the design, and, on the floor below, two corridors with interior windows that would allow views onto the swimmers. The top floor included two master bedrooms, an access platform to the pool, and a dining room linked to the ground-floor kitchen by a lift. The corridors beside the pool linked a large salon, for parties and receptions, to a more intimate salon and a "café" in the turret.

The most striking aspect of Loos's design for Josephine Baker is the way that it disrupts, or inverts, many of his basic architectural principles, especially those concerning the relationships between interior and exterior, and private and public. Loos's usual starting point for domestic architecture was the premise that space is experienced sensually, rather than a concern with the way a building looks. He designed for the body, not just for the eye. The architect's first task, he believed, is to enclose and cover a body, and a dwelling should be constructed so as to fit comfortably: "Carpets are warm and liveable. He decides for this reason to spread one carpet on the floor and to hang four to form the four walls. But you cannot build a house out of carpets. Both the carpet on the floor and the tapestry on the wall require a structural frame to hold them in the correct place."

It is because he started from this phenomenological perspective that Loos was especially concerned with the movement of bodies within, and through, the interior of a house. This is where architecture touches on dance. Loos designed domestic interiors around what he called the *Raumplan*, or "plan of volumes." Rather than working from definitive drawings, he would often make decisions about the design of a building onsite, as he responded to the emerging form and character of its constituent spaces, rather as a dancer responds to the rhythm of the music and to the movements of other dancers. The construction would lead him, as much as he led it. Movement, adaptation, and improvisation were built into the experience of a Loos house, and to enter one would often entail a kind of choreography. One might confront a closet facing the front door, which would make one pause just inside the doorway. The way into the living room would be off-center, prompting first a shimmy and then a twist to align oneself with the axis of the room on entering it. A description of a residential house that Loos designed and built in Prague in 1930, the Villa Müller, exemplifies the kind of dance he built into his architecture: "The many different levels make it necessary for anyone who wants to get from the dining room to the study, for example, to go down two steps to a landing, climb another eight from there, descend a further four steps again in the room itself." In a Loos interior, too, a person would repeatedly be stopped by the layout of the house, and have their body turned around to face the space they had just crossed, rather than the space ahead or outside its windows.

As the Baker design was to house one of the world's most famous dancers, it comes as a surprise, to begin with, that it contains none of this choreographed stop and go, or turn and twist, no dance of expectation and shock. Nor is there any sign of Loos's usual tactile, sensual approach to the way that spaces and materials should envelop the body. The front door opens directly onto a broad staircase, leading straight up to the main public space, as in a cinema or theater. Interior windows are used not to create mystery, opacity, or anticipation, but to ensure transparency and clarity. Loos's occasional touches of theatricality in his domestic interiors, whereby the person living in the house would be placed, as it were, in a theater box and given the opportunity to watch the performance of guests in the artfully arranged stage set, here take precedence over the functions of enclosure and movement. The organizing principle behind the arrangement of rooms, framings, and sight-lines in the house thus turns out to be, not just the idea and the presence of Josephine Baker, but rather an almost cinematic *mise en scène* for presenting Josephine Baker to others: Baker the hostess in the public salon at the top of the grand stairway, Baker the glamorous star descending that stairway, Baker the fetishized, exotic body in the pool. Kurt Ungers, Loos's assistant on the project, confirmed that the arrangement of the large salon, small lounge, and circular café on the first floor, around the swimming pool, was deliberately "intended not for private use but as a miniature entertainment centre," and that the corridors with windows onto the pool were designed to create the effect of "an underwater revue." In short, the interior of the Baker house was based on principles that Loos normally used for public, rather than private, buildings. Specifically, the movement from the entrance, up the grand stairway, past the first-floor entertainment salon, then up the arcing stairway to the mezzanine outside the main bedrooms, and finally to the display area around the pool, was derived from plans that Loos had made, in 1925, for an exhibition hall, hotel, and theater complex in the northern Chinese city of Tientsin.

Even if the interior of the Baker house had become a public space, it does not follow that the exterior became "private"; or, at least, if it did, it did so in an idiosyncratic way. For Loos, the exterior of a private residence should, like Georg Simmel's blasé self-presentation, give away as little information as possible about what is going on within, not least in order to protect an interior space that is the setting for the complex creative and sexual dynamics of subjective life: "The house does not have to tell anything to the exterior; instead all its richness must be manifest in the interior." The same discretion need not constrain a public building conceived as a work of art. "The work of art is a private matter for the artist," Loos had argued in 1910. "The house is not." The function of a house is to provide shelter and comfort, whereas the aim of a work of art is "to draw people out of their state of comfort." "The work of art is revolutionary, the house is conservative."

In the Baker design, the shape, the material, and the finish of the exterior all have the provocative and disorientating quality of a work of art. It is less clear whether the geometry of its volumes, the contrast of the turret against the flat roofs, the expanse of largely windowless walls, and those black-and-white marble stripes were intended to signify anything more specific and, if so, what. From the 1960s onwards, it is possible to cite example after example of architectural criticism asserting that, if the feminized interior reveals Loos's voyeurism and fetishism, then somehow, among the aftershocks of *l'art nègre* and *le tumulte noir* in late 1920s Paris, the exterior must constitute an instance of modernist primitivism, and/or colonialist ideology, that invokes Baker's negritude. These observers comment on the exoticism of the building, occasionally seen as Mediterranean, but more often as "mysteriously," "more or less," or "vaguely" evocative of "Africa." If they have any grounds for seeing "Africa" in the Baker house, it is probably because Loos may have been playing, teasingly, with architectural and cultural codes, rather than invoking any geographical specifics. If the house connotes "Africa," it does so rather as Baker conjured up "Africa" for audiences in Paris; that is, through chains of arbitrary associations sparked off by a purely formal relationship between the signifiers "black" and "white," rather than through any actual links between either the fabric of the house, or the person of Josephine Baker, with the continent or the history of Africa. Loos was making something new, not reconstituting an ethnographic exhibit, let alone peddling colonialist fantasies or ideologies.

As someone born, in 1870, in Brünn in the province of Moravia, which became Brno in Czechoslovakia and now finds itself in the Czech Republic, Loos's practical experience of empire was limited to the increasingly anachronistic Austro-Hungarian Empire, whose rule ran only to the European land mass and which owned no overseas colonies. He regarded the empire he lived in as peripheral and backward, not least because of its inadequate and willfully belated response to modernization. (When he started *Das Andere* early in the century, he promoted it as "A journal for the introduction of Western culture into Austria.") In short, Loos would have been an unlikely apologist for expansionist colonialism. Nevertheless, he clearly did think in terms of a racially inflected and evolutionary hierarchy of cultures, which he deployed to polemical effect. "The Papuan and the criminal ornament their skin. The Indian covers his paddle and his boat with layers and layers of ornament," he

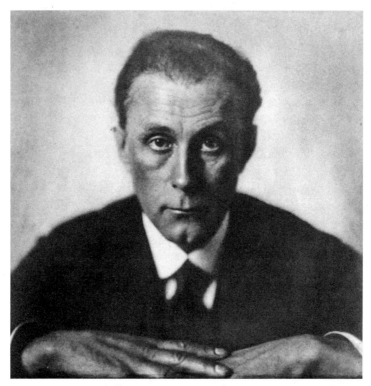

Adolf Loos, c. 1922 (Trude Fleischmann)

would argue, "But the bicycle and the steam engine are free of ornament. The march of civilization systematically liberates object after object from ornamentation." "We must seek to overcome the Red Indian within us," he would assert. He would provoke audiences by asking them, "Why do the Papuans have a culture while the Germans don't?" In this imagined taxonomy, "Papua New Guinea," "Turkey," "China" and "the Balkans" represent backwardness or underdevelopment. The Western culture that he hoped to introduce into liminal Austria linked "classical antiquity" to modern "England" and "America." Sitting uneasily between the backward and the modern were "Germany" and "Japan," both of which he believed had the potential for significant cultural renewal or destruction. Notably absent from Loos's cognitive atlas was "Africa."

In his mid-twenties, in the 1890s, Loos had been greatly influenced by the three years that he lived and worked in America. When he returned to Vienna, at a time of considerable anti-American sentiment, he became notorious as a champion of American styles and values, and throughout his career, his imagined and idealized "America" continued to evoke the possibilities of modernization, rationality, social cohesion, and industrial efficiency. It is, therefore, more likely that the public face Loos wanted the Baker house to present to Paris would be characterized by deliberate connotations of a modern "America," rather than vague evocations of a primitive "Africa."

When the *Chicago Tribune* announced a competition, in 1922, to find a design for a new headquarters, Loos had submitted an entry. His monumental design was dominated by a huge Doric column, standing on top of an eleven-story base of brick and terracotta, which he intended to act as a symbol for Chicago, equivalent to the Eiffel Tower in Paris or the leaning tower in Pisa. The column was to be made of black polished granite which, when juxtaposed with the building's windows, would produce a visual effect of layering or striping. There was a degree of playfulness in this monumental design: a knowing juxtaposition of twentieth-century American mass media against classical Greek architecture, the *Tribune* standing tall as a pillar of society, or embodying Loos's punning response to the challenge, "What kind of building should journalists work in?"—"In a newspaper column, of course!" The relevance to the Baker house is that just as Loos recycled his Tientzin exhibition complex design for its interior, so the elevation of the Baker turret represented a proportionally exact miniaturized version of the *Tribune* Tower—which also provided a prototype for the black-and-white banding of the house.

It may be that Loos was adapting plans from unsuccessful tenders to economize on a project, which he knew might well not come to fruition. Pragmatism aside, the sheer vivacity of the design for Baker suggests that he was allowing his imagination free rein, in response to the question, what would it mean to build a modern house for a black American star in Paris? A clue might be found in that black-and-white cladding, which commentators have been so quick to compare to African zebra stripes or Papuan tattoos. In terms of Loos's own work, the stripes echo the banding on the *Tribune* tower. More directly, they also recall the exquisite American Bar (originally Kärntner Bar), which he designed in Vienna in 1908. Its façade features the stripes of the American flag and a blue square where the stars would normally be. Using that analogy, it is reasonable to suggest that the Baker façade may be another allusion to the American flag. With that in mind, it can be seen that the asymmetrical windows on the corner, diagonally opposite the turret, are placed roughly where the stars should be in relation to the stripes. Given the way that Loos equated construction with clothing, maybe the Baker house exterior is another of his architectural puns: How do you dress an American star? In stripes!

This is speculation, of course, but the inventiveness and wit of the design invite the response. The building is a performance, an improvisation on the theme of Josephine Baker that spins a fabric of erotic spectacle, glamorous surfaces, and spatial rhythms around its referent, its nominal occupant, and its star. The plans reveal Adolf Loos's ingenuity and passions, and also his prejudices, his blind spots, and the limits of his imagination. The rendering of Baker's public persona is brilliant, affectionate, and, ultimately, conventional. There are signs that he intended the building to be dialogic. It was his provocation to Baker to perform as "Josephine Baker," in a space that was somewhere between cinema and salon: neither quite public nor wholly private. From Loos's point of view, the design may have promised a creative transgression of the boundaries between black and white, masculine and feminine, European and American. In the end, though, it turned out to be more about him than about her. Josephine Baker did not want to be on show at home, and Loos was wrong to assume that she would want a house that excluded the possibility of family life. She may have been the object of avant-garde fascination, but she was no revolutionary. She desired, in principle if not in practice, a more conventional and simply *ordinary* home life than his designs would have allowed. In dedicating an artwork to her, in the form of a house, Loos made, in his own terms, a category error.

"Since I personified the savage on the stage," wrote Baker, "I tried to be as civilized as possible in daily life." That personal civilization seems to have included a preference for conservative domestic architecture. She did not want to live in a jazz house. In 1929, she bought Le Beau Chêne (Beautiful Oak), a thirty-room neo-Gothic mansion, built at the turn of the century and set among parklands, lakes, and streams in the wealthy suburb of Le Vésinet, to the west of Paris. It was elaborately decorated with the kind of ornamentation Adolf Loos would have loathed: pointed turrets, fussy dormer windows, and mock medieval shields. Baker planned the interior decor herself.

Pierre Jeanneret, Le Corbusier, Josephine Baker, and (on the right of the group) Pepito Abatino aboard the Lutétia, *1929*

Three Dances for Josephine Baker

Le Corbusier's dance sequence for Josephine Baker exists only as jottings in his sketchbook.

Ballet:

Oval cylinder / one could also eliminate the cylinder completely

    1. entrance 2 showgirls, made up with tattoos, 1 negro on stage

Sound: one step or pure negro tam tam without music

    2. 1 negro carrying a banana tree
    3. a modern man and woman + New York dancing only 1 step holding each other slowly
    4. the cylinder is lowered Josephine descends dressed as a monkey
    5. she puts on a modern dress she sits down
    6. goes forward on a podium and sings
    7. last solemn song; the gods rise

background meandering sea of Santos and at the end a big ocean liner / words translated on programme

This is familiar territory: another trip from tattooed primitivism to the whitewashed modernity of an ocean liner. Jazz meets social Darwinism one more time, with primitivism predictably returning in the plangent rhythms of the machine age. However, the scenario does have a Purist edge to it that recalls *Ballet mécanique*. Le Corbusier wanted the scenario to be choreographed and staged with "machine-like precision" and "classical economy," which are just the kind of modern iterations of timeless aesthetic laws and classical virtues—severity, restraint, unity, and order—that he and Amédée Ozenfant sought, through Purism, to reassert against the anarchy, relativism, and self-obsession of the postwar period. The Purists' journal, *L'Esprit nouveau*, had reprinted Loos's "Ornament and Crime," with its diatribe against tattoos, in 1920, and it illustrated Le Corbusier's manifesto for white walls in its first issue, with the photograph of a liner, like the one that appears at the end of the scenario. Although the Purists shared their enthusiasm for *l'art nègre* and jazz with the Dadaists and the Surrealists, what they valued in them was less any celebration of primal instinct or sacred possession, than the resource these forms provided for a new classicism. Le Corbusier took the same optimistic view as his brother, Albert Jeanneret. In jazz, Albert had argued, physicality and instinct might interact with mathematics and technology in a way that would "orient our musical creation toward a new sentiment of order and economy." After visiting New York in 1935, Le Corbusier would likewise conclude that: "In an excited Manhattan, the Negroes of the USA have breathed into jazz the song, the rhythm and the sound of machines."

What the scenario's specifically Purist configuration of primitivism, mathematics, and this new "sentiment of order and economy" reveals about Le Corbusier's perception of Josephine Baker can be clarified by comparing his dance with two others from around this period, for which she was also the inspiration.

The first was dreamed up by Harry Kessler, the aristocratic German aesthete and diplomat, who had seen her dance in Berlin in 1926. Kessler belonged to Loos's generation, rather than Le Corbusier's, and his attitudes and tastes had been formed in the Decadence and Nietzscheanism of the 1890s. He was interested in progressive social causes—he was known as "the red Count"—as well as the arts, music, and dance. Kessler collaborated with the poet Hugo von Hoffmannsthal on the scenario for Richard Strauss's *Der Rosenkavalier* and, in 1912, he proposed a ballet to Diaghilev for the Ballets Russes and persuaded Strauss to write the music. A year after the riotous opening of *Le Sacre du printemps* at the Théâtre des Champs-Élysées, and only months before the outbreak of the Great War, *La Légende de Joseph* had its first performance at

Harry Graf Kessler

the Grand Opera in Paris in 1914, with Strauss conducting and the rising star Mjassin dancing the title role. (Better known in the West as Léonide Massine, Mjassin replaced Nijinsky in the Ballets Russes, and became Diaghilev's principal choreographer between 1915 and 1921.) Although this may not have been obvious at the time, the elite premiere of Kessler's ballet represented not only the last hurrah of a by now anachronistic fin-de-siècle aesthetic culture, but also the passing of a prewar cosmopolitan ethos.

In 1926, Kessler organized a dinner for Josephine Baker, expressly so that she could dance for his guests. To begin with, no doubt overwhelmed by so many men in dinner jackets—she was still only twenty—she sulked in a corner and refused to perform. Anxious that he might have put her in an embarrassing situation, Kessler began to describe his scenario for her. As he did so, Baker brightened up.

> My plot is how Solomon, handsome, young, and royal (I have Serge Lifar in mind), buys a dancer (the Shulamite, Miss Baker), has her brought before him, naked, and showers his robes, his jewels, his entire riches upon her. But the more gifts he lavishes, the more she eludes him. From day to day he grows more naked and the Dancer less perceptible to him. Finally, when it

Aristide Maillol, La Mediterranée, *1905*

is the King who is altogether naked, the Dancer utterly vanishes from his sight in a tulip-shaped cloud, first golden in colour and composed of all the jewels and stuffs of which he had stripped himself to adorn her, then turning black. At the end of the scene, in the semi-gloom, there enters the young Lover, wearing a dinner jacket and...

For the present, Kessler told his guests, he would keep the rest of the story to himself. As he narrated this tale, Baker had begun to dance around the white marble statue that was the centerpiece of his apartment, Aristide Maillol's *La Méditerranée*, which shows a woman sitting on the ground with one elbow resting on an upraised knee. Baker's movements, recalled Kessler, were "vigorous and vividly grotesque," as she appeared to become preoccupied with the sculpture. She "stared at it, copied the pose, rested against it in bizarre postures, and talked to it, clearly excited by its massive rigor and elemental force. Then she danced around it with extravagantly grandiose gestures, the picture of a priestess frolicking like a child and making fun of herself and her goddess." By now, Baker appeared to have forgotten her audience. "Genius (for she is a genius in the matter of grotesque movement) was addressing genius."

Comparing Kessler's incomplete scenario with Le Corbusier's notes reveals the differences in sensibility between the two men: Le Corbusier's Purist modernism versus Kessler's overripe aestheticism. Both of them invoked ancient worlds to uncover the contours of modernity, but whereas Le Corbusier opted for a cartoon evolutionism, Kessler evoked a fantasia of Bible stories, replete with exotic sets, fabulous jewels, and ornate fabrics. Both signified modernity through clothing. Le Corbusier had Baker donning a modern dress (perhaps like the one she wears in a caricature he drew of them in Rio de Janeiro, with himself trailing along behind her—see Plate 8), whereas Kessler's "young Lover" enters in Loos's symbol of modern masculinity, the dinner jacket. Whereas Kessler did not reveal the outcome of his narrative, Le Corbusier's decision to follow Baker's "jazz" performance with the ascension of African gods, at the same time as a liner appears on the horizon, suggests the recurrence of the primitive in the modern. In the end, what is most striking is the similarity of the *form* in which two such different men responded to their encounter with Josephine Baker. Both Kessler and Le Corbusier were inspired by her, in the sense that they felt compelled to decode and re-enact, in dance, the cultural narratives that they perceived her to embody.

In the third scenario, the only one that was actually produced, Josephine Baker does not appear. Instead, she functions as an implicit but unmistakable point of reference. This is the "Hot Voodoo" number performed by Marlene Dietrich in Josef von Sternberg's 1932 film *Blonde Venus*—itself an allusion to Baker, the "Black Venus." The film as a whole is an almost delirious exercise in transatlantic modernism, a story about desire, fantasy, obsession, sacrifice, and domination. It works through, in fictionalized form, Marlene Dietrich's transformation from German cabaret performer to Hollywood star, by playing on the audience's assumed knowledge about her relationship to Sternberg and her decision to move her daughter with her to the United States, while leaving her husband in Germany. As a kind of counterpoint, it also silently alludes to Josephine Baker's ascension to stardom, which entailed a move in the opposite direction, from the United States to Europe. Thus, in the film, a German immigrant chorus girl remakes herself as an American housewife and mother, Helen Faraday, who then becomes a Harlem cabaret performer and hits rock bottom, after leaving her husband and losing her son, before re-emerging in Paris as the cosmopolitan *vedette* Helen Jones, who finally crosses the Atlantic yet again to end up, implausibly, as a dutiful mother in New York. Through its layers of allusion, parody, masquerade, doubling, and metamorphosis, *Blonde Venus* represents both a playing out of Dietrich's struggle with Sternberg for mastery over her image and her career and an attempt to redeem her ambiguous and transgressive sexuality—her Europeanness—in such a way that she could become a fully-fledged American star.

In "Hot Voodoo," against the backdrop of a nightclub stage set featuring "jungle" foliage, "African" drums and "primitive" teeth-filled masks, and accompanied by a chorus line of blacked-up "native" women, Dietrich performs a weird striptease. Hidden in a gorilla suit, she first removes one hairy paw and then the other to reveal her slim, manicured white hands. Next she takes off the costume head, replaces it with a huge platinum blonde Afro wig, and lifts herself out of the gorilla body. Revealed to be wearing a shimmering black bodice, trimmed below the waist with (shades of Baker) boa feathers, she launches huskily into her song: "That African tempo has made me a slave, hot voodoo—dance of sin, hot voodoo, worse than gin, I'd follow a cave man right into his cave." The obvious parallel between Sternberg's Hollywood

The "Hot Voodoo" number in Blonde Venus, *1932*

number for Dietrich and Le Corbusier's shipboard scenario for Josephine Baker is that both present the modern woman—white or black—emerging from a gorilla or monkey suit that signifies, parodically no doubt, the stain of primitivism and the alignment of woman—white or black—with nature and instinct, rather than culture and reason. What is revealed, in both cases, is the same ultramodern primitivism that Harry Kessler had spotted in Baker's dancing in Berlin. And as with Baker's nudity, the striptease in "Hot Voodoo" is less a matter of revelation, than of "putting on" a skin—in Dietrich's case, a "white" skin that has taken on the fetishized exoticism of Baker's "black" skin. To the extent that Dietrich is "aping" Josephine Baker, she "apes" the quality that observers like Le Corbusier and Kessler—as well as Ivan Goll and e. e. cummings in Paris—found so hard to tie down definitively, but which certainly incorporated the "ultramodernity" of Baker's invented yet rejuvenating primitivism. What is revealed is not some primordial truth, either about race or about female sexuality, but the artifice—the self-parodying performativity—of race, gender, and sexuality as categories of modernity, and so the modernism of their invention, subversion, and reinvention. (Josephine Baker was more down-to-earth: "That German cow has copied me all my life," she grumbled. "The only thing left for her to copy will be my funeral.")

Kessler, Sternberg, and Le Corbusier were all, in their different ways, modernists, and the dances that they constructed around the connotations they inferred from Josephine Baker each revealed both an aesthetic predisposition and a degree of personal or libidinal investment. Like Loos's house, Le Corbusier's Purist dance scenario was an inventive response to her persona, her body, and her music. From these, Le Corbusier extrapolated two chains of association. One linked Baker's negritude and sexuality to Africa (the banana tree), primitivism (the monkey, tattooing), and the elemental (the African gods, the sea). The other aligned Baker, through the dress she puts on and the song she sings, to America (the New York couple dancing) and to modernity (the ocean liner). These associations, and this configuration of modernity, exoticism, and sexuality, provide an illuminating framework for understanding the subsequent evolution of Le Corbusier's approach to urban planning.

Algiers

The "primitive" connotations that Le Corbusier projected onto Josephine Baker were symptomatic of his sexual fascination with women of color, especially Arab women, that dated back at least to his early twenties, when he spent five months touring around Turkey, Greece, and the Balkans, in 1910 and 1911. In his record of that trip, *Le Voyage d'Orient*, written at the time but not submitted for publication until a couple of weeks before he swam out to sea to his death in 1965, Le Corbusier fantasized, in an indulgently masochistic mode, about the sexual allure of incarcerated Eastern women. To the young Charles-Édouard Jeanneret, his head no doubt full of the eroticism that was synonymous with "the Orient" in French culture, the possibility that the houses on the quiet streets of Istanbul might be "prisons of odalisques" was enough to provoke the same feelings as "a lightly painful, melancholic, beneficent poem." He daydreamed about seraglios filled with "divine, thrilling odalisques," with gold and jewels snaking around "their naked ankles and arms": "Loaded with gold and their nails painted in vermillion, they suffocated from waiting so long in their magnificent cages."

This eroticism spilled over into his perception of the landscape and vernacular architecture of the region, and especially the way that the play of light on white walls intensified the sensual impact of the color of things and people. Color, for Le Corbusier, "exists for the caress and for the intoxication of the eye." This is not an unhealthy, regressive sensuality, he assured himself, but (in an early example of the thinking that would later emerge in Albert Jeanneret's account of jazz, as well as in his own reaction to Josephine Baker) a proper physical and instinctual foundation for the abstraction and mathematical precision that must be the basis for creative renewal and transformation in the machine age. "The art of the peasant is a striking creation of aesthetic sensuality," Le Corbusier wrote. Art differs from the sciences, because "it stimulates sensuality and awakens profound echoes in the physical being." Traditional art thus "gives to the body—to the animal—its fair share." On this "healthy base," a creative synthesis between the sensual relationship to the land and "the magic of geometry" might produce "an astonishing union of fundamental instincts and of those susceptible to more abstract speculations." For Le Corbusier, it was the white wall of vernacular architecture that embodied both sides of this *astonishing union*. It signified an erotic relation to sunlight, color, space, and place: "Each spring, the house that one loves receives its new coat: sparkling white, it smiles the whole summer through foliage and flowers that owe to it their dazzle." At the same time, the white wall was the means through which architecture controls and moralizes that sensuality, while yet remaining rooted in it.

The same ambiguity between mastery and sexuality resurfaced in Le Corbusier's projects for the redevelopment of Algiers in the 1930s and 1940s. His first trip, in the spring of 1931, was the prelude to what he described as "twelve years of uninterrupted study" of the city. The occasion was a conference to mark the centenary of the colonization of Algeria in 1830, with the objective of deciding how best to renovate Algiers prior to making it the capital city of French Africa. This prospect inspired him to undertake, without client or commission, a sequence of extraordinarily ambitious plans, which demonstrate both his vision of urban society and the shift in his work away from a purely machine-based, mathematical aesthetic, toward one that acknowledged more explicitly its sensual substrate. As part of this process, Le

Corbusier did attempt to incorporate a dialogue with Islamic culture into his schemes, but that aspiration was constrained both by his unwavering commitment to the principle of *la grande France* and its *mission civilatrice*, and by the way that his infatuation with non-European women shaped his perception of the culture.

The political context in which Le Corbusier was working in North Africa had been established by an exceptionally subtle and effective colonial administrator, Hubert Lyautey, created a Marshal of France in 1921 and governor-general of Morocco between 1912 and 1925. In the year of Le Corbusier's first visit to Algiers, Lyautey was the main organizer of the Exposition Coloniale Internationale in Paris, which he used to promote his conviction that colonial power was most effective when it did not try to assimilate colonized peoples and their cultures. Lyautey's starting point, strategic as much as ethical, was the need to respect cultural difference and particularity: "Vex not tradition, leave custom be. Never forget that in every society there is a class to be governed, and a natural-born ruling class upon whom all depends. Link their interests to ours." This type of association was the precondition for social intervention into indigenous societies, through welfare provision and economic development, the segregation of populations, and urban planning. "A construction site is worth a battalion," Lyautey proclaimed, and his tenure as governor saw major, and often quite experimental, developments in Rabat, Fez, and Casablanca. Le Corbusier and Lyautey shared not only a belief in urbanism as a way of managing populations, but also their admiration for the vernacular architecture of the Islamic Mediterranean and a preference for modernist aesthetics. "Islam gave me a taste for great white walls," declared Lyautey in 1931, "and I could almost claim to be one of the forerunners of Le Corbusier."

These aesthetic preferences and political principles did not mean that Lyautey wanted to raze the existing Arab quarters, or medinas. On the contrary, for reasons that combined the political, the aesthetic, and the economic, he wanted to preserve and develop them alongside new, modern cities built for European settlers. Lyautey extolled the "charm and poetry" of the Arab town and the sophistication of the culture that produced it. "Yes, in Morocco, and it is to our honour, we conserve," he declared. "I would go a step further, we rescue. We wish to conserve in Morocco Beauty—and that is no small thing." But politics and aesthetics required the rigid segregation of indigenous and European populations: "Large cities, boulevards, tall façades for stores and homes, installation of water and electricity are necessary, which upset the indigenous city completely, making the customary way of life impossible."

When Le Corbusier arrived, therefore, Algiers was a city divided in two. The French had developed *Alger la blanche*—a reference to the walls, supposedly, rather than the people—over the decades as a modern European city with broad boulevards and avenues running parallel to the sea. The Casbah, originally the fortress-palace of the precolonial city, was an Arab town embedded within it, built on an outcrop of rock overlooking the bay. By the 1890s, two thirds of the city's population was of European origin. In 1926, almost eighty per cent of the Muslim population lived within the limits of the old, pre-occupation city, and two-thirds of them lived in the Casbah itself. In the wealthier European areas, less than 3 percent of the population was Muslim. In his reaction to the Casbah, Le Corbusier again echoed Lyautey. It was "beautiful" and "adorable." It must "never, no, never be destroyed." What is more, as a "place of European and Muslim life during centuries of picturesque struggles," its mixture of aesthetic charm, heritage appeal, and exoticism gave it "gigantic" potential for economic growth through tourism. At the same time, it was hugely overpopulated, with many of its inhabitants living in far from picturesque poverty. A quarter of a century later, Frantz Fanon saw the division, but not the charm: "The *colons'* town is a town of whites, of foreigners. The colonized's town is a town that squats down, a town on its knees, a town that wallows. This is a town of niggers, a town of *bicots*." From a colonial or planning perspective, then, the Casbah needed to be purified and reorganized, and its population reduced and, where necessary, evicted and relocated.

As he started to play with ideas for reshaping the city, Le Corbusier was driven in part by the mathematics of topography, demographics, density, and economics. At the same time, the sensuality of his relationship to the place asserted itself. He visited the brothels of the Casbah, where he admitted to being "profoundly seduced by a type of woman particularly well built," and where he claimed (with Josephine Baker's body apparently forgotten or disavowed) to have discovered "the nobility of the nude thanks to the plastic structures of certain females of the Casbah under the intense but nuanced light of Algiers." A bemused witness to all this was Jean de Maisonseul, who later in life became director of the Musée des Beaux Arts d'Alger. As an eighteen year old, he had acted as Le Corbusier's guide. He recalled how, in the side streets of the Casbah, Le Corbusier was fascinated by two young girls, one Spanish and the other Algerian: "They brought us up a narrow stairway to their room; there he sketched some nudes on—to my amazement—some schoolbook graph paper with coloured pencils; the sketches of the Spanish girl lying both alone on the bed and beautifully grouped together with the Algerian turned out accurate and realistic; but he said they were very bad and refused to show them." Le Corbusier also bought "horrible" postcards, which Maisonseul recalled as being "in raw colours, pinks and greens, representing *indigènes nues* in an oriental décor." Although, years later, Le Corbusier claimed that the notebooks containing the sketches had been lost or stolen in Paris, he appears to have used both his drawings and the postcards as source material for several paintings. In *Fathma* (1939), a woman sits on a roof terrace, surrounded by objects with stereotypical Algerian connotations. Like the Baker persona in his dance scenario, she reveals two aspects: not primitivism and modernity in this case, but a unique mingling of French and North African eroticism that divides her between the veiled (the hidden and mysterious female) and the nude (an occupied and prostituted population). A painting from a year earlier takes its title from Delacroix's 1833 picture *Femmes d'Alger*, the pre-eminent symbol in French art of the conquest of Algeria. Le Corbusier continued to study the Delacroix exhaustively and to make sketches of it that removed the "exotic clothing" and "Oriental décor" to reveal its formal structure. These different strands and obsessions were all eventually supposed to feed into a monumental, but never completed, project that haunted him between his first return from Algiers and his death over thirty years later. It was to have been called *Femmes de la Casbah*.

This eroticized vision informed the way that Le Corbusier perceived Algiers as a space: "Algiers drops out of sight like a magnificent body, supple-hipped and full-breasted," he rhapsodized from a liner, heading toward France, in 1934. "A body which could be revealed in all its magnificence, through the judicious influence of form and the bold use of mathematics to harmonize natural topography and human geometry." It also resurfaced in his sketches for his plans, where he liked to include pictures of veiled women to add local color and to highlight the presence of two distinct populations in the city. Even in his diagrams, he consistently used the veil as shorthand to represent the Casbah. His first set of proposals, the Obus plan of 1932, made the links between colonial mastery and feminized space quite clear. His plan was to preserve the upper Casbah, while restricting population and housing densities and imposing changes on the way that buildings were used. Some residential buildings would be converted into arts and crafts centers, for example, both to thin out the population and to act as a catalyst for an indigenous cultural renaissance. The slums of the lower Casbah would be demolished, with only mansions of heritage interest being preserved and converted into museums, and new parks and gardens being introduced. Arching over this purified, but still segregated, Arab quarter would be a huge "bridge" linking European residential districts in the hills to the business district in the Marine quarter. In some sketches Le Corbusier depicted the link as a household broom with its head in the port and its handle resting on the hills.

The first conference on the future of Algiers that Le Corbusier attended, in 1931, had agreed on the need for a "green belt" around the old city. In Le Corbusier's reworked vision, this principle of retaining a zone of undeveloped and seminatural land had become a green artery in the sky, an extraordinary structure that would serve three purposes. First, it would be green in the sense that it would act as a cordon sanitaire, contributing to a healthier environment within the Casbah but also, in effect, quarantining it from its European neighbors. Second, and as a result, it would maintain and even reinforce the segregation between the Arab and European populations: "This artery will be separated entirely from the indigenous town, by means of a level difference."

And, third, it would introduce the possibility of constant surveillance of an indigenous colonial population within a miniaturized Casbah, refashioned as a heritage park for tourists. At the same time, the curvilinear forms Le Corbusier proposed for structures to be built in developments outside the Casbah celebrated his obsession with Algerian women and his attempt to embrace more "natural" forms in his plans: the forms, it would appear, of Josephine Baker's buttocks and the "plastic structures" of the prostitutes in the Casbah.

Le Corbusier's relationship to Algiers thus elucidates what was implicit in the "primitive" images and associations in his scenario for Josephine Baker. A voyeuristic, and perhaps slightly masochistic, fascination with non-white women was bound up, in some way, with a fetishization of indigenous Islamic culture. These feelings were then displaced onto, or rationalized into, the plans for surveillance over a colonized population and the French colonial modernization of Algiers. This North African connection is only half the story, however. The other narrative leads once again to America.

America

In 1935, at the invitation of the Museum of Modern Art in New York, Le Corbusier embarked on a three-month lecture tour of major American cities. His brief was to expound his views on the need to return to the social and architectural optimism of a time when medieval European cathedrals were "white because they were new," not "black with grime and worn by centuries," and when "thought was clear, spirit was alive." His book about the trip, *When the Cathedrals Were White*, was not published in English until 1947. It was subtitled *A Journey to the Country of Timid People*. Le Corbusier's jibe about Americans' "timidity" was, in part, a reaction against their reluctance to offer him new commissions. More fundamentally, he believed that American modernity was constrained by excessive sexual repression, a "timidity" that arrested it in a state of cultural immaturity and hobbled its potential dynamism. In America, then, as in Algiers, Le Corbusier perceived architecture through an optic of sexuality. He celebrated the energy of the "architectural spirit which is manifest in everything, skyscrapers, machines, objects, bars, clothes," but equally he bemoaned the timid disavowal of that vigor evident in the gloomy black of men's suits and the black facing of the Empire State Building.

Le Corbusier's gloom at America's misdirected energy, and its cultural denial of sensuality, sent him in search of naked female bodies. "On Broadway, divided by feelings of melancholy and lively gaiety, I wander along in a hopeless search for an intelligent burlesque show in which the nude white bodies of beautiful women will spring up in witty flashes under the paradisiac illumination of the spotlights." Again, he was disappointed. Although, on the street, "the night streams with mobile lights," behind the billboards the "the burlesque shows, movies, revues, are never joyous, but rather tragic or desperately sentimental." The same morbidity pervaded the city's public spaces: "In the entrances of skyscrapers, in the halls of skyscrapers, in the lobbies of moving-picture palaces and theatres, a funereal spirit reigns, a solemnity which has not yet succeeded in coming alive."

In contrast to the need to control the potential unruliness of a colonized population in Algiers, which was linked, in Le Corbusier's imagination, to the sexuality of Islamic women, in the United States the problem was the mutually reinforcing formation of the sexually inhibited American man and the dominant American woman—a type he found "magnificent." Le Corbusier blamed this architecturally and psychologically disabling gender imbalance largely on the spatial separation of the central business district from distant suburbs in American cities. The potential solution was a force that would reintegrate the calculative genius of American capitalism with its more instinctual substrate, the technological with the sensual. In Le Corbusier's mind, this mechanism was jazz: "Negro music has touched America because it is the melody of the soul joined with the rhythm of the machine." Although he does not mention Josephine Baker, he was invoking the same mixture of primitive and modern that he had intuited in her. Jazz was "American music, containing the past and the present, Africa and pre-machine age Europe and contemporary America." Louis Armstrong was "mathematics, equilibrium on a tightrope," and his music represented "the melody of the soul joined with the rhythm of the machine". The "Negro orchestra" represented a Purist ideal. It was "impeccable, flawless, regular, playing ceaselessly in an ascending rhythm: the trumpet is piercing, strident, screaming over the stamping of feet. It is the equivalent of a beautiful turbine running in the midst of conversations. Hot jazz." For Le Corbusier, the sexual charge of jazz should have been powerful enough to undo the excessive Puritanism of America, evident in its funereal architecture. The technologies of gramophone and radio that allowed the "immense and splendid body of black music" to be heard in American homes, and so to touch American women, should have reanimated the inhibited energy of the culture and reconnected people to the healthy sensuality, which he had celebrated a quarter of a century earlier in *Voyage to the Orient*. True to the Purist view of jazz and its powers of classical regeneration, he saw the music as an American phenomenon that might inspire a new American architecture: "Jazz, like the skyscrapers, is an *event* and not a deliberately conceived creation." Together, they represented the "forces of today," although the jazz was ahead of the architecture: "If architecture were at the point reached by jazz, it would be an incredible spectacle. I repeat: Manhattan is hot jazz in stone and steel."

Louis Armstrong, 1932

It is at this point that the "modern" associations in Le Corbusier's scenario for Josephine Baker join up again with its "primitive" dimension. The dance, his plans for Algiers, his cultural analysis of America, and his investment in jazz all turned on the idea that, if it was to fulfill its social and human potential, the machine age had to find a way of containing—that is, of embodying and controlling—both the physical sensuality of the premachine past and the abstracting, mathematical rationality of the twentieth century. Le Corbusier's call to revive the white skin of medieval cathedrals and vernacular Mediterranean architecture was underpinned by a mythology, if not quite of the noble savage, then at least of a blackness and a sexuality that were, in some sense, healthier, more authentic, and more elemental than anything to be found in contemporary European or American culture.

This fantasy of a redemptive black sensuality would have been part of Josephine Baker's fascination for Le Corbusier. It certainly informed the little ballet he wanted her to perform. His scenario projected onto her fetishized body a primitivism that was linked to the inexhaustible, excessive, and so potentially lethal sexuality he fantasized about in Islamic women. Translated into a social reality, that erotic force was the anarchic danger perceived in the indigenous colonial population of Algiers, which had to be watched and

tamed though the rationality of Le Corbusier's architecture and planning. At
the same time, the modern Baker, who sang Negro music and wore designer
dresses, betokened a potentially virile America, as opposed to its current
debilitation by a repressive culture that had lost contact with the sensual and
sexual roots of its vigor. This, then, was a society that needed hot jazz and Le
Corbusier's architecture in order to de-repress, energize, and liberate it.

Homecoming

In 1929, when the *Lutétia* reached France after their South American adventures, Josephine Baker and Le Corbusier, with no apparent regrets, went their
separate ways. At the end of 1930, Le Corbusier married Yvonne Gallis, a
beautiful young Monégasque fashion model of gypsy descent. Five years later,
on the evening he returned home from his trip to New York, Yvonne played
him the record of a Parisian *java*. He realized that what he had learned from
his engagement with the United States was not just a clearer perception of his
own culture, but a more profound appreciation of it: "My ears still full of hot
jazz, here I am in the presence of the real originality of the *java*; I find in it
mathematical France, precise, exact; I find in it the masses of Paris, a society
worthy of interest, so measured, precise, and supple in its thought. A controlled sensuality, a severe ethics." Le Corbusier persisted with his plans for
Algiers. The coming of the Second World War saw the break-up of his architectural practice in Paris. His cousin and partner, Pierre Jeanneret, and some
of his other colleagues joined the Resistance. Le Corbusier opted to seek work
with the Pétain government. In June 1941, he returned to Algiers to develop
one last proposal, now less ambitious and on a smaller scale than earlier versions, which he completed a month later in Vichy. Like all its predecessors,
it was rejected. By this time Josephine Baker had started working for French
military intelligence and then, courageously, for De Gaulle's Free French.
She, too, spent much of the war in North Africa where, despite ill-health, she
danced and sang for French and Allied troops near the front line.

PLATE 1   *Paul Robeson by Winold Reiss, 1924.*

PLATE 2 Survey Graphic, *featuring Winold Reiss's portrait of Roland Hayes, 1925.*

PLATE 3 *Poster for* La Revue négre, *Paul Colin, 1925.*

PLATE 4   *Josephine Baker, Paul Colin,* Le Tumulte noir, *1927. Coloured lithograph.*

PLATE 5 *Josephine Baker, Paul Colin, Le Tumulte noir, 1927. Coloured lithograph.*

PLATE 6 *Fernand Léger,* Élement méchanique (Mechanical Element), *1924. Oil on Canvas, 146 x 97cm.*

PLATE 7   *Fernand Léger, Jazz (Variente), c. 1930. Ink on paper, 31.2 x 23 cm.*

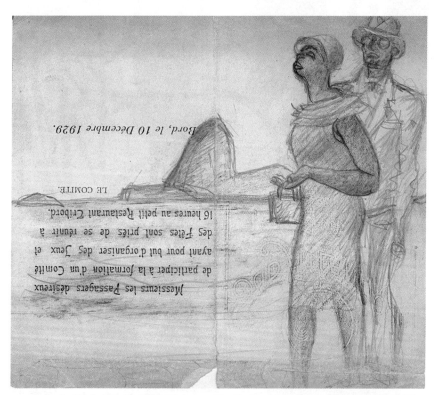

Bord, le 10 Décembre 1929.

LE COMITÉ.

16 heures au petit Restaurant Cribord.
des Fêtes sont priés de se réunir à
ayant pour but d'organiser des Jeux et
de participer à la formation d'un Comité
Messieurs les Passagers désireux

PLATE 8 *Le Corbusier,* Josephine Baker and Le Corbusier in front of the Sugar Loaf, *Rio de Janeiro, 1929. Pencil on paper, 12 x 13.8cm.*

Kenneth Macpherson filming Paul Robeson in Borderline, *Territet,*
Switzerland, 1930 (H.D.)

Borderlines

RACE, COSMOPOLITANISM, AND
THE MODERN UNCANNY

Between concert engagements in Europe in March 1930, Paul and Eslanda
Robeson found themselves with a couple of weeks to spare. They used the
time to visit the picturesque town of Territet in Switzerland, where they had
been invited to work on an experimental film with some avant-garde intellectuals with a passion for cinema. Collectively styling themselves POOL,
the group had a nucleus of three people. The expatriate American poet H.D.,
Hilda Doolittle, had been given her acronymic by Ezra Pound, to whom she
had been briefly engaged; later she would write about her analysis with Freud.
The English author Annie Winifred Ellerman took the pen name of Bryher,
after her favorite of the Scilly Isles. As it happened, she was heir to the fortune
of the richest man in England, the shipping magnate Sir John Ellerman, and
she used her money to support the group's creative projects, as well as many
other writers and initiatives that helped to define interwar European modernism as a movement. The third member was a talented, if sometimes feckless,
young Scot, Kenneth Macpherson. In Territet, this "menagerie of three," as
H.D.'s biographer has called it, played out an intricate minuet of sexual relationships, while reflecting on the depth and complexity of their emotions.
H.D. and Bryher were already in a lifelong sexual relationship when H.D. met
and embarked on an affair with Macpherson, sixteen years her junior, in
1926, the year in which her autobiographical novel *Palimpsest* was published.
Macpherson, in turn, wrote his own novel about the relationship, which bor-
dered on being a pastiche of his mistress's voice: *Poolreflection*. Bryher married
him, and both women tried to give direction to his undoubted but undisci-
plined talents. In 1927, Bryher gave Macpherson an expensive Debrie camera
and POOL embarked on a number of film experiments, at the same time as
they launched, as they proclaimed, the first journal devoted to film as an art.
This was *Close Up*, which promised "Theory and analysis: no gossip."

The film in which the group had persuaded the Robesons to appear was to be titled *Borderline*. It would deal with the "borderline" neuroses and perversions of a civilised white couple, contrasted against the characters played by Paul and Essie Robeson, described in H.D.'s pamphlet on the film as "another borderline couple of more dominant integrity." These two "have a less intensive problem, but border; they dwell on the cosmic racial borderline." The POOL group's interest in black America had already surfaced in a special issue of *Close Up* on "The Negro in Film," in August 1929, and H.D. returned to it in "Two Americans," a short story about the group's reactions to the Robesons, written in April 1930, just weeks after the shooting of *Borderline*.

How best to explain the dynamic between race, authenticity, and belonging that was being played out not only in the journal issue, the film, and the story, but also in the relationship between the Robesons and the POOL group? The approach taken here draws on ideas from the time about the uncanny and cosmopolitanism.

The Uncanny and the Homeless

A *borderline* sounds like a place where the uncanny belongs. Although it is supposed to define where one space ends and another begins, "borderline" more often connotes an intermediate and uneasy zone between contiguous states, a no-man's-land both politically and existentially. The territorial metaphor has limitations, however, at least when applied to psychological states. What these limitations are can be exemplified by a reading of Freud's 1919 essay "The 'Uncanny,'" in which he attempts to draw a conceptual borderline around what is specific and unique to the *Unheimlich*. The "unhomely" or the "uncanny," he acknowledges, has something to do with categories like fear, dread, and horror, but that set of associations is too fuzzy: "we may expect that a special core of feeling is present which justifies the use of a special conceptual term. One is curious to know what this common core is which allows us to distinguish as 'uncanny' certain things which lie within the field of what is frightening." This desire to mark the limits of the concept leads to Freud's opening digression into the etymology of *heimlich* and *unheimlich*. Although the opposition between the two concepts makes it tempting "to conclude that what is 'uncanny' is frightening precisely because it is *not* known and familiar," Freud discovers, of course, that the relationship between the two is not one of a boundary, or an outer limit, where the ontological security of the known and the familiar abuts the strangeness and danger of the unknown, imagined as another space.

Instead, the *Unheimlich* turns out to be a kind of viral incursion within the *Heimlich*: "*heimlich* is a word the meaning of which develops in the direction of ambivalence, until it finally coincides with its opposite, *unheimlich*.

Unheimlich is in some way or other a sub-species of *Heimlich*." The uncanny thus implies a convoluted yet constitutive dislocation in being, rather than being in another place. For Freud, it was a *temporal* dislocation—a recurrence from the past—that disrupts the *spatial* metaphor of the home. He cross-referred the *heimlich/unheimlich* ambivalence to Schelling's definition: "According to him, everything is *unheimlich* that ought to have remained secret and hidden but has come to light." Typically of the movement of the essay, Freud later narrowed down this recurrence to a dynamic of Oedipal repression:

> It often happens that neurotic men declare that they feel there is something uncanny about the female genital organs. This *unheimlich* place, however, is the entrance to the former *Heim* of all human beings, to the place where each one of us lived once upon a time and in the beginning. There is a joking saying that "Love is home-sickness"; and whenever a man dreams of a place or a country and says to himself, while he is still dreaming: "this place is familiar to me, I've been here before," we may interpret the place as being his mother's genitals or body. In this case too, then the *unheimlich* is what was once *heimisch*, familiar; the prefix "*un*" ["un-"] is the token of repression.

Freud thus saw ambivalence about belonging, or feeling-at-home, as one symptom, among others, that might lead to a diagnosis of neurosis, and specifically of masculine neurosis. Thinking about Angst in the second half of the 1920s, Martin Heidegger picked up on this same theme of uncanny dislocation, or the origin that had become alien and discomfiting. He treated it not as a pathology, however, but as an ontological issue. "Anxiety (*Angst*) pulls Dasein back from its falling-away emergence in the 'world'," he wrote, in *Being and Time*. "Everyday familiarity collapses. Dasein is isolated, but isolated *as* Being-in-the-world." In this light, the uncanny appears as an insecurity that defines the nature and experience of being: "Being-in enters into the existential 'mode' of the '*not-at-home*.' Nothing else is meant by our talk about 'uncanniness.'"

Heidegger explained the anxiety of the uncanny as a symptom of Being-in-the-world. More specifically, it was a symptom of being part of the strange, mediated world that was everyday modernity: a symptom that presented as an experience of not being at home there. The definitive uncanniness of subjectivity, perceived by Freud and Heidegger, resulted from that coincidence of being *both* "within the world" *and yet* "not at home." It is Heidegger who drew the more radical inference and offered the more fundamental explanation: "*From an existential-ontological point of view, the 'not-at-home' must be conceived as the more primordial phenomenon.*"

For Freud, analytically, the symptomatology of the uncanny led to neurosis. For Heidegger, philosophically, the experience of the modern uncanny led to an account of *Heimat*, or homeland, as something that, far from being a secure and nourishing origin, is, in fact, uncannily familiar, in the sense of rendering the "more primordial" insistence of the "not-at-home" in Dasein's own Being. In a sense, both Freudian and Heideggerian conceptions of the uncanny might be seen as tragic interpretations of the unhomely, at least when contrasted with the more joyous embrace of the "not-at-homeness" inherent in modern being to be found in Friedrich Nietzsche's *The Gay Science*. There, Nietzsche interpreted the alienation of an origin not as the result of *repression*, but as a principled *rejection*, by the self-elected homeless, of the peremptory claims of cultural and political belonging: "We, who are homeless, are too manifold and mixed racially and in our descent being 'modern men,' and consequently do not feel tempted to participate in the mendacious racial self-admiration and racial indecency that parades in Germany today as a sign of a German way of thinking." Nietzsche's ethical alternative to *Heimat* was neither Heidegger's banal everyday "world," nor an abstract humanitarianism, but, rather, self-creation through affective social relationships. Although moderns like him may not have been good Germans, Nietzsche insisted that they were, very much, "good Europeans," with "Europe" here connoting less a geographical territory, a historical imperialism or a cultural identity, than the *universalism* of Europe's philosophical discourse and the possibility of translating that universalism not only into a politics but also into ways of being in the world.

Here the borderline between *Heimat* and *Heimatlos* evaporates, like the opposition between *Heimlich* and *Unheimlich*. Apparent opposites shade into one another. The uncanny and the cosmopolitan present themselves as two instances of feeling-not-at-home as a specifically modern experience of being-in-the-world.

Close Up

In the late 1920s, the POOL group no doubt considered themselves to be, in some sense, "borderline." They were obviously bohemian in their interests, tastes, and affiliations, and assuredly cosmopolitan in their restless shuttling around Europe and across the Atlantic. From Territet, they would take the train not only to Paris, but also to Vienna for Bryher's analysis with Hanns Sachs; to Berlin to dine with the director G. W. Pabst, who encouraged Macpherson's career and indulged the group's fanciful hope that H.D. might be a potential rival to Louise Brooks; or to London, in 1927, to see Paul Robeson in *Show Boat*. They were introduced to Robeson and Essie by a fourth, nonresident, member of the POOL group, the journalist and poet Robert Herring, who wrote about film for a literary monthly, the *London Mercury*. Herring shared Macpherson's passion for jazz, and the two men sailed to Harlem together, to visit its music clubs and to mingle with Carl Van Vechten's Manhattan set.

The group's restlessness meant that, at the same time as they attempted to create a modernist art of film, as well as literature, their engagement with a primarily literary European avant-garde was mediated through an awareness of the different, distinctively American modernism of the Harlem Renaissance. This interest gave their aesthetics a political edge, and sharpened their awareness of interracial dynamics in Paris and London, as well as New York. It also inflected their ethical self-creation as, in Nietzsche's sense, "homeless." The POOL group were, without doubt, "modern men" and "modern women." Their lives were complicated enough, and mobile enough, to count as psychologically and morally *manifold*, and they were certainly "mixed" sexually, if not racially. Apart from the long-standing relationship between H.D. and Bryher, Herring was gay, and Macpherson was bisexual, and he went on to have a series of relationships with young black men. In such ways, the POOL group became alert to the fluidity and porousness of sexual and racial boundaries. This perception, which was no doubt also a desire, was then translated into the attempt to represent cinematically the vicissitudes of cosmopolitan being-in-the world: *Borderline*.

Prefiguring themes in the film, the *Close Up* issue on "The Negro in Film" was prompted, at least in part, by 1929's vogue for "all talkie" feature musicals that were also "all negro"—most notably Paul Sloane's *Hearts in Dixie* from Fox, featuring Stepin Fetchit, and King Vidor's *Hallelujah!* Drawing on their networks in New York, the editors solicited contributors from people like the NAACP's Walter White, Elmer Carter, who succeeded Charles S. Johnson as editor of *Opportunity*, and Geraldyn Dismond, a journalist best known for her "society" columns. Their short articles showed a particular interest in the opportunity that the films seemed to promise for black performers and black-owned production companies to flourish in the sound era. A contribution promised by Paul Robeson failed to materialize.

Several of the journal's regular writers were more interested in the sound dimension of the films, as the absence or presence of recorded sound was then a question at the heart of *Close Up*'s attempts to define a modernist aesthetic for film. The "Negro in Film" issue marks an important step in their gradual move away from militant opposition to talkies and mourning for the lost universal visual language of silent cinema—"the art that died"—and toward an accommodation with sound cinema's aesthetic and ethical potential. In his editorial, Macpherson acknowledged that, for all that it had destroyed, synchronized sound had at least had the virtue of allowing more intimate access to "the Negro": "Talking films took films from us but they have given us a glimpse of him." Even the novelist Dorothy Richardson, the most obdurate of *Close Up*'s columnists in her resistance to sound, admitted (in the following issue) that the singing and the "lush chorus of Negro-laughter" in *Hearts in Dixie* might be "the noble acceptable twin of the silent film"—although she still recoiled from the recorded speech as "annihilating." The American Marxist Harry Potamkin set the appearance of "negro films" in the context of the Harlem Renaissance, but then attributed the timing of the fashion explicitly to sound technology.

> The present vogue for negro films was inevitable. The film trails behind literature and stage for subject-matter. There has been a negro vogue since the spirituals were given their just place in popular attention. Many negro mediocrities have ridden to glory on this fad. Many white dabblers have attained fame by its exploitation. The new negro was suddenly born with it. Cullen and Hughes were crowned poets, but Jean Toomer, a great artist among the negroes, has not yet been publicly acclaimed. He first appeared before the hullabaloo was begun. The theatre took the negro up. First Gilpin and eventually came *Porgy*. Now the film. *Sound has made the negro the "big-thing" of the film-moment.*

What is not clear is whether Potamkin believed that that sound somehow *caused* the wave of "all negro" musicals, or that there was an affinity between black performers and sound cinema—and, if the latter, what the nature of that affinity might be.

A commonly accepted explanation of the supposed compatibility, at the time, was a technical one. The quality of recording meant that voices on the screen did not sound great, and the timbre of "negro" voices—their "rich resonance . . . in speech and in song," as Elmer Carter called it in his contribution to *Close Up*—was widely supposed to make for more accurate and pleasing recordings. Typical of this view, but symptomatic in revealing that more than sound quality was at stake, was a comment by the *New Yorker's* film critic, Robert Benchley, in a review of *Hearts in Dixie* for *Opportunity*: "Voices *can* be found which will register perfectly. Personalities *can* be found which are ideal for this medium. It may be that the talking-movies must be participated in exclusively by Negroes, but, if so, then so be it. In the Negro the sound-picture has found its ideal protagonist." The more fundamental question about sound, to which "the Negro" was supposedly the ideal, and possibly only, answer, turned out to be that cinema audiences found the experience of mechanically reproduced speech difficult and disquieting.

This brings us back to the uncanny. It has been argued that a frisson of the uncanny is generated when a machine, such as a talking automaton or a "talking picture," produces something so inalienably human as a speaking voice. The effect, speech, becomes dissociated from either human or mechanical origin. The simulacral voice becomes, as it were, the ghost making itself heard from within the machine. In the early decades of the twentieth century, the creation of mechanically produced sounds and disembodied voices, through the gramophone, the telephone, radio, and talkies, disseminated a widespread new experience of the *acousmatic*; that is, the phenomenon of hearing sound, without being able to see its originating cause or body. The anxiety, or sense of uncanniness that this experience produced—Marcel's first telephone conversation, in *The Guermantes Way*, is an example—was what, in cinema, the presence of "the Negro" on screen was somehow supposed to remedy, or at least displace.

But, again, why "the Negro"? Two strategies for the use of black actors, or two sets of presuppositions, have been identified in Hollywood's early sound films. One strategy was to use the bodies and voices of black performers, and their supposedly "inherent" or "natural" talents, to show off the cinematic apparatus's power to capture and reproduce—to embody, almost—those talents and those performances. The other strategy was to emphasize what has been called the *hyperpresence* of black bodies, to draw attention away from the mechanical apparatus and its clunky artifice, and to compensate for its mimetic shortcomings—and so, also, to mitigate the uncanniness produced by modern subjectivity's technological mediation.

It is this hyperpresence that, in *Close Up*, provides the link between "sound," "the Negro," and the question of authenticity, or being-in-the-world, and the uncanny. Macpherson and his colleagues understood and rejected the condescending primitivism and cultural appropriation that had characterized much of the vogue for *l'art nègre* earlier in the decade. He was dismissive of films in which black characters were simply a projection of a white social conscience: "Confronted with an instability (his own) which he calls a Race Problem, the white man is always going to portray the negro as he likes to see him, no matter how benevolently." Rather than representing difference within a white paradigm, Macpherson wanted "the negro" to become "his own historian" and "his own agitator." But the limit to Macpherson's approach was an inability to think outside the paradigm of cultural eugenics, in which blackness recurs, either as degenerative and malign, or (as for him) as benign and rejuvenating. That is why, following the example of Alain Locke's "cultural racialism," he still looked to a cinema that could present an authentic "race mind" to counter the "mendacious racial self-admiration and racial indecency" that Nietzsche had predicted for Europe: a cinema that would embody difference from the inside out.

This constrained and compromised ideal is what Macpherson tried to express in his editorial for "The Negro in Film" issue of *Close Up*. When he asserted that attempts at "universal cinema" have failed, and that the only hope lies in a "strictly racial cinema," he was drawing a contrast between an inauthentic cosmopolitanism, which he was already sheeting home to Hollywood, and an embodied existential authenticity, which he discerned in Stepin Fetchit's performance and 'splendour of being" in *Hearts in Dixie*.

Stepin Fetchit as Gummy, Hearts in Dixie, *1929*

There is more than promise in the jungle, lissom lankness that slams down something unanswerable in front of what we let go by as beauty. . . . Fetchit waves loose racial hands and they, like life, touch everything that the world contains. They are startling with what nobody meant to put into them, but which is all too there—histories, sagas, dynasties, Keatsian edges off things make a voiceless trouble back of the eye and the recording mind. Only afterwards you are really beset by them. They are not Fetchit's hands, they are the big step we have not yet taken. First of all these so utterly not incantationish gestures are unselfconsciousness, perfectly inherited great-ness of race and race mind. It only begins there. We can scrap every trained toe waggle of a ballerina for the very least of these movements. Making this greatness articulate for the cinema is the fascinating pioneer work of somebody.

Robert Herring revealed the eugenicism of the perspective more explicitly, in his article "Black Shadows." In "Negro art," he claimed, "you will find a new life, very rich, very swift, intense, and dynamic, unlike ours, but full of things which we cannot help knowing we lack." And yet this vitality and this "differ-ence" were distressingly absent from existing "Negro films." Herring wanted

"Negro films made by and about them. Not black films passing for white, and not, please, white passing for black. We want no Van Vechtens of the movies." Herring suggested that the potential authenticity of "Negro art" would transcend even the mechanical artifice of sound: "Now that it has been discovered that Negroes have voices, let it be found too that they have something to say." He knew that it would not be found by way of Al Jolson:

> And we don't get it by blacking our faces and wearing white gloves, and I don't think we get it from real Negroes having to live down to the pleasant banjo-strumming, cotton-field singing idea we have of them. We want the real thing, always, and the cinema demands the real thing, and heaven knows there is enough reality waiting there, if black shadows might move on our screens in their own patterns, and have their own screens, too, to do it on. And not rely on white patronage to do it with. For surely they are as tired of all that as of white, yellow, white—nothing but white—films; and heaven knows I am.

Harry Potamkin too wanted more authentic blackness, and found, inevitably, that it could never be authentic enough or black enough. He took aim at King Vidor's casting of the light-skinned Nina Mae McKinney—"a good-looking yaller girl"—as the *femme fatale* in *Hallelujah!* and demanded, instead, something "as rich as the negroes" in *La Croisière noire*, Léon Poirier's documentary film about André Citroën's expedition to central Africa: "I shall be assured of the white man's sincerity when he gives me a blue nigger." Potamkin expressed his desire for an authenticating, unalienated origin as a brutal nostalgia: blackness in cinema, blackness and cinema, as *Heim*: "I am not interested primarily in verbal humour, in clowning nor in sociology. I want cinema and I want cinema at its source."

Borderline

The not-quite-articulate sense of "the negro" as the existential cure to the cultural wound represented by the *Unheimlich*, evident in many of the contributions to the *Close Up* issue, is worked through again in the POOL group's 1930 film *Borderline*. The ambition was to make a psychoanalytic film, or to make a film psychoanalytically, and, as in most POOL writings, the relationships to be explored were ones that existed between the members of the group. Here the fraught relationship between H.D. and Macpherson was center stage, fictionalized as a neurotic white couple: a cerebral and over-civilized older woman, Astrid, played by H.D., using the pseudonym Helga Doorn, and an alcoholic younger man, Thorne (Gavin Arthur). H.D. had aborted the child she was carrying by Macpherson in 1928, and the aftermath of that trauma may explain the lethal intensity of the spiral of dependency, jealousy, and resentment in which Astrid and Thorne are trapped. (H.D.'s abortion may add another dimension to the otherwise heavy-handed Oedipal imagery of the knife, with which Astrid taunts and nicks Thorne, and with which he then kills her.) The film's narration is fragmented and elliptical. Rejecting the "simplicity" of most films, and the laziness of most audiences, Macpherson wanted *Borderline* to embody the "complexity" of the issues and relationships that it was addressing. The effect he was aiming at, he wrote, was "unexplainedness—like something seen through a window or key-hole." Hence, the film starts *in medias res* and eschews establishing shots, a linear time structure, or any clear demarcation between the representation of events, thoughts, or memories. Its main structuring device is less a narrative sequence of events, than the externalization of the destructive relationship between the white couple and its projection onto the social and psychological impact on the town made by the presence of the black couple, Pete and Adah, played by Paul and Essie Robeson.

Despite the opacity of the narration, the underlying story is quite straightforward, as a "libretto" handed out to the audience at the film's first screening makes clear. Pete works in the town's hotel bar, a location that holds together the spatial organization of the film. Adah, "who had left him some time previously, has arrived also in the same town, although neither is aware of the presence of the other," and rented a room with Thorne and Astrid. "Thorne

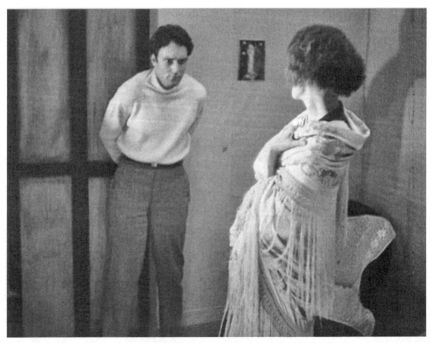

Astrid (H.D.) and Thorne (Gavin Arthur)

Pete (Paul Robeson) and Adah (Eslanda Robeson)

is a young man whose life with Astrid has become a torment to them both. Both highly strung, their nerves are tense with continuous hostility evoked by Thorne's vague and destructive cravings. He has been involved in an affair with Adah, and the film opens with the quarrel which ends their relationship." As a racially borderline figure, Adah, described in the libretto as a "mulatto," crosses sexually from the black man, to the white man, and back to the black man. Her betrayal of Pete with Thorne provokes, in Astrid, first jealousy and then a self-loathing, which erupts as a racism—"They are niggers, my dear!"—that chimes, all too easily, with the proto-Nazi prejudices of the locals. When Thorne is acquitted of Astrid's murder, Pete is made a scapegoat and expelled from the town.

At the heart of the film's narrative and psychological strategy is the contrast between Thorne and Pete; or, rather, the subjective splitting and fantasy of wholeness that, in combination, they represent. There are only two occasions on which Thorne and Pete appear in frame together, but both are crucial to the racialized logic of the film. The first occurs at the end of a sequence when Thorne appears threateningly at the threshold of Adah's room, after she and Pete have resumed their sexual relationship. For the most part, the sequence is structured as a series of shots and reverse shots, which highlight the point of view of each man in turn, while Thorne is held back by the hotel's cigar-smoking manager (Bryher) and its Pete-infatuated

Borderline, *1930*

piano player (Robert Herring—"an enlightened film critic in the guise of a nance pianist," as one contemporary observed.) The eyes of these choric onlookers flick between the two men, like spectators at a tennis match. Thorne, his forehead sheened with alcoholic sweat, appears disheveled and impotently outraged, whereas Pete comes across as, at first, a little disconcerted, then quizzical, then self-assured, and finally (through Thorne's eyes) as sexually triumphant and insolently contemptuous. When the two are shown confronting each other in profile, it is very much as a tableau of black and white tonalities, with a brightly lit patterned white curtain dividing the screen between them. The white-shirted Pete's face is wholly in shadow, whereas a dark-jacketed Thorne, being restrained by the manager, whose face appears as a blob of white, has his downcast gaze lit in dramatic chiaroscuro. A closer shot shows only the profiles of the two men, Thorne at the extreme left of the frame brightly lit and humiliated against a dark wooden background, Pete at the right edge of the frame smiling but still in shadow against the light fabric of the curtain.

Toward the end of the film, a reconciliation between Thorne and Pete repeats the tableau shot. Both are now in light, but Thorne is foregrounded against the light fabric, with Pete set against a dark flower-patterned wallpaper. In a close shot-reverse shot, each man's smiling face connotes a transracial masculine camaraderie, which is emphasized by the extreme close up of their handshake.

Just before this reconciliation, the hotel manager passes on the letter of expulsion to Pete. In the process, three intertitles play on the easy slippages between personal pronouns. In the first, Pete asks: "What do you think?" In the second, the manager distances herself from the racism of the town, but then acknowledges her own inescapable complicity in it: "Sorry, Pete! What

Thorne and Pete

The handshake

makes it worse is that they think they're doing the right thing. We're like that!" In the third, bitterly expanding the referent of that *we*, a deflated Pete replies: "Yes, we're like that." As he leaves, the forlorn piano player takes Pete's photograph from the music rack, puts it in his wallet and pockets it. After the reconciliation between Pete and Thorne, a quick shot of the piano's keys is followed by a head-and-shoulders "portrait" of an overcoated Pete and then a comparatively long sequence of him waiting at the station for a train, the very sign of cosmopolitan mobility, counterposed elementally against a sublime Alpine backdrop.

Intercut into the shots at the station are the pianist's gesture of *bon voyage*, the return to the bar of a racist old woman expressly intended to embody "public opinion," the manager drawing up the hotel's accounts, shots of Thorne sitting pensively in grassy mountainside meadows, and the hotel's barmaid wistfully rediscovering the now-dead rose that "poor old Pete" had laughingly put behind his ear, a few nights earlier. In the closing shot the manager, pen in mouth, closes her ledger.

This conclusion resonates with a striking feature of Heidegger's account of the uncanny in *Being and Time*: that is, its interaction with his thinking about the call of conscience. The conscience that can be satisfied does not do the work that Heidegger wants conscience to do. Doing the right thing by such a conscience can lull people into feeling at peace with themselves—at

Robert Herring as the pianist

Bryher as the hotel manager

home—whereas Heidegger clearly wants the not-at-home to be acknowledged as primordial. In the slippage between *they* and *we*, in the abjection of Pete, and in the settling of accounts, it seems as though the POOL group were trying to distance themselves from their white background, and its manifestation in the locals' pathological racism, through the valorization of "the negro," as the embodiment of authentic, healthy humanity. As one publicity handout, most likely written by Bryher, put it: "The whites are neuroses; the negroes, nature." At the same time, however, and in the same gesture, they can be read as trying to make amends (even if unconsciously) for white oppression, as trying to make peace—to square the ledger—with their own consciences in the hope that they can be at home with themselves.

The cosmopolitan and uncanny connotations of the borderline are evident in the pamphlet that H.D. wrote about the film. Although she emphasizes the neurosis of the white couple, using "borderline" almost in a clinical sense, she identifies the central ambiguity about being-at-home and not-feeling-at-home-in-the-world:

> There are in Europe, many just such little towns as this particular borderline town of some indefinite mid-European mountain district. There are trains coming and trains going. One of these trains has already deposited the half-world mondaine Astrid with Thorne, her lover. They have come here because of some specific nerve-problem, perhaps to rest, perhaps to

recuperate, perhaps to economise, perhaps simply in hope of some emotional convalescence. They live as such people do the world over, in just such little social borderline rooms as just such couples seek in Devonshire, in Cornwall, in the South of France, in Provincetown, United States. *They are borderline social cases, not out of life, not in life*; the woman is a sensitive neurotic, the man, a handsome, degenerate dipsomaniac. Thorne has not reached the end of his cravings, may step this side, that side of the border; Astrid, the white-cerebral is and is not outcast, is and is not a social alien, is and is not a normal human being, she is borderline.

This existential and psychological instability is then both ascribed to, and represented by, a tangle of racial as well as sexual borderlines, and the complicated patterns of desire and hostility they engender. H.D. argued that *Borderline* treats "race" as a boundary—"the cosmic racial borderline"—rather than as an essence, and explained how, in constructing the film, Macpherson deliberately played on the narrative displacements and dislocations between the semiotic, the psychic, and the sociological that "race," as a trope, allows. In doing so, she implies, the film's portrayal of Pete and Adah escapes both stereotypical thinking and condescending benevolence: "Their problem is not dealt with as the everlasting black-white Problem with a capital. It remains however a motive to be counted on; though threads are woven in and through the fabric, white into black and black into white, Pete and Adah must inevitably remain 'borderline', whether by their own choice and psychic affiliation or through sheer crude brute causes."

In recent decades, critics have often lamented that, even if H.D. and Macpherson were able to spot the limits and arbitrariness of other people's racial logics, they still unwittingly repeated their pathology of alienation, fantasy, and projection. It has been objected, very reasonably, that *Borderline*'s black-and-white cinematography, and its narrative juxtaposition of hyperactive whites against Robeson in repose, repeat "the white alienation versus blackfolks spirituality opposition that runs through discourses on blackness in the twenties and thirties"; that the effect of its "modernist aesthetic" was "to freeze Robeson into a modernist ideal of the Negro male, outside of history"; and that the film reproduces the distinction between the "natural" and the "civilized," with "its apparently explanatory account of cultural attainment and neurosis," as "a white/black binary." It is worth noting, however, that these latter-day objections reiterate, with different emphases, what Macpherson himself said in his *Close Up* editorial: "the white man is always going to portray the negro as he likes to see him, no matter how benevolently." The critics also echo Essie's own more light-hearted judgment: "Kenneth and H.D. used to make us so shriek with laughter with their naïve ideas of Negroes," she confided to her diary, "that Paul and I often completely ruined our make-up with tears of laughter, had to make up all over again."

The risk in focusing solely on the film's manifest inadequacies in representing the experience of being-black-in-the-world is that of overlooking what
Borderline can reveal about the experience of being-a-white-cosmopolitan-in-
the-world at the turn of the 1920s and 1930s. "Anxiety is anxious in face of the
'nothing' of the world," Heidegger asserted at that time, and that anxiety was
the source of the uncanny sense of not-feeling-at-home. For the makers of
Borderline, as for the theorists in the *Close Up* issue, the embodied—although
still silent—*presence* of "the negro" functions as the sublime force that figures the forlorn desire for the opposite of that anxiety: an unalienated or
"homely" being-in-the-world. In his chapter on cinema in Nancy Cunard's
huge, ground-breaking anthology, *Negro* (1934), Macpherson admitted
how, in thinking through the question of "The Negro and Film" and in his
response to Robeson, he felt that he "had seen, perhaps I should say I had
been haunted by, a sense of *virility or solidarity of being* which was at once discernible as imperatively Negroid." The logic of H.D.'s pamphlet is the same:
"Mr. Robeson is obviously the ground under all their feet," she writes, emphasizing less his virility, than the way he manages to be both grounded and
sublime. "He is stabilized, stable, the earth," but, at the same time, this "giant
negro is in the high clouds, white cumulous cloud banks in a higher heaven".
This contrasts with the white characters in *Borderline*. "Conversely, his white
fellow-men are the shadows of white, are dark, neurotic."

Robeson and clouds

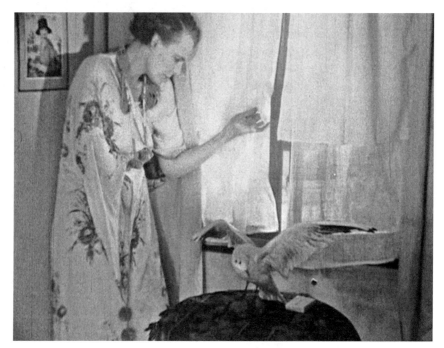

H.D. and seagull

Macpherson, Bryher, and H.D. were under no illusions that *Borderline* constituted a fully worked representation of contemporary black subjectivity, or even of a black experience of racism. In turning to "the negro" as the cure for their unhomeliness, however, they did demonstrate, in practice, the inescapability of the uncanny. A psychoanalytic account might link "the ground under all their feet" to mother earth, and then to the maternal landscape, and so (as Freud concluded) to that place, both *heimisch* and *unheimlich*, "where each one of us lived once upon a time and in the beginning." But that would repeat the kind of over-neat explanation that mars the "Uncanny" essay. Even though *Borderline* was made by Freudian true believers, and remains constrained within their own historically located paradigms of racialized thinking, H.D. did intuit, in Macpherson's cinematic vision, a way of imagining the solaces and costs of cosmopolitanism, as an alternative strategy for living homelessly. Whether or not her answers are palatable or persuasive, her questions at least reveal an awareness of the scale of the existential fluidity and self-reinvention that were needed to become cosmopolitan. Seen thus, *Borderline* reads as a variation on Nietzsche's theme of the *ethical* courage needed to be homeless. "When is an African not an African?" speculates H.D. "When obviously he is an earth-god. When is a woman not a woman? When obviously she is sleet and hail and a stuffed sea-gull. He says when is white not white and when is black white and when is white black? You may or may not like this sort of cinematography."

Two Americans

H.D.'s story "Two Americans" revisits the themes of *Borderline*, but views them this time through the prism of the social interactions and psychodynamics between the POOL group and the Robesons. Questions of exile, homelessness, and nostalgia are worked through the erotic fascination with Robeson that H.D. shared with Macpherson, and her anxious reaction to Robeson's easy friendship with Macpherson as two fellow artists, despite their racial difference; a camaraderie in which she felt that, as a woman, she could not participate. In the story, Raymonde Ransome believes that her earlier affair with Daniel Kinoull is one reason for that exclusion, and she therefore now experiences the relationship as a wound: as a "steel pin" or (perhaps with a nod to the Thorne character in *Borderline*) as a "silver thorn" in her side.

Such metaphorical allusions to materials like steel and silver recur throughout the story: "Weather-worn marble, Raymonde Ransome, faced Saul Howard, seared bronze." This imagery underlines the affective materiality of symbolic differences, which are elsewhere articulated in terms of a racial masquerade: "Their faces remained faces yet for all that, those faces had turned now forever into static symbols, they were mask on contrasting mask, the one white, the other, as it happened, black." The interpolation into that sentence of the apparently bland phrase "as it happened" is less innocent or redundant than it first appears. The obvious implication is that this meeting is purely contingent, a singular event. This happened, and it happened to happen like this. At the same time, however, the phrase implies an awareness that *this* event, however apparently trivial and fortuitous, has been overdetermined by all the historical and cultural forces implicit in the lexicon of nation, cosmopolitanism, home, and being-in-the-world. "White" confronting "black" is never just happenstance. This is made clear as H.D. goes on to portray Robeson (in the persona of Saul Howard) as a mythical figure, as a pagan life-force contrasting (perhaps in another implicit reference to the abortion of Macpherson's child) with her own sterile puritanism and, again, as the embodiment of that fullness, which both reveals and promises to heal her own wounded, inadequate and inauthentic being.

> They met in a field of honour, herself entirely defeated, himself yet to be acclaimed for some kingship the world is not ready to recognize. He was no black Christ. He was an earlier, less complicated symbol. He was the Dionysus as Nietzsche so valiantly struggled to define him; possibly she stood vaguely for counter balancing Nietzschean Apollo, though where he was complete, she was strikingly deficient. She was deficient, even, you might say, crippled in some psychic song-wing; his song flowed toward all the world, effortless, full of benign power, without intellectual gap or cross-purpose of hypercritical consciousness to blight it. There was no swerving from the beginning, the root, the entire deep in-rooted power of

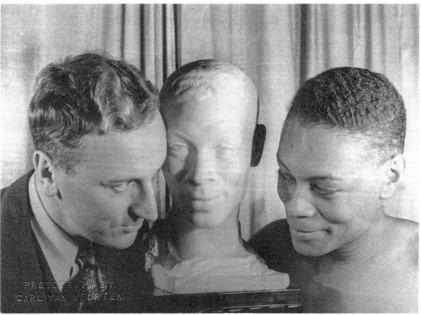

Kenneth Macpherson and Jimmie Daniels, with Richmond Barthe's unfinished bust of Daniels, 1938 (Carl Van Vechten)

his gigantic Being. He was really no person at all. Seated opposite him, on
the orange-lacquered low wooden seat that Gareth [*Bryher*] had had spe-
cially designed for just that fireside corner, Raymonde knew that. She let
her own personality harden, "fix" as it were; now she would be this forever.

It is at this moment in the story that H.D. evokes the uncanniness of Robeson's
voice, as, for the first time in the whole cycle of *Close Up, Borderline,* and "Two
Americans," Robeson speaks.

> For her, the "voice" was speaking. It spoke to the world, every gramophone
> window displayed Saul Howard's records. The voice spoke on everybody's
> wireless. Howard himself was, in fact, on his way back to London, stopping
> off here from his concert in Vienna. The voice that spoke on everybody's
> wireless, spoke now to her intrinsically. It said, "Daniel is a lovely fellow."

What is uncanny about Saul Howard/Robeson's voice is not so much the
extraordinary timbre of his basso profundo, as the way that H.D.'s description of its effect undermines the logic which assumes that the discovery of
the human speaker behind an apparently disembodied, mechanically reproduced voice will annul the acousmatic anxiety discussed earlier. Such a reso-
lution turns out to be impossible. The supposed dissipation of the acousmatic
uncanny inevitably fails to restore the *integrity* of body, subject, and voice. The
vocal utterance, even when anchored in a human body, continues to enact an
uncanny disjuncture between the appearance of a person and the sound of a
voice. In doing so, it exposes a kind of structural *ventriloquism*. It is this ventriloquism that H.D. appears to disavow, through the peculiar selection of the
adverb *intrinsically*, in the sentence "The voice that spoke on everybody's wireless, spoke now to her intrinsically." Far from being *intrinsic*, however—that
is, far from being an integral feature of Robeson's body—H.D. repeatedly
acknowledges that the voice remains quite autonomous: the voice that "spoke
now to her" is one that "spoke to the world" and "spoke on everyone's wireless." It is not *he*, the man, who speaks, but rather the ventriloquized voice: "*It*
said, 'Daniel is a lovely fellow.'"

Once Saul Howard (or his voice) has spoken, the relationship between
his presence in the world and his agency, and no longer just his symbolism,
becomes an issue: "His least movement was so gracious, he didn't have to
think things out. Nevertheless, with an astonishing analytical power, he did
think. That was the odd thing about Saul Howard, he did think. He had a
mind, a steadfast sort of burning, a thing that glowed like a whole red sunset
or like a coal mine, it was steady, a steady sort of warmth and heat, yet all
the time intellectual; he thought not as a man thinks." In contrast to Saul's
elemental being, his wife, Paula, displays a brittle veneer of civilization: Paula
"thought more as white folks, consistently, being more than half white." This
representation of Essie/Paula, and the narrator's identification with Robeson/

Saul against her, reveals how envy and desire—"she showed up horribly her deficiencies beside Saul"—can become entangled with historically specific categories and taxonomies of "race." Paula's flaw for H.D., like Nina Mae McKinney's for Harry Potamkin, was that she is not black enough: "Paula was Paris, was striking, yet, all the time, she made it very clear that she was not to be confounded with the tribe who had given jazz to Europe. She had attained something for which something had been sacrificed." Her compromising "whiteness" makes her prey to the wound of civilization: "For the very valour of her achievement, someone should warn her just what it was she left out. Yet who was there now to warn her and what really had she lost?" To be not black enough is to fail to manifest the intensity or "hyperpresence"—Macpherson's *solidarity of being*, H.D.'s *ground under all their feet*—which was supposed to cure the alienation, anxiety, and uncanniness of modern being-in-the-world.

Although "Two Americans" thus repeats the same existential investment in "the negro" as *Heim* that is evident in the *Close Up* issue and in *Borderline*, here that wish is overlain by a more mundane desire for "home." The result is an ambivalence between home as essential and home as contingent, which enables Raymonde to grasp both her rootedness in "America," and also the necessity of her cosmopolitan exile if she, like Saul Howard, is to operate effectively as an artist. The question of their shared Americanness arises first, when "Bennie" (modeled on Robert Herring) tells the story of Paula and Saul's courtship: " 'She said the four most likely young bucks of Harlem wanted her. She said, then I saw Saul Howard strolling along Broadway with a Phi Kappi Nu key and a gold football trophy dangling from his watch chain, and I said *now that's my man!*' Raymonde interpreted, 'It wasn't Broadway and it wasn't Phi Kappi Nu and Paula would never have said "now that's my man." ' Bennie said, 'Don't swank, Raymonde, just because' (he was being funny) 'you and Saul and Paula are Americans.' " This is the context in which H.D. told the story of the visit to see Robeson, bleached by the footlights, sing "one of his incredible spirituals in the middle of a shocking musical comedy": "Saul Howard interpolated oddly into that London music hall, was oddly not that. His heart that afternoon had not been in the thing that he did. Nevertheless, across that packed house, there was ripple of delicate blue grass, there was a flight of cardinal butterflies. Oddly and for almost the first time, in her tragically rooted London war-consciousness, Raymonde Ransome felt that America was her home."

At one level, Raymonde's "tragically rooted London war-consciousness" refers to personal traumas that H.D. had suffered during the war: the still-birth of a child, the death of her father and brother, the nervous collapse of her husband. Beyond that, it refers, historically, to the existential changes that came with the war and its aftermath, and also to the changes in the psychosensory experience of the twentieth-century world. By evoking that broader history, Raymonde's "tragically rooted London war-consciousness" also underlines how central to this modern experience—this experience of modernity, of being modern—were the question of home and the anxiety of being not-at-home. For H.D., this constitutive uncanniness was given an added twist through the contrast between the cosmopolitanism of London, Switzerland, and Europe, and the sudden nostalgia for America. The phrase "as it happened," with all its ambiguous resonances of inevitability as well as contingency, reappears in the final paragraph of *Two Americans*, as H.D. draws together the story's antinomies between white and black, female and male, and home and exile: "'Mohammed and the mountain,' said Raymonde, facing, as it happened, the ridge of the French Grammont, 'did or didn't it come to him? It's come to me anyway. I mean,' she said, 'America.'"

Plaza Cinema, Lower Regent Street, London, 1937

Down the River of Dreams

SONGS OF EXILE AND NOSTALGIA

Close Up ceased publication in June 1933. The indifference with which *Borderline* was received, even more than the hostility, effectively killed off Kenneth Macpherson's lingering interest in cinema. Although he occasionally speculated about new projects, if only as an excuse to dun Bryher for more funds, his time was by now increasingly taken up with drink, café life, and sexual adventures. During the Second World War, he lived for a while in New York with another heiress, Peggy Guggenheim. In March 1933, H.D. began her analysis with Freud. Bryher soldiered on, but *Close Up* had run out of steam. Times had changed, and cinema no longer seemed to matter in quite the way it had, in 1927. "A year ago this June I returned from Berlin," wrote Bryher, capturing the mood, in the penultimate issue. In Berlin, police cars with machine guns raced around the streets, and groups of brown uniforms waited at each corner. "The stations had been crowded: not with people bound for the Baltic with bathing bags, but with families whose bundles, cases or trunks bulged with household possessions. (The fortunate were already going into exile.) Everywhere I had heard rumours or had seen weapons." Back in London, people still asked her about cinema. "They asked questions like, 'what is Pabst doing now' or 'will there be another film like *Mädchen in Uniform*?' I said 'I didn't go to cinemas because I watched the revolution' and they laughed, in England."

Borderline's combination of aesthetic experimentation, political radicalism, and negrophilia was already passé by the time the film was first screened in 1930. Encroaching fascism, economic depression, the success of sound cinema, and the spread of radio cemented the divide between committed art and escapist entertainment. If she had gone to the cinema in Paris or London in the years after *Close Up* had folded, however, Bryher might still have encountered old acquaintances and familiar themes. The director of *Zouzou*, Josephine Baker's first sound film, made in France in 1934, was Marc Allégret, who had been one of *Close Up*'s Paris correspondents, apparently as a result of tutoring Bryher's younger brother in England. In *Song of Freedom*, a British film directed by J. Elder Wills two years later, in 1936, Bryher's *Borderline* collaborator, Paul Robeson, was again deployed to embody the theme that H.D. identified as "the cosmic racial borderline" and to expose the social and existential problems confronting "black people among white people." In a third film, with affinities to both *Zouzou* and *Song of Freedom*, Julien Duvivier's popular 1937 success, *Pépé le Moko*, Bryher might have perceived another variation on the "cosmic racial borderline" theme. Jean Gabin's Pépé is no neurotic cosmopolitan aesthete, stuck in a small Swiss town, but a charismatic gangster hiding out in the Arab quarter of Algiers. Even so, he is still one of H.D.'s "borderline social cases": trapped in the Casbah, Pépé is "not out of life, not in life."

Zouzou, Song of Freedom, and *Pépé le Moko* all share with *Borderline* a concern with the dynamic tension between the insistence of "race" and the possibility of "home." Unlike the POOL experiment, however, these three films approach the "race/home" nexus explicitly through the relationship between European metropolitan centers and their exotic colonies—the French Antilles, sub-Saharan Africa, and the Maghreb, respectively—and so also address, however fantastically, the representation and status of colonial subjects within the culture of the metropolitan power. The colonial logic of *Zouzou* is initiated by the question: Where, and how, does the heroine, the daughter of a clown from Martinique and a French mother, belong in metropolitan France? The answer is framed by the ideology of *la plus grande France*—the principle that all overseas and colonial subjects could become free and equal citizens of the republic—and narrated as the story of Zouzou's partial, but incomplete, *assimilation* into the metropolitan culture. In *Song of Freedom*, John Zinga (Robeson) is a black British citizen feeling out of place in the metropolitan heart of empire, accepted in London but longing for his "home" in Africa. Again the question is, where does he belong? The film sprawls from Africa to Europe and then again to Africa, while shifting temporally from past, to present, and then "back" to underdevelopment. In doing so, it evokes the British colonial strategy of *development* and *indirect rule*: Zinga ends up combining the roles of European administrator and African law-giver, promising to deliver the benefits of metropolitan modernity, while perpetuating indigenous culture. In *Pépé le Moko*, there is no doubt about where the hero belongs. Even sequestered in Algiers, Pépé remains utterly metropolitan, Parisian to the tips of Jean Gabin's elegant boots. The film's narrative of belonging, displacement, and loss is triangulated around the Casbah as Arab enclave, Algiers as French colonial city, and Paris as French metropolis. It presents an affective geography that gives form to Marshal Hubert Lyautey's colonial principle of *association* with *difference*.

Although *Zouzou, Song of Freedom,* and *Pépé le Moko* are full of assumptions about race, colonialism, and modernity, the aim of this chapter is less to excavate their ideological underpinnings, than to consider how they might have operated as iterations of a vernacular modernism, and how they might have determined what it felt like to live at the heart of two great, if troubled, empires in the mid-1930s. If asked, most fans would probably have said that they went to these movies because they wanted to enjoy the celluloid performances of Josephine Baker, Paul Robeson, or Jean Gabin. Even so, they would have encountered more than just a star turn in an escapist narrative. Through the phenomenology of cinema, audiences engaged, willy-nilly, with ingrained, even visceral ways of understanding the cultural significance of modern colonialism.

Context

As the film's producer, Pepito Abatino thought of *Zouzou* as, above all else, the first major star vehicle for Josephine Baker, and he was determined that the movie should match her status as a *vedette* of the Casino de Paris. He therefore set about finding suitably prestigious collaborators, several of whom had roots in the avant-garde of the 1920s. Carlo Rim, editor of the cultural journal *Jazz*, was brought in to develop the screenplay. One of the cinematographers was the Russian émigré Boris Kaufman, youngest brother of Dennis (Dziga Vertov) and Mikhail, who filmed *The Man with the Movie Camera*. Boris had shot all Jean Vigo's great films, including *L'Atalante* earlier in 1934. Marc Allégret was also well connected. Apart from writing for *Close Up*, he had a background in avant-garde photography and art. He was born into a family of Protestant intellectuals in northern France, where his father, Élie Allégret, a Presbyterian priest and missionary to Africa, was not just an old friend of André Gide's, but also something of a spiritual mentor to the novelist. When, in 1917, Élie left his friend in charge of his children, while he went on holiday, Gide, then fifty-two, and Marc, who was seventeen, became lovers. In Paris, Gide introduced Allégret to artists and writers like Cocteau (a potentially dangerous influence, Gide worried), Valéry, Picasso, and Satie, and he encouraged his protégé's interest in photography—as did Man Ray, with whom Allégret worked on Marcel Duchamp's film *Anémic Cinéma* (1926).

When Gide went to the Congo in 1926 to investigate the conduct of European mining companies and the Belgian administration, Allégret traveled with him, as his secretary. The trip marked the end of their sexual relationship, and Allégret experimented with the pleasures of prepubescent African girls, cheaply bought. Gide wrote his denunciation of the colonial powers, *Voyage au Congo*, and Allégret used the same title for a documentary film. Putting aside the controversial questions Gide raised in his book, the film combined a

Marc Allégret with André Gide in the Congo, 1926

quasi-anthropological record of indigenous customs with a lyrical story about a developing sexual relationship between a young African couple. Above all, Allégret was mesmerized by the beauty of African bodies in movement and the aesthetic play of light on black skin. By the early 1930s, Allégret's ambitions had led him into mainstream, commercial cinema. On *Zouzou*, his experience in Africa, combined with Carlo Rim's residual negrophilia, ensured that the film took at least an ironic distance from France's colonial and racial ideologies. There are also stylistic traces from his avant-garde days, in the lighting of Baker's dance numbers, and in Kaufman's use of location shooting, tracking, superimposed shots, and lap dissolves, when Zouzou walks, emotionally distraught, through the streets of Paris, at the climax of the film.

In 1936, Paul Robeson was at the height of his popularity in Britain, and *Song of Freedom* was tailored to exploit his public persona. The film trades on his success in *The Emperor Jones*, not just by reprising the storyline of a black working man, who becomes ruler of an exotic island kingdom, albeit benevolently, but also by incorporating, as *The Black Emperor*, extracts from Louis Gruenberg's 1933 operatic adaptation. From Robeson's point of view, the critical recycling of the "Brutus Jones" character enabled him to publicize his self-identification as African. Over the previous couple of years, he had written a series of articles on black culture, most of them in the *Spectator*, and had given several newspaper interviews about his "discovery" of Africa. "I am proud of my African descent," he said in one, and in another: "We are a great race, greater in tradition and culture than America." He announced his intention to "produce plays, make films, sing chants and prayers, all with one view in mind—to show my poor people that their culture traces back directly to the great civilisations of Persia, China, and the Jews."

This enthusiasm for Africa led to one terrible error of judgment, Robeson's participation in the Korda brothers' film *Sanders of the River*, in 1934. After a personal screening of ethnographic material shot on location by Zoltan Korda, Robeson had been convinced that the film would present an accurate portrait of African life and customs. "For the first time since I began acting," he enthused to the *Observer*, before shooting started, "I feel I've found my place in the world, that there's something out of my own culture which I can express and perhaps help to preserve—for I'm not kidding myself that I've really gotten a place in Western culture, although I have been trained for it all my life." In the event, *Sanders* turned out to be a paean to British colonialism. Robeson's response to the ensuing controversy was confused. As usual, he insisted that he had a right to accept whatever roles were offered him, but, at the same time, he blamed the Kordas for slipping in the imperialist slant over the last few days of shooting and during post-production. Given the script and the *mise en scène* of the film as a whole, Robeson's defense was weak, and it failed to convince even his friends. "The picture was an out and out betrayal of the African colonials, whatever may be said of your good intentions," the American Communist Ben Davis told Robeson, "and the imperialist twist came about in more than the cutting of the film. You became the tool of British imperialism and must be attacked and exposed whenever you act in such pictures or plays." Robeson acknowledged his error and set out to redeem himself: "In my music, my plays, my films I want to carry the central idea: to be African."

Robeson worried about reconciling his professional success as "a singer and an actor," as "primarily an artist," with this cultural and, increasingly, political affiliation to Africa. "Had I been born in Africa, I would have belonged, I hope, to that family which sings and chants the glories and legends of the tribe," he ruminated. "I would have liked in my mature years to have been a wise elder, for I worship wisdom and knowledge of the ways of men." After the backlash against *Sanders*, he welcomed the role in *Song of Freedom*: an ordinary man of the people, who turned out to be just such a "wise elder." It offered him "a *real* part for the first time." He described *Song of Freedom* as "the first film to give a true picture of many aspects of the life of the coloured man in the west. Hitherto, on the screen, he has been caricatured or presented as a comedy character. This film shows him as a real man." In equating the representation of "the coloured man" in *Song of Freedom* with his own role, Robeson failed to mention either the caricatured witch doctors, whose "superstitious nonsense" keeps Africa "backward, uncivilised, impoverished," or his comic sidekick, Monty, played by Robert Adams, who goes from being Zinga's fellow worker to acting as his dresser in his concert career, and finally becomes his manservant and bag-carrier on the trip to Africa.

The English press reviews, in any case, failed to notice any radical perspectives on class, race, or imperialism. "Robeson comes into his own," judged *Film Pictorial*, in a film that *The Era* found "thoroughly entertaining," but which seemed "sentimental, overcoloured and unreal" to *The Bystander*. There were extrinsic reasons for this distracted response. Between the shooting of *Song of Freedom*, in the spring of 1936, and its premiere in March 1937, Oswald Moseley's British Union of Fascists had marched down Cable Street, in the very part of London portrayed in the film; the Jarrow Marchers, protesting against the rise of unemployment, had reached the capital from their mining communities in the north of England; Mussolini's troops had occupied Ethiopia; the Spanish Civil War had broken out; the Jesse Owens Olympics had been staged in Berlin; and King Edward VIII—the jazz-loving Prince of Wales of the 1920s—had abdicated to marry Wallis Simpson. A month after the film's release, Guernica was bombed. In the United States, the black press, which had often been highly critical of Robeson's choice of film roles, was more attentive. The "finest story of coloured folks yet brought to the screen," the Pittsburgh *Courier* called it; "a story of triumph." Langston Hughes wrote to Essie Robeson that "Harlem liked 'Song of Freedom.' "

In France, the three years between *Zouzou* and *Pépé le Moko* witnessed the rise of the Popular Front and, to all intents and purposes, its fall. In 1934, economic depression and the extent of government corruption revealed by the embezzlement scandal known as the Stavisky Affair had encouraged widespread political cynicism. Agitation by antirepublican forces, like Action Française and the protofascist Croix-de-Feu, provoked antigovernment demonstrations, which culminated in a riot outside the Chamber of Deputies that left fifteen people dead and many more injured. When the resignation of the government created the conditions for a far-right putsch, a number of left and center-left parties came together to form the Popular Front. This coalition soon established itself not just as the basis for a "national unity" election ticket—the Front was elected to government in June 1936 and Léon Blum became France's first socialist prime minister—but also as a mass-cultural movement, which challenged many of the country's social, cultural, and educational traditions. The Popular Front government fell after barely a year in office. The broader movement lasted longer, until it too unraveled after a series of strikes in November 1938, just ten months before France declared war on Germany. Julien Duvivier and Jean Gabin's 1936 film *La Belle équipe* was a celebration of the Popular Front ethos. It did not do well at the box office. Their follow-up was a more commercial proposition: a gangster movie, set in France's North African colonies. The Maghreb provided an exotic location for a stream of novels, plays, and songs, as well as films, in the years between the Colonial Exhibition, in 1931, and the outbreak of the Second

World War. Jacques Feyder's 1934 Foreign Legion story, *Le Grand Jeu*, was typical of the way that an "Arab" setting provided an overheated, melodramatic and feminized correlative to a narrative of masculine European guilt, exile, and redemption. It also prefigured not only several elements of *Pépé le Moko*'s plot, but also its "poetic realist" style.

Pépé le Moko has always appealed to intellectuals. Jean Cocteau called it a "masterpiece," and Graham Greene praised it as "one of the most exciting and moving films I can remember seeing." For the adolescent Italo Calvino, growing up in the Italian town of San Remo, it typified the earthiness and eroticism of a French cinema "heavy with smells," in contrast to Hollywood films "light with Palmolive, polish and antiseptic." After seeing the Casbah in *Pépé le Moko*, the novelist recalled, "I would look at the streets of steps in our old town with new eyes." This reaction helped Calvino to understand "realism" in cinema as the effect of "establishing a special link between the places I knew from experience and the places of the elsewhere." Cinema, that is, offered a prism through which to experience the world at hand, not a mimetic representation of distant places—as Simone de Beauvoir was to discover. In 1948, she and Jean-Paul Sartre visited Algiers because, she recorded, "we wanted some sun and we loved the Mediterranean." They were disappointed. In contrast to the picturesque romance they fondly recalled from *Pépé le Moko*, the Casbah proved to be a place of "wretchedness and rancour." Beauvoir had got it the wrong way round. Rather than offering accurate information for tourists, cinema, in Calvino's words, satisfied "*a need for disorientation*, for the projection of my attention into a different space, a need which I believe corresponds to a primary function of our assuming our place in the world." Cinema provided an alternative, imaginary perspective on the everyday. It created the subjective conditions for "an expansion of the boundaries of the real, for seeing immeasurable dimensions open up all around me, abstract as geometric entities, yet concrete too, crammed full of faces and situations and settings, which established an (abstract) network of relationships with the world of direct experience."

Following Calvino's account, cinema can be understood as a medium that renders abstract, relational forces ("colonialism" and "race," for example) in concrete form: a crowd of faces (Baker, Robeson, Gabin), a patterning of situations and settings (stories and narration), the *mise en scène* of space and location (Paris, London, Africa, Algiers)—and, of course, sounds, voices, music, and movement. In *Zouzou, Song of Freedom*, and *Pépé le Moko*, the affective power of cinema to make audiences perceive the world otherwise is encapsulated, and reinforced, by the strategic deployment of a number of songs. Three, in particular, combine narrative function with sensory impact. In *Zouzou*, Josephine Baker sits on a swing, inside a giant birdcage, in a grand Parisian music hall: an American expatriate playing a French-born orphan of Martinician descent, sings a lament

Josephine Baker and Jean Gabin in Zouzou

for a lost homeland, "Haiti." In *Song of Freedom*, Paul Robeson's London docker, having expressed his anguish at being separated from "our people" in Africa, sings a lullaby, "Sleepy River," over an idealized montage of working-class London. In *Pépé le Moko*, the *chanteuse réaliste*, Fréhel, plays a madam trapped, like Pépé, in the Casbah. Mourning both her lost youth and her lost home, she gazes at a photograph of her glamorous younger self, as she sings along with a gramophone recording of "Où est-il donc?," a celebration of Paris, made in her heyday as a music-hall star. All three songs have a haunting quality to them. All are evocative of their uneasy times. With the wisdom of hindsight, they might be interpreted as a requiem for

Zouzou dances

a society that would not survive the world war of 1939 to 1945. The aim here is to understand their affective power for audiences at the time, and their ability to translate ideas and emotions into sensory images. The first task, therefore, is to explain how the songs function cinematically.

Narrative Space

Zouzou interweaves two stories. One story is about the heroine's thwarted passion for Jean (Gabin, on the cusp of stardom), the adoptive brother who loves her only as a sister, and how she loses him to her best friend, the blonde Claire (Yvette Lebon). The other narrative charts Zouzou's rise to stardom. What links them is Zouzou's partial, or conditional, assimilation into French society. Success in her career, allied to her self-sacrifice, enables Jean and Claire to become a couple. What drives the film's narration is Zouzou's progress along a number of trajectories through different spaces. One is geographical: her move from provincial Toulon to metropolitan Paris. A second is institutional. As a child, Zouzou lives and works in a circus, a disappearing form of communal entertainment. She gets her break in the more commercial and hierarchical music hall. And she performs her big set pieces in an impossible theatrical space that silently acknowledges the defining medium of twentieth century modernity: the film studio where her performances were actually staged and the cinemas in which they were viewed. The third trajectory charts Zouzou's career as a performer. Here, Josephine Baker's bid to become a movie star, through her role in *Zouzou*, is displaced onto a story about Zouzou's transformation from a circus performer into a music-hall star, or *vedette*.

Although she made her name as a dancer, in *Zouzou* Baker sings two songs, twice each, but dances only once, on the occasion of her "discovery." Having delivered the star's laundry to the music hall, where Jean works as a lighting technician, Zouzou is persuaded to try on a sparkling leotard, and she goes on stage in this costume, to show herself to Jean. A sequence of extreme close ups, in slightly soft focus, sculpt her skin and muscles, emphasizing the gleam from her teeth, eyes, and waxed hair. Jean gets her to pose, to test his spotlight. When she starts to dance, Zouzou is entranced by the huge silhouette she casts on the backdrop behind her. She manipulates it by contorting her body into grotesque shapes and movements, doing animal walks, and mimicking military poses. Jean raises the curtain so that the theatre manager, desperate for a new star to save his show, can also see her perform.

Baker first sings "C'est lui," in comic parody of the established music-hall star, at the laundry run by Claire's mother. As she does so, the film cuts to Miss Barbara, a statuesque East European blonde (Illa Meery.) As she rehearses the song, she first mangles the words and then forgets them altogether—to the fury of the desperate manager, but with the indulgence of his partner, Miss Barbara's deaf sugar daddy. The film cuts back to Zouzou, who faultlessly finishes the song. In this sequence, the lyrics are subservient to Zouzou's clowning and the star's ineptitude. In narrative terms, the performance signals that Zouzou will displace Miss Barbara. When "C'est lui" is reprised toward the end of the film, Baker, wearing a magnificent satin gown adorned with sequins and feathers, delivers it in torch-song style, with a jazz trumpet prominent in the orchestration. "For me there's only one man in Paris," Baker sings. "It's him," even though he is "so dumb" and "hasn't understood a thing." The song not only recapitulates the plot about Jean's insensitivity to Zouzou's feelings, it also enacts her continuing disavowal of the narrative's inevitable outcome. She performs it after she has ensured that the imprisoned Jean will be set free, but before a scene in which, out of sight, she will watch Jean's release and his departure with Claire.

The two performances of "Haiti," written by Vincent Scotto, bookend the sequence that shows Baker singing "C'est lui" and the scenes at the prison gate. The first, a long song-and-dance production, intercut with the narration of Jean's release, features outsize bedroom furniture, including the giant bird-cage, which is uncovered to reveal Baker, decorated only by a few ostrich feathers, sitting on a swing. She sings about the beautiful forests and wide horizons of that blue, distant land, Haiti. At the end of this performance, Baker throws

Josephine Baker and the Paul Colin poster, Zouzou

open the cage door and dives, from a height of a couple of meters or more, onto the linked arms of two waiting chorus boys, who sweep her athletically onto the stage. The brief reprise follows Jean's release and Zouzou's emotional collapse in the streets of Paris, which ends as she comes to halt in front of a billboard advertising herself, ostentatiously signed by Paul Colin. A billposter plasters a notice announcing "100th performance" across it. Inside the music hall, the camera tracks back across the elaborate staircase on which Zouzou sang "C'est lui," where in extreme long shot a couple embrace, past a veil, and then to Zouzou herself, in close up, in the cage. As she sings the song's last two lines—"Mon désir, mon cri d'amour, Haiti / C'est de te revenir un jour, Haiti"—she looks wistfully through the bars of the cage, and the film ends.

Like *Zouzou, Song of Freedom* recounts the rise to stardom of an obscure but naturally gifted performer. Its narrative falls into four stylistically distinct segments, linked through a sequence of implausible coincidences and, more importantly, through excuses for Paul Robeson to sing. A brief prologue establishes the imperial context. Until 1700, the African island of Casanga had escaped the attention of slave traders, but it suffered the tyrannical rule of a hereditary queen, Zinga. Her son and his wife flee the island with a carved medallion, which had been worn by all the island's rulers, only to turn themselves over to slavers. A historical montage runs through the miserable passage to England and the abolition of the slave trade, ending in the present of 1936 London. The second segment introduces John Zinga, a docker whose legacy includes the medallion, a musical theme that haunts him "somewhere at the back of my head," and a longing to "return" to Africa. He also has an amazing bass singing voice, which (first coincidence) is overheard by the outlandishly camp opera impresario Donozetti (Esme Percy), as he disembarks from a transatlantic liner. Donozetti tracks Zinga to an East End pub, and turns him into an international concert-hall star. The third segment opens with a travel montage, showing the great European capitals and Zinga's triumphant performances, and ends with a shot of the poster for "*The Black Emperor*, A Negro Opera featuring John Zinga." An anthropologist in the audience (Bernard Ansell), the only white man to have visited Casanga and lived to tell the tale, recognizes the musical theme that haunts Zinga (second coincidence) and explains the significance of the medallion. Turning his back on a contract in New York, Zinga travels to Africa, the setting for the fourth segment of the film. Greeted with hostility and abuse, he despairs at the "primitive" conditions in Casanga. "But they're your people, John," his long-suffering wife, Ruth (Elizabeth Welch), reassures him. "The worse things are, the more you can help them." It is only when Ruth's life is threatened that (final coincidence) Zinga dredges up from his racial unconscious not just the music, but also the indigenous "words" of the tune that has haunted him. It is the sacred song of Casanga's rulers, and Zinga's knowledge of it persuades his subjects to accept him and his "better magic": Western medicine, irrigation, and other modern "wonders." The final image shows John Zinga back on the European concert circuit, stripped to the waist and surrounded by African statues, singing to raise money for development projects.

Throughout the film Zinga is asked, or asks himself, where he comes from. "Do you come from Africa?" asks a sailor early on. "I wasn't born there," replies Zinga earnestly; "but most of us coloured folks come from there originally." ("Yeah, we got rhythm deep down inside," mocks Monty, in a rare moment of eye-rolling, hand-waggling subversion.) Zinga's search for home is articulated through the movement of the film from Africa to the London docks, from East End community to the jungle setting of the West End opera, through the montage of Zinga's European tours, to the "return" to Casanga, and finally the London stage again. Zinga's final home lies not, as he imagines, in Africa, but in his acceptance of an ambivalent relationship to both Africa and England. When he finally reaches Casanga, even his one ally, the village elder Mandingo (Ecce Homo Toto), tells him: "Although you are of our colour, you are not of us." At one level, at least, Zinga accepts the interpellation. "In *the country where I come from*, people are saved from fevers much worse than that," he assures the villagers. His role, in effect, is to deliver modernization, and thereby to act as a native administrator on behalf of the colonial powers. "I have more than jungle ways to bring to you. I have learned much from the people across the sea. Their wisdom. Their government. Their medicine."

The "Freedom Song" embodies the narrative's motivating enigma—its MacGuffin. Zinga irritates his workmates by constantly humming the theme. After his operatic triumph, he sings it as his encore. "I hear the voice of my people," he extemporizes. "They are calling for freedom." In Casanga, at his moment of greatest crisis, the "authentic" version speaks through him to reveal his true status as king. "People bow down to the might of the sea and the king," he sings, reverting to English. "From the shadow of darkness, I lead my people to freedom." Other performances, including the extract from Gruenberg's opera, are less significant in narrative terms. They are placed to make good the promise of Paul Robeson as star, rather than Paul-Robeson-as-John-Zinga, as the film's main attraction.

The narrative geography of *Pépé le Moko*—a space that is symbolic and political, as well as physical—is elegantly established in an introductory sequence, lasting a little under two minutes, in which the colonial police instruct a colleague from Paris about the reality of a socially and racially divided Algiers. The opening shot shows a map of Algiers and then moves to a sweeping panoramic shot of the Casbah, the vast and impenetrable labyrinth of "dark winding streets running down to the sea." This is the perspective of the *dieu voyeur*—a Lyautey, perhaps, or a Le Corbusier—which conceives urban space as a set of problems to be made amenable to government action. A montage of rapid cuts moves the perspective from that overhead, all-encompassing vision

The geography of the Casbah in Pépé le Moko

down to the level of the Casbah's exotically named streets, its claustrophobic alleyways, and its crowded cafés. The explanation switches from the space of the Casbah to its *people*, although still retaining a focus on potentially soluble problems: "It is inhabited by forty thousand people of all origins, where there should be ten thousand." But colonialism's administrative discourse slides seamlessly into a taxonomy of "races": "Some of them come from a barbaric past and ancient traditions mysterious to us: Kabyles, Chinese, Gypsies, stateless people (*Heimatlos*), Slavs, Maltese, Negroes, Sicilians and Spanish—and women, women of every country and shape." A sexualized ethnography, in turn, mutates into a concern with Arab domestic architecture: "Big ones, fat ones, little ones, ageless, and shapeless ones so gross no one would touch them. Houses with inner courtyards without ceilings echoing like wells inter-communicating by means of terraces which are reserved to the Arab women. But Europeans go there." This sexualization of space draws together

Jean Gabin as Pépé; Mireille Balin as Gaby

two strands in the French colonial discourse of the time. One was Lyautey's strategy of *association*, which entailed the need to respect the indigenous cultural concern for the "integrity" of private and domestic life: "You are familiar with the narrow streets, the façades without opening behind which the life of the family spreads out and which must therefore remain sheltered from indiscreet looks." The other was the Orientalist strand in French popular culture, which offered a more prurient interpretation of Muslim domestic architecture. Pierre Loti's popular turn-of-the-century tales, like the novella *Three Women of the Casbah*, often told of naïve Europeans being seduced by alluring Arab women, or being unable (farcically or tragically) to tell the difference between a home, a harem, and a brothel in the Casbah. In *Pépé le Moko*, the link between the description of the Casbah's architecture and the catalogue of prostitutes, in effect, folds Lyautey's colonial surveillance in with Loti's voyeurism.

The colonial backdrop to *Pépé le Moko* is thus established as the tension between the colonial administration's fantasy of spatial transparency and social order, and the anthropological *fact* of the Casbah, with all its illegible activities and messy human interactions. "And somewhere in this maze Pépé is at home." Pépé is *le caïd des caïds*, the boss of underworld bosses, but trapped in the Casbah, disgruntled by his exile from Paris and smothered by his clinging gypsy mistress, Inès (Line Toro). Into this claustrophobic world comes a group of French tourists, including the beautiful Gaby (Mireille Balin), a Parisienne kept by a champagne magnate. The immediate sexual frisson between Pépé and Gaby is articulated through the motif of their shared love of Paris. When Gaby and Pépé discover that they both come from the same working-class district of les Gobelins, they launch into an antiphonic call and response of Métro station names, hers charting the luxury shopping streets and bright lights of Paris, his its rougher areas. The exchange ends when, at the same moment, they both utter "la place Blanche"—home to the Moulin Rouge, and where the underworld met the Parisian elite. These shared Parisian origins, and their mutual recognition as doubles, as well as lovers, are reinforced by the unusual similarity in the *mise en scène* of Gabin and Balin. Pépé's masculinity (his beauty, his violence, his vulnerability) is as lovingly etched by lighting and camerawork as Gaby's femininity (her beauty, her glamour, her dependence). For Gaby, Paris is part of Pépé's appeal, but he also represents the Casbah, at least the aspect presented to tourists from mainland France. Asked what Pépé is like, Gaby answers that he is attractive, and then, after a pause, "and frightening." Danger is linked to the exotic: "I'd like to know what he thinks, how he landed in the Casbah—so picturesque." For Pépé, Gaby is Paris, recollected from exile in the Casbah. Even her jewels and her glamor are no match for his overriding nostalgia. "You're covered in silk, full of gold," he tells her in their last conversation, "and you remind me of the Métro, *frites* and cups of *café-crème* on café terraces."

This story of desire and recognition intertwines with the film's thief-taking narrative through the figure of the Arab policeman, Slimane (Lucas Gridoux). Slimane introduces Gaby to Pépé, he informs Kleep about their affair, and then tells Gaby the lie that Pépé has been killed. His concocted message, supposedly from Gaby, lures Pépé out of the Casbah into the *colons'* Algiers, where he is finally arrested, and slashes his wrists as he watches Gaby's ship sail for France. Slimane is a socially marginal figure, isolated from other Arabs, despised as lazy and devious by his colonial masters, and obsessed by Pépé and by his relationship with Gaby. However, it is the ambivalence of his in-between status that makes Slimane central not just to the film's plot development, but also to its colonial ideology. He has a freedom of movement, socially as well as spatially, denied to any other character. He slips at will between the bureaucratic perspective of colonial power and a native understanding of the Casbah's secrets that is denied to the European police. When he says that military-style solutions will not work in the Casbah, an abortive police raid proves him right. Slimane uses subtler tactics to achieve his masters' ends, exploiting human desires and frailties. In doing so, he embodies the limits to official rhetoric about the rule of law, universal rights, and respect for cultural particularity, and exposes colonialism's dirty little secrets: its systematic exploitation, deception, and violence.

Lucas Gridoux as Slimane

In *Pépé le Moko*, these disavowed truths are implicit in the curiously flirtatious dance of death between Slimane and Pépé. The two men amiably exchange vows of hostility, as they stroll through the Casbah together. Pépé strokes Slimane's cheek and chucks him under the chin. Slimane jokes about Pépé's sex-appeal ("Women will be your undoing"), and Pépé teasingly accuses Slimane of wearing mascara and perming his hair. Slimane's repeated promise to catch Pépé, "slowly, slowly," smacks as much of courtship as of a manhunt. He lurks in the street outside the room where Pépé and Gaby make love. There is an edge of personal malice to his betrayal of Gaby to her rich lover. The homoerotic hints in Slimane's deference towards Pépé's masculinity are the obverse of the native's *sly civility* toward his masters—a cultural posture rendered physically in his deferential stoop, his ingratiating smile, and his wheedling tone of voice.

There are two songs in *Pépé le Moko*. About an hour into the film, on the morning after he has first made love with Gaby, Pépé sings "Pour être heureux dans la vie," an up-tempo, up-beat rumba by Vincent Scotto. The *mise en scène* refers back the film's opening sequence, but this time the Casbah is shown not through the lens of colonial administration, but as a functioning community. Toward the end of the film, Fréhel's "Où est-il donc?" operates as a narrative hinge. The song is placed just before a sequence, in which Pépé beats the truth about Slimane's stratagems out of the informer, l'Arbi (Dalio), and then walks down through the Casbah toward the sea and his death. Pépé has sent the thuggish Carlos (Gabriel Gabrio) with a message for Gaby, and he waits for news with Carlos's woman, Tania (Fréhel). When Carlos fails to return, Tania tells Pépé how she copes at such moments, escaping into a different time and place by listening to songs she recorded in happier days. As an exile's thoughts about Paris from abroad, "Où est-il donc?" echoes Pépé's desperate nostalgia and so, indirectly, the dynamic of his relationship with Gaby. The lyrics, written by Vincent Scotto long before the film was made, mention the "Moulin de la place Blanche," about which Pépé and Gaby waxed sentimental, and the reference to "mon bistro du coin" echoes Pépé's evocation of cups of *café-crème* on café terraces. The song offers a condensed version of "the story so far" and motivates the denouement to follow. As it ends, Inès and l'Arbi enter with news of Carlos's arrest.

Dream-Work

Cinema satisfied Italo Calvino's "need for disorientation." When he explains that watching films achieved this "disorientation" through "the projection of my attention into a different space," he evokes Freud's concept of the *andere Schauplatz*, that "other scene" created in the process of dreaming. And when Calvino talks about cinema enabling him to see "immeasurable dimensions open up all around me, abstract as geometric entities, yet concrete too, crammed full of faces and situations and settings," this, too, equates to the experience and mechanisms of dreaming. In analyzing how dreams work, Freud was certainly hoping to explain how (Calvino again) "an (abstract) network of relationships" is established "with the world of direct experience." Freud's answer was that dreams (like jokes, slips of the tongue, and behavioral symptoms) are structured primarily by a process of distortion, or *Entstellung*, and its component mechanisms of displacement (*Verschiebung*) and condensation (*Verdichtung*). Calvino's beguiling equation between cinema and dreaming prompts the question of whether Freud's mechanisms of condensation and displacement might help to elucidate the affective power, or the haunting quality, of "Haiti," "Sleepy River," and "Où est-il donc?"

Before looking at the songs in that light, a brief explanation of Freud's analysis of dreams may be useful. His starting point was that the psychical material motivating dreams does not present itself straight. It goes through a process of hallucinatory translation, so that we can acknowledge desires and fears that trouble us but, at the same time, deflect the need to confront them for what they are. Freud went further. Rather than aiming just to excavate a hidden layer of truth from beneath the fiction of the dream—unscrambling its raw materials, as it were—he argued that what is important in dreaming is the productivity of the actual process of transformation. In a note added to *The Interpretation of Dreams*, in 1925, he expressed his concern that, although the primacy of latent dream-thoughts over the manifest content of dreams had been widely understood, "the distinction between the latent dream-thoughts and the dream-work" was still being overlooked. Fundamentally, dreams are nothing other than "a particular *form* of thinking, made possible by the condition of the state of sleep." It is the *dream-work*, and neither the manifest nor the latent content, that is "the essence of dreaming." It is because he was more interested in the *how* of dreaming, than in the *what*, that Freud paid special attention to *distortion*. *Entstellung* has a number of connotations. To distort is not only "to change the appearance of," but also "to wrench apart" or "to put in another place." In dreaming, distortion involves the transformation of *feelings* into *images*. "The waking mind produces ideas and thoughts in verbal images and speech, but in dreams it does so in true sensory images." It involves the creation of a dream *space*. "The scene of action of dreams is different from that of waking ideational life." Distortion thus produces that *andere Schauplatz*, to which Calvino alludes. Within this dramatic arena, the sensory images present not a mimetic reproduction of the wishes that generate them, but a dream *narrative*. They "construct a *situation* out of these images; they represent an event which is actually happening." The images "dramatize" an idea. Like cinematic *mise en scène*, the dream-space acts as more than just a setting for the dream-narrative. This other space is an alternative psychical reality that provides an encompassing mood, and whose affect is produced

Zouzou in her cage

through the narration of the dream-*events*. The events produce the space, just as much as the setting amplifies and valorizes the events.

Verdichtung, or condensation, connotes not only a process of concentration or reduction, as water droplets coalesce from steam, but also the process through which light is compressed or focused into a beam. Freud used the analogy of a telescope. The telescope's disposition of lenses produces an image that has some relation to objects beyond the apparatus, but the image remains a virtual entity, wholly determined by the construction of the telescope and its mechanisms. In his revisionist gloss on *Verdichtung*, Lacan emphasizes the element of *surimposition*: the way that different associative chains are superimposed on each other in a single image. Such "overdetermined" representations—which can be expressed in the form of the nodal point of a dream, a composite person, or a montage—again allude to other ideas, while excluding them from the dream, joke, utterance, song, or whatever.

The puzzle about the staging of "Haiti" in *Zouzou* is why, at the climax of her first major movie, the dancer Josephine Baker is immobilized inside a cage. In what sense is this image overdetermined? The motif does pick up on a line in the song ("Far from your shores," even the "most beautiful cage" is "nothing but a prison") and the cage also recalls an earlier scene in which Jean, back from the sea, strolls arm-in-arm with Zouzou, through the markets of Toulon. When she sees caged birds for sale, to the fury of the shopkeeper, she releases them. The metaphor is banal enough: Zouzou wants to let her desire fly free. Set this image against the placing of the two performances of "Haiti," around "C'est lui" and Jean's release from jail, and the symbolism is transparent: Jean gets out of jail, Zouzou goes back behind bars. Despite these diegetic motivations, and following the logic of the transformative work of dream-images and the superimposition of allusions within a single image, a more likely inspiration can be found in *Le Tumulte noir*, Paul Colin's 1929 portfolio of lithographs, which includes an image of a near naked Baker performing a "wildly indecent dance" behind bars—less a portrayal of a woman or a dancer, according to Colin, than an attempt to convey "something as exotic and elusive as music" (see Plate 5). At the level of its manifest content, the image, which looks very little like Josephine Baker, has been accused of representing "the most condescending and dehumanizing racist side of negrophilia," the familiar primitivist condensation of blackness with primitivism, animality, and voracious female sexuality. True enough, but looking at *how* the image is produced, the art-*work*, reveals a curious feature about the painting of the bars. They have been added on last, and they are painted so thinly that it is possible to see through them. This is not so much a portrait of Josephine Baker in a cage, then, as an image of a sexualized black woman over which bars have been painted, apparently as an afterthought. These superimposed bars may, therefore, signify less containment of Baker's ferocious sexuality, than the observer-artist's gesture of anxious self-censorship.

Colin's bars bring to mind Sartre's account of looking and objectification in *Being and Nothingness*, which was picked up and developed by Lacan. Sartre's premise was that, in any act of looking, there is always a duel between one consciousness and another. Only one can emerge as a true subject: the other will become the object of that subject's more powerful look. Sartre explained the insight with a parable. A voyeur is kneeling, absorbed, at a keyhole, peering at the object of his look. Suddenly, he is alarmed by a rustle of branches behind him, or footsteps followed by silence. A third person has caught him out. The voyeur feels ashamed, not just because he has now become the object of a more powerful look, but, more profoundly, because he realizes that he exists as the potential object of the gaze. From this vignette, Lacan drew the lesson that the structure of the imaginary is not dyadic (Paul Colin painting Josephine Baker) but triadic (Paul Colin's image of Josephine Baker viewed within a field of social, and sexualized, visibility). Compared with Colin's dancer, "arms high, belly thrust forward, buttocks quivering," Baker's performance of "Haiti" is remarkably demure. A tame songbird, she does not even dance. She swings gently back and forth, her body hardly moving. At one level, the cage evokes the "primitive" old "black" Josephine, while actually presenting the "sophisticated" new "French" one. At another level, the scene may reveal how censorship works. The allusion to the eroticized primitivism of Colin's "Josephine behind bars" shows what cannot be spoken. The inter-action between desire, shame, and censorship is folded into the very *process* of looking: the act of looking, in this case, at a beautiful black woman, in the anxious era of Popular Front colonialism.

In *Pépé le Moko*, mechanisms of layering, superimposition, and displace-ment are evident in Fréhel's performance of "Où est-il donc?" Here too there is an artful fit between star mystique and fictional role, this time intensified by the overlayering of several different time frames in the one scene. When the character "Tania" refers back to her heyday as a music-hall artiste, the audience sees a photograph of the young Fréhel. When "Tania" sings a nos-talgic song, she duets with one of Fréhel's earlier records. The past is not just recalled in thought and language, it is made sensually present through cam-era and phonograph. These technologies invoke a third mechanism of the dream-work, which Freud called the *Rücksicht auf Darstellbarkeit*, the con-siderations of representability. When he translated the term into French as *égards aux moyens de la mise en scène*, Lacan evocation of *"mise en scène"* underscored the cinematic nature of the dream-work.

Duvivier's cinematic *mise en scène* concentrates on three elements: the machinery of reproduction, the connotations of the performer, and the con-voluted nature of time. From Tania/Fréhel walking across the room in long shot, there is a cut to an extreme close up of her hand cranking the phono-graph, and then, as she describes how she used to make her stage entrance, a pan to show the photograph on the wall. The camera pulls back to show Tania's hand dropping the needle and the record starting to play. The move-ment resumes, presenting her framed in medium close up, looking off-screen left. This set-up is maintained, as she listens to the record. When it reaches the phrase "dreaming of Paris," a cut-away shows Pépé lying thoughtfully on his bunk, looking distractedly at Tania. The previous set-up is resumed, but now as a strange duet between Fréhel's younger, but already quite metallic, voice, distorted further by the primitive recording, and the worn, huskier voice of the mature woman on screen. The unwavering focus is on Fréhel's *presence*—her physical presence here and now, with the fictional characteriza-tion overlaid by the trace of the past Fréhels heard in the recording and seen in the photograph. The mechanical reproduction reinforces the irretrievabil-ity of the past.

The minimalism of the staging assumes the audience's familiarity with Fréhel, both as an exponent of the *chanson réaliste* and as a woman with a well-publicized past. After a difficult childhood, she had been a star of the *café-concert* in the years before the First World War. In Colette's novel *La Vagabonde* (1910), Fréhel appears as the eighteen-year-old Jadin, new to the stage and "flabbergasted at being able to earn two hundred and ten francs a

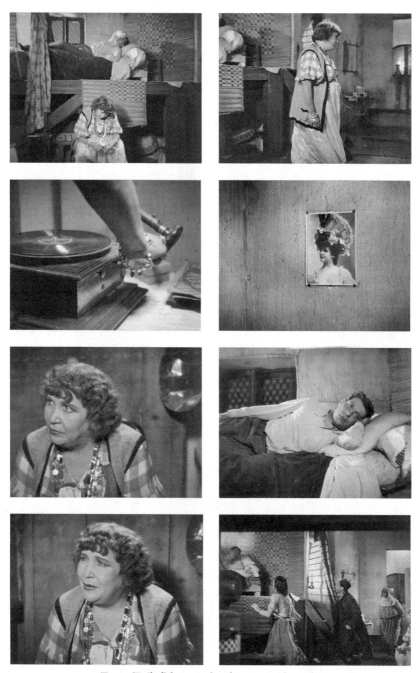

Tania (Fréhel) laments her fate in Pépé le Moko

month by singing." She sang "like a little seamstress or a street singer," and she had "the face of a pink and sulky young apache." The public adored her "just as she is, with her dress that is too long and bought goodness knows where, her light brown hair not even waved, her hunched shoulder which looks as if it were still lugging along the laundry basket." After an unhappy affair with Maurice Chevalier, the death of a child, and addiction to alcohol and cocaine, Fréhel left France for ten years or more, touring in Asia and Eastern Europe. In the 1920s, she managed a comeback, no longer Colette's "radiant and exultant" young performer, but the bloated and tragic woman in *Pépé le Moko*. Of course, this is just gossip, but it is gossip that taught the audience how to "read" Fréhel: as the embodiment of morality tales about class and destiny, public success and private tragedy, beauty and decay, and desire and loss.

These connotations transform "Où est-il donc?" into something more than a reverie for the past or an expression of regret. The song actually opens by looking forward, conjuring up Parisians who want to migrate to America, because of "what they've seen at the cinema." The lyrics then predict, in a kind of future imperfect, that those who leave will soon grieve for the city. The words in the second half of the song are attributed to these expatriates, struggling to make a buck in Depression New York, but they are also sung by Fréhel/Tania, exiled to the Casbah. The imagery evokes the way of life that will have been lost: the *tabac*, the *bistro de coin*, the *copains*, the *bals musettes* with their *javas* to the accordion, the free *galettes*. Within and beyond the film narrative, the performance alludes to desires and anxieties that haunt vanished pasts and possible futures: who I used to be and what I am now; what I might have been and who I fear I shall become. When the record ends, Tania weeps. The sound of an opening door motivates a cut, to show the whole room. Inès and l'Arbi enter, marking a return from the complex imaginary interweaving of past, future and present, to the ordered linearity of narrative time.

It could be said that, in "Où est-il donc?," Tania is mourning a lost home. In his essay on "Mourning and Melancholy," however, Freud restricts the term "*mourning*" to the painful but necessary process of working through of the loss of a loved person—or, presumably, a place—and finding a replacement. An essential aspect of mourning is the need to acknowledge that the beloved object had a separate existence and so, more fundamentally, that the world exists independently of the mourner. This separation is something Tania cannot manage. Because she cannot let go of the past, she cannot mourn. She remains trapped in *melancholy*, which entails a repressed feeling of aggression toward the lost object that is turned inward against herself. "According to the analogy with mourning," observes Freud, "we have to conclude that the melancholic has suffered the loss of an object, but from his expressions, it results from the loss of his own self." The melancholic transforms the nothingness of a disenchanted world into a nothingness of the self.

This suggests that there may be something more than pangs of colonial displacement to the *melancholy* of "Où est-il donc?" or the *nostalgia* evoked by "Haiti" and "Sleepy River." *Homesickness* is part of their affect, but it manifests itself, less as a desire to be somewhere psychologically more comfortable than the uneasy place and time in which one happens to find oneself, than as an awareness, at some level, that *home* is a place impossible to get to. In these films, home exists as somewhere unknown, yet supposedly familiar from the past (Josephine Baker's Haiti), as a hoped-for place of return in the future (Paul Robeson's Casanga in *Song of Freedom*), and in the recognition that homecoming is impossible (Fréhel and Jean Gabin in the Casbah). The nostalgia of the songs might then be seen as an emotional defense against an experience of displacement and disorientation, which is integral to the modern idea of home as *inaccessible*. This suggests the next link in the affective chain: from melancholy, to nostalgia, to the uncanny. As Freud was at pains to explain, the *Unheimlich* is implicit in the *Heimlich*, it is not its opposite. The uncanny that haunts these films, in the form of lost or never-known homes, does not do so as the trace of an actual place that once existed, that might exist somewhere else, or that could exist in the future. Rather, this uncanny is an experience of radical existential displacement, which is part of the experience of being in a place, even as it forecloses the possibility of making that place a home. The key to the *haunting* evocation of home in the three songs may, therefore, be that there was "no there there" to be mourned in the first place.

Melancholy, nostalgia, and the uncanny all bring out the *temporal* nature of the modern relationship to home. Zouzou, John Zinga, and Pépé hover between an uncomfortable present, a fantasized past, and an idealized or dreaded future. Not only are they "out of place," they are at once behind themselves and ahead of themselves, caught in what Freud termed the "wrinkled time" of human experience. This is what, in the films, gives the places that the characters desperately try to get to, or get back to, a dreamlike, out-of-reach quality. Where does the "Paris" of Fréhel and Pépé exist, other than in desire and deceiving memory? What is Zouzou's "Haiti," except a figment of defensive imagination? And John Zinga's "Africa" is not to be found in this world. "We will find our haven at last," sings Ruth Zinga, near the end of *Song of Freedom*, "When our long, long journey is past / Down the river of dreams."

The Refrain

In "1837: Of the Refrain," in *A Thousand Plateaus*, Gilles Deleuze and Félix Guattari propose three anthropological functions for music. Music can keep up our courage, and show us the way home, in an unfriendly world: "The song is like a rough sketch of a calming and stabilising, calm and stable, centre in the heart of chaos." (This is the comfort that "Où est-il donc?" offers Tania.)

Second, we use music to create a home, to claim a space where we belong, and which we own: a child humming while doing homework, in Deleuze and Guattari's examples, or a housewife having a radio on in the background. This is about *making* a home, not *being at* home: "it was necessary to draw a circle around that uncertain and fragile centre." "Sonorous or vocal components" create "a wall of sound, or at least a wall with some sonic bricks in it." Third, Deleuze and Guattari describe how music sustains a home in our

Song of Freedom

hearts, as we make our way in the world. "One launches forth, hazards an improvisation," they write, as if with John Zinga's variations on the "Freedom Song" in mind. "One ventures from home on the thread of a tune."

For Deleuze and Guattari, "the refrain" is neither a particular form of music, nor an element of music. Rather, it evokes the capacity of music to bring things or forces together—they talk about *assemblage*—and so to define, claim, disrupt, or remake a "territory," by which they mean a field of understanding and possible action. They speak of a refrain "when an assemblage is sonorous or 'dominated' by sound." They call it a "glass harmonica": a prismatic apparatus of *glass* that can, like Freud's telescope lenses, compress and refract abstract forces (for Freud, desires and anxieties) into something new (dream images). It is a glass *harmonica* because the *aural* mechanisms of transformation can "assure indirect interactions between elements devoid of so-called natural affinity, and thereby . . . form organized masses."

In *Song of Freedom*, John Zinga has returned home after a day's work on the docks and a drink in the pub with his mates, Bert, a white Cockney, and the comic Monty. As John gazes at a map, Ruth chides him for his obsession with Africa. "That's my home; that's where we come from," he replies, and tells her about a sailor he met in the pub, who was reluctant to set sail for Africa that night: "It's natural. He's leaving his people to go out among strangers. He'll be sort out of place. Lonely, maybe. However hard I try, I feel the same here. Out of place." The scene ends with an iris wipe to Bert, a shrimp of a man, and his large wife, Nell, in their parlor, where Monty has just broken a piece of crockery. Bert stands laughing, while Nell scolds Monty as the two of them kneel, picking up the pieces. On the soundtrack, Robeson starts to sing "Sleepy River": "There's a sleepy river I know." With the second line, "Down that sleepy river we'll go," there is a cut to a street scene, a chiaroscuro studio recreation of a London, reminiscent of Daumier's etchings. Street lamps are placed center-frame in the distance and right foreground, with busy market stalls and cloth-capped men walking to and fro. John and Ruth are shown by their window, as he sings the next three lines, followed by a shot of Bert, Nell, and Monty, entranced by Robeson's voice, for two lines, and then back to John and Ruth for the repeated line, "Down our river of dreams." The second verse reverts to the street, with a thinner crowd suggesting that the evening has passed. Over the second line, "As we sail to lullaby land," a fair-haired, white mother sits knitting, with a baby in a crib at her feet. Domestic imagery continues to accompany the next four lines: a black couple opening a door, a shot from their point of view of three children asleep in a bed, the mother putting her finger to her lips, and the two adults closing the door again. On "Follow the tide wherever it goes," there is a cut to John and Ruth, this time through their window, from the exterior. They lean forward to look outside. In what could be a reverse shot, a woman—dark haired, apparently Jewish— gazes up wistfully from her window ("Let the world go sleepily by"), followed by a Middle Eastern couple and, to end the verse, Bert and Nell embracing contentedly at their kitchen table. The camera pans right to Monty, looking out of his window, and then cuts to John and Ruth, humming the refrain in harmony. The spatial relationship between the two positions is revealed: Monty, in the foreground, is gazing at John and Ruth, across the way. A final shot of the street, now more tightly framed, shows it almost deserted, with one or two late-night pedestrians bidding each other goodnight, lights being turned off, and a down-and-out rummaging through a dustbin. Finally, two shots show Tower Bridge, at night, with a cargo ship moving left to right, and the camera panning slightly right to left.

Although this description cannot convey the full sensory impact of the sequence, it does suggest the crystallizing power of music and reveals two competing versions of community that are in play. John Zinga's yearning for Africa assumes that being authentically *at home*, or *in place*, entails not just a common racial identity, but also settlement in a space shared with nation, tribe, clan, or kin. Wherever you happen to be living, you really belong with "your people": "It's natural." The montage, in contrast, displays a different kind of assemblage: an urban, migratory, and transitory community, in which ethnic markers are neither easily read nor especially important. This community is "territorialized" as a network of contingent and transient connections. It is an unstable location of being, rather than belonging; a plural community in which finite being is exposed to finite being. Crucial to the affect of the sequence is the way that this second version of community is achieved, less by the words of the lullaby or by the film images, than by the timbre of Robeson's voice. This is the "wall with some sonic bricks in it," which draws a circle around an "uncertain and fragile centre." It is in this sense that Robeson's rendition of "Sleepy River" functions as a refrain.

A similar "sonorous assemblage" is enacted in Jean Gabin's song, "Pour être heureux dans la vie," in *Pépé le Moko*. The two men's voices are quite different. Robeson's is a deep, enveloping bass, Gabin's a light, music-hall tenor. The songs also contrast in style, rhythm, and tempo. Robeson's lullaby helps the young to sleep and soothes their elders as night falls; Gabin's energetic rumba celebrates the morning of a bright new day. "Sleepy River" is set against a gloomy mock-up of the East End; "Pour être heureux" mixes location footage with brightly lit staged shots, in a montage of Casbah inhabitants, cut to the rhythm of the song. The sonic "circle" of Gabin's song encompasses an old woman sifting grain, a young woman delousing her son, prostitutes enjoying the morning, a young girl sifting grain, a shoe mender beating a shoe in time, and women dancing. Like Robeson, Gabin is present primarily through his voice. He is not seen until well into the song, and then only in a few long shots on Inès's terrace, and reflected in a mirror.

These versions of community can be read through a colonial prism, as illustrations of how particularity and difference are embraced by the "mother country," or *la plus grande France*. But something else shows through, in their rhythms of displacement, marginality, and urban adaptability. Deleuze called this the "complicated time" of a people-to-come: a community of singularities, relationships, and possibilities not yet pre-empted by the "gross statistical categories" of race, sex, and gender. The forces from which our lives are composed are always more complicated than social taxonomies of "identity." In his more utopian moments, Deleuze hoped that they might be transformed, through music, to create other spaces, other times of living.

In amongst their bewildering array of anthropological, ethological, and philosophical examples of music's powers of assemblage, Deleuze and Guattari included a schematic history of European music. What romanticism added to classicism, they assert, was new concepts of "people" and "territory," understood in terms of roots and identity. In romantic music, and in the lullabies, folk songs and *Lieder* which romantic composers reworked, they hear an articulation of the "affect proper to the natal": that is, "to be forever lost, or refound, or aspiring to the unknown homeland." Deleuze and Guattari left open the promise of modernist music to remake this romantic equation of people with birthplace and create new spaces for a "people to come." They speculated how "the bad or mediocre refrain" might act as a springboard, as a means of creating something more generative. Beginning from "popular and territorial *melodies* that are autonomous, self-sufficient, and closed in upon themselves," they asked, "how can one construct a new chromaticism that places them in communication, thereby creating '*themes*' bringing about a development of Form, or rather a becoming of Forces?"

Colonial Melancholy

One set of answers to the question of what *Zouzou, Song of Freedom*, and *Pépé le Moko* reveal about the way that colonialism and "race" were experienced in 1930s Europe would be, quite rightly, that they clothed the wretched fact of colonialism in an aura of racially legitimated national destiny, that they tell us nothing about the economic, political, and military realities of British or French colonial rule, and that they offer no clue about what it was like to be a colonial subject. (That would have to wait for Gillo Pontecorvo's cinematic rereading of the Casbah in *Battle of Algiers*, in 1966.) Coming at the question from a different angle, and concentrating on the affect of the films and the songs within them, another answer might be that they do hint at something about the relationship between colonialism, "race," and the postromantic experience of home: "to be forever lost, or refound, or aspiring to the unknown homeland." In doing so, they suggest, at least, why "the colonies" seem to have operated in the mid-1930s as "another scene" for metropolitan audiences, a fantasy space onto which could be projected the paradoxical overinvestment in a home that never was and never could be there. This can then reveal something about the psychological roots of modern racism.

In these films, the incomplete mourning for an impossible home returns as the haunting quality of popular music and song. The sense of not belonging, or of something being missing, is symptomatic of the melancholic nothingness of the modern self; and it is this *nothingness* that fantasmatic racial identities are supposed to transform into the *something* of imagined collectivities. They offer a way of justifying life when universal values have fled the world, and when death has become an arbitrary end rather than the completion of a life. The experience of secular modernity creates a sense of disorientation so disturbing, and an anxiety about the possibility of living a meaningful life so profound, that ersatz gods and new myths of belonging have to be invented to provide some promise, however spurious, of human insurance against extinction. "Race" tells us where we come from, taking at face value the conflation of geography with biology, which Freud identified in the "home-sickness" joke about a familiar place and the mother's genitals. Promising membership in a larger collective destiny, "race" tells us that we are not merely mortal and alone. It holds out the lure of psychic wholeness, the sense of a selfhood that might escape the ravages of historical contingency.

That structure of fantasy, grounded in a belief that the claims of racial or ethnic identity are absolute, is undeniably present in *Zouzou, Song of Freedom*, and *Pépé le Moko*. However, Deleuze's hope that "in all art, for all art, the people is never given and must be invented anew" suggests a different, more "convivial" answer, one that focuses less on the films' investment in established colonial attitudes and categories of race, than on their convoluted temporalities and on their performance of alternative ways of being, or becoming, together. In the collaborative arts of cinema and music, and in at least one aspect of the vernacular European response to Josephine Baker and Paul Robeson, it is possible to find affirmations of the forces of multiplicity, improvisation, and modernity. In these moments, there is no promise of a home to be found in the lost arcadia of Haiti, the Paris of one's youth, or the primordial utopia of Africa. There are no promises of any sort, and certainly no recourse to claims of collective identity or destiny. Rather, in the "other space" of cinema, there are glimpses of might-have-been, could-be community: Josephine Baker's trust, as she leaps from the cage into the arms of the dancers; the tempo of Jean Gabin's rumba for the Casbah; the grain of Paul Robeson's voice cradling the fantasy of a universally hospitable London.

Paul Robeson leaving Waterloo Station, London, on the boat train The Majestic, *1935*

Here I Stand

PERFORMING POLITICS

Both Paul Robeson and Josephine Baker were swept up by the political currents of the twentieth century, and both on occasion became embroiled in political controversy. Robeson achieved a degree of political significance, first as an embodiment of the New Negro and later as a hero of the international Left and an embattled critic of American policies during the Cold War. Baker was less self-consciously, or less self-definingly, political. Early in her career, in 1931, she had a brush with politics when Marshal Lyautey invited her to become "Queen of the Colonies" during the great Exposition Coloniale in Paris; the invitation was withdrawn after objections that that the United States was not a French colony and that she was not a French colonial citizen. Baker has been described as "backing into politics," because her political views were less ideological than emotional and reactive. Even so, she came out of her experience of working for General De Gaulle's Free French during the Second World War with decided opinions. From then on, she took a consistently principled public stand against racism and discrimination, she was active in a number of antiracist campaigns, and she embarked on her own living experiment in utopianism by adopting twelve children of different races from around the world to create her multicultural Rainbow Tribe.

Here, the focus is less on Baker's and Robeson's political beliefs or activities than on the way that, on occasion, they quite literally *performed* politics, just as they performed in song, dance, or drama. The aim is to explain how, when, and where they did so, and to understand the motivation and consequences of those events. Their political performances are therefore explained and judged as performances like any other. What work went into them? Where did they take place? On which narratives and imagery did they draw? How did they trade on the performers' celebrity and public images? How were the performances disseminated? What was their historical context?

Paul Robeson, the Royal Albert Hall, June 1937

On June 24, 1937, a year into the Spanish Civil War, three months after the release of *Song of Freedom*, and just weeks after the bombing of Guernica, Paul Robeson appeared at a rally at London's Royal Albert Hall to raise funds for Basque refugee children. The Republican cause enjoyed widespread progressive support. Sponsoring this event were W. H. Auden, Jacob Epstein, Sean O'Casey, E. M. Forster, H. G. Wells, Rebecca West, and Virginia Woolf. Even the venue lent an air of respectability. Opened in 1871, the Albert Hall was a monument not only to the nineteenth-century ideals of scientific progress and public enlightenment, but also to the morbid sentimentality of the Victorian era. By the mid-1930s, it had become a forum for national ceremonies and community events. Just a year before the Robeson event, for example, it had witnessed a massive celebration of the British Empire to mark the centenary of the birth of Joseph Chamberlain, the imperialist politician and father of the recently installed prime minister, Neville Chamberlain.

In the run-up to the rally, Robeson had been vacationing at the Soviet spa of Kislovodsk, and he had promised to transmit his contribution by radio from Moscow. When the Albert Hall management began to dither about whether to include it, and rumors spread that the German government was threatening to jam the link, Robeson dashed to London by plane and swept majestically onto the platform. He sang to the packed audience of 6,000 people and then delivered a passionate speech. "Like every true artist, I have longed to see my talent contributing in an unmistakably clear manner to the cause of humanity," he began.

> I feel that tonight I am doing so. Every artist, every scientist, must decide *now* where he stands. He has no alternative. There is no standing above the conflict on Olympian heights. There are no impartial observers. Through the destruction, in certain countries, of the greatest of man's literary heritage, through the propaganda of the false ideals of racial and national superiority, the artist, the scientist, the writer is challenged. The struggle invades the formerly cloistered halls of our universities and other seats of learning. The battlefront is everywhere. There is no sheltered rear.

Robeson had learned to link art to politics in the Harlem Renaissance, but he had moved beyond Alain Locke's strategic "cultural racialism." Now he framed "the struggle for Negro rights" as part of the "wider antifascist struggle." At the same time, he made it clear that politics had become, for him, a *personal* matter. His rhetoric is heroic not only in the way that it evokes a grand historical narrative, but also in the way that geopolitical conflicts are articulated in terms of his own destiny.

> The artist must elect to fight for Freedom or Slavery. *I have made my choice. I had no alternative.* The history of this era is characterized by the

degradation of my people—despoiled of their lands, their culture destroyed, denied equal protection of the law, and deprived of their rightful place in the respect of their fellows.

Robeson had no doubt that this uncompromising declaration of political commitment marked a turning point in his life. He saw it as an act of self-reinvention: his way of becoming his own man. Many recent scholars share that judgment. They too see it as the moment when he managed to break away from the constrained imaginings of "the black modernist nationalism of the 1920s and the white primitivist modernism of Greenwich Village," including the roles he had played in such anxious explorations of masculinity as Eugene O'Neill's *The Emperor Jones* or Kenneth Macpherson's *Borderline*. Rejecting any "cultural aesthetics that denied or disguised their political implications," Robeson was finally able to take on his destined role as "an international New Negro rebel." The general view is that he thus transcended "years of self-doubt and floundering" and found "a clear-cut moral and ethical direction, a passion that satisfied his need for a higher calling, a passion that added a new and compelling spiritual dimension to his life."

Six months later, at a second pro-Republican rally at the Albert Hall, organized by members of the Labour Party, Robeson affirmed his new identity, when he sang for the first time his own lyrics for "Ol' Man River." Reworking Oscar Hammerstein's doleful pastiche as a defiant credo, Robeson claimed the song as his own. The voice is no longer that of the lazy stevedore, Joe, but of Paul Robeson the anti-Fascist, antiracist and anticolonialist activist. Joe landed in jail because he got a little drunk; Robeson "shows a little grit." Joe got weary and sick of trying; Robeson keeps laughing, instead of crying. Whereas Hammerstein ended with exhaustion and despair—"tired of living and scared of dying"—Robeson now sang: "I must keep fighting / Until I'm dying."

In Harlem, Robeson had been embraced as a hero because he appeared to embody the struggle of black Americans to gain recognition as full citizens of the United States. He was the "New Negro" incarnate. Having that destiny thrust upon him had not always sat easily with his sense of self or, more prosaically, with his career ambitions. That discomfort was one of the reasons why Robeson and Essie, along with their newborn son Paul Jr. (Pauli), migrated to London in 1927. Initially, Robeson flourished in England, not least because the racism he had encountered daily in New York seemed to be absent. Looking back in *Here I Stand*, the autobiography-cum-manifesto he published when the Cold War was at its iciest, he acknowledged that he had "found in London a congenial and stimulating intellectual atmosphere in which I felt at home." Even as his fame and his wealth grew, however, he ran up against the limits of London's welcome. He may have been treated "as a gentleman and a scholar" in "the most aristocratic circles," but his role at smart social occasions was still to provide the entertainment or to add a touch of exoticism. In 1929, he fell foul of London's resurgent racism, when he was refused entry to a dinner hosted by Lady Colefax at the Savoy Grill, where he had been welcomed many times before. At around the same time, he left the Drury Lane Theatre after a matinee of *Show Boat* to be confronted by a group of Welsh miners, who had marched to London after being locked out of their colliery. Moved by their stories and songs, he arranged for food and clothing to be sent to their valley. Such experiences were part of a radicalizing political journey that culminated in the Albert Hall appearance.

So, too, was the informal education he was receiving in socialist and anti-colonialist ideas. "I learned my militancy and my politics from your Labour Movement here in Britain," Robeson told *Reynolds News* in 1949. "I realized that the fight of my Negro people in America and the fight of the oppressed workers everywhere was the same struggle." In 1956, when asked by the House Un-American Activities Committee whether he had studied Marxism in Moscow, Robeson responded that he learned it in England, so that the committee should not "blame that on the Russians. You will have to blame that on the English Labour Party." He would have had in mind his conversations not only with Labour politicians, but also with authors like George Bernard Shaw and H. G. Wells, and with new acquaintances from the Caribbean, Africa, and India, including C. L. R. James, George Padmore, Jomo Kenyatta, and Jawaharlal Nehru. Robeson learned from them that London, for all its seductive comforts, was still the hub and heart of empire: "it was there that I 'discovered' Africa. That discovery, which has influenced my life ever since, made it clear that I would not live out my life as an adopted Englishman, and I came to consider that I was an African." In constructing an *African* American identity for himself, Robeson enrolled to study African languages at the School of Oriental and African Studies. Even so, C. L. R. James lamented that Robeson "never really understood Britain's imperialism," insofar as he failed to grasp fully the difference between being a black American citizen and a colonial subject. Paul Robeson Jr. would later share this harsh judgment. He believed that, at this time, his father was living "a pampered, aristocratic life, far from the racial humiliations endured daily by even the highest-ranking blacks in the United States." Such privilege sowed the seeds of pride: "occasional high-handedness had emerged in his personality." With that arrogance came hubris: "an incipient feeling of license" and even "grandiosity in his speculation about his godlike status."

This background helps to explain both Robeson's hubristic focus on himself and the emotional urgency of the desire for commitment evident in the Albert Hall speech. To proclaim that "I have made my choice" was to answer to the question, *who am I?*, not just for a hostile world but for himself. The reason that Robeson needed such an answer can be inferred from a chance meeting in Bloomsbury one spring morning in 1932, when, on his way to the British Museum, C. L. R. James bumped into Robeson. In James's experience, Robeson

C. L. R. James, March 1944 (Carl Van Vechten)

was "never upset about anything." On this occasion, however, Robeson fretfully asked whether James had heard the press gossip about an affair between "a coloured singer and a member of the British Royal Family"—widely known to be Lady Edwina Mountbatten. "It's not me, James," Robeson declared "passionately." James laughed. Robeson was indignant. James reassured him. As "a Negro from the United States" living in England, there was no disgrace in being linked "to a member of the British Royal Family." Hence his reaction: "I laugh because you seem so upset about it. That is very funny." Robeson was intractable. "They got the wrong Nigger in the woodpile, this time James," he protested. "It's not me—Hutch maybe—but not me!" Robeson had probably not slept with Edwina Mountbatten and he was certainly right about her less than discreet affair with Leslie Hutchinson. But whether the gossip was true is less significant than the intensity of Robeson's response. Most men he knew, reflected James, would have been secretly flattered by the rumor of "an illicit relationship with a member of the British Royal Family." Not Robeson. "For some reason or other, which I cannot go into here but which I think should be remembered about Paul, is his passionate statement: *'James, it isn't me.'*"

The "some reason or other" that was making Robeson so anxious may provide a clue to his thinking about "who he was" at this time. What was the ascribed *"me"* that he was abjecting so passionately? Pragmatically, Robeson would have been worried about the damage such gossip could do to his career. He would have sensed that the rumor must reinforce the dull, relentless habits of mind that rendered him always and only the embodiment of black, masculine sexuality. In Harlem, he had been accused of reinforcing white perceptions of black sexuality when he appeared in *All God's Chillun Got Wings*, Eugene O'Neill's play about a destructive mixed-race marriage. Now, in London, he was again being ensnared by demeaning assumptions about his race and sexuality: "That Mr Robeson should be stripped to the waist is my first demand of any play in which he appears," was the *Daily Graphic* reviewer's response to his *Othello*. ("It is still true, alas," James Baldwin would write in 1961, "that to be an American Negro male is also to be a kind of walking phallic symbol: which means that one pays, in one's personality, for the sexual insecurity of others.") Even if it "wasn't him" in the case of Edwina Mountbatten, Robeson knew that his many erotic adventures exposed him to the stereotype of the sexually voracious black man.

Closer to home, his marriage was in trouble. In 1930, on the eve of his premiere in *Othello*, Essie had published her biography, *Paul Robeson: Negro*. Its purpose, as she frankly confided to Carl Van Vechten, was to "work out

Eslanda (Essie) Robeson and Paul Robeson, 1933 (Carl Van Vechten)

exactly the picture of Paul I want people to have." She therefore depicted Robeson as "Harlem's special favourite" in the 1920s, and recounted how he appeared to find a home in London under her tutelage. In its final chapter, however, the book veers off in a new direction. Essie gives a fanciful account of a walk on Hampstead Heath and a fireside heart-to-heart, in which she acknowledges and forgives Paul's sexual "lapses," and he responds "with eyes full of tears, and full of immense relief". In reality, negotiations about their marriage were more painful, more protracted, and less easily resolved than this fiction allowed. Shortly after the book was published, Essie opened a love letter to Paul from the actress Peggy Ashcroft, who was playing Desdemona to his Othello in the West End. "I feel now that he is just one more Negro musician, pursuing white meat," she seethed in her diary. "I suppose it's a curse on the race." Although they remained friends, the affair with Peggy Ashcroft was short-lived. More threatening was his relationship with a less distinguished actress, Yolande Jackson, whom he had met in 1930. When C. L. R. James ran into Robeson in Bloomsbury, the affair was at its height and he had been living apart from Essie for some time. His divided affections and loyalties would have been another reason for his discomfort. Later in 1932, when Robeson returned to New York for a revival of *Show Boat*, Yolande traveled with him. At a press conference, he conceded that he and Essie had separated, that he hoped to marry an Englishwoman and that she was neither Nancy Cunard nor Peggy Ashcroft, but he threatened to quit the United States forever if the relationship provoked any racist abuse. One answer at that press conference goes a long way to explaining the unease he betrayed to James: "I desire above all things to maintain my personal dignity." By the end the year, for whatever reason, the relationship with Yolande Jackson was over, but that only intensified Robeson's search for a public persona and a sense of self that he could live with.

Robeson was exasperated and hurt by Essie's biography. Again, he felt that it presented a version of him that *wasn't him*. His son suggests that its publication made him decide to dismantle Essie's "sense of ownership of him" and to "free himself from his dependency on her." This suggests another reason for the vehemence of his "*it isn't me*" to C. L. R. James, which resurfaced in the Albert Hall performance. Robeson was experiencing an exhausting dissociation between his troubled emotional life and the ever more demanding expectations of "Paul Robeson," the public figure. Professional, social, and personal anxieties were interacting to create an ethical crisis. "I refuse to live under the sword of Damocles all my life," he told the *Manchester Guardian* in 1934. He wanted to get out from under the world's determination to trap him within an ill-fitting and destructive public role and to make himself anew. "I want to be where I can be African and not have to be Mr. Paul Robeson every hour of the day."

Yolande Jackson, 1930 (Bassano Ltd.)

By the time Robeson appeared at the Albert Hall rallies in 1937, the dogmatism of "*The artist must elect to fight for Freedom or Slavery*" had become existentially necessary as well as politically opportune. His performance was an expression of his need to claim his experience, to make it his own, and not to be told who he was by others. It represented, apart from anything else, a wager on political commitment as the path to personal redemption: "*I have made my choice.*" This new "Paul Robeson" provided the script by which he lived the rest of his life.

Paul Robeson's Odyssey

Although Robeson's appearances at the Albert Hall rallies had their own integrity, they also constituted episodes in a larger biographical narrative. However much Robeson thought of his socialist and anticolonial radicalism as a new beginning, the terms in which he articulated it were familiar from the Harlem Renaissance. Although he now spoke not just of "my Negro people in America," but of "oppressed workers everywhere," he still cast himself as the protagonist in a victimized people's struggle to triumph over bondage and despair and to realize a dream of redemption, liberation, and collective self-formation. The difference was that Robeson now threw off his earlier hesitations about accepting the burden of heroic leadership.

Temperamentally, Robeson was well suited to play the hero. Against many modernist conceptions of masculinity—Baudelaire's image of the dandy or the flâneur as a kind of cool participant observer, for example, or Simmel's account of the blasé attitude of the metropolitan male—Robeson's personality is best described by a psychological term taken from classical Greek: *thymos*. Thymos denoted a quality of engaged and driven spiritedness that interacted in the masculine soul with its rational, or calculating, capacity and with the more instinctual desires and appetites. It was heroic insofar as it manifested itself as a man's ambition to do great deeds and to be recognized for them, a will to achieve fame that also entailed a capacity for rage, if dealt with unjustly, for distress, when he or those he loved were injured or slighted, and for shame, when he fell short of his own self-evaluation. The thymos of the hero provides an apt way of describing the style in which Robeson acted out his politics. The tendency to hubris noted by his son stemmed from the way that he saw politics through the prism of his own destiny, and he was motivated as much by his discomfort when his reputation or dignity was impugned, as by his anger at the many injustices of his contemporary world.

Culturally, thymos was embedded in the genre of the epic. The career of the epic hero, which is also a working through of thymotic drives, follows a conventional arc: departure from home, a series of adventures that are also tests, and finally a return home and the founding of a people, of whom the hero is embodiment and leader. This homecoming—the *nostos*—marks not just survival, but also maturity, insofar as "home" represents a place where double consciousness might be replaced by an undivided "I." That "home" is both the point of departure and the final destination for the hero's journeys is especially apposite for understanding the roles that defined Paul Robeson's political career. His experience of finding a home in London, for example, strolling through its parks, gazing at the Thames and even (according to Essie) watching cricket at Lord's, soon gave way to a concern that he was being seduced away from his heroic destiny by the city's enervating embrace. Like the character he played in *Song of Freedom*, Robeson felt a nagging sense of being "out of place" in London. He fantasized about setting up home in Africa. He visited the Soviet Union and said, "This is home to me." He supported Spanish antifascism and said, "To me Spain is another homeland." In the end, neither London, Africa, the Soviet Union, nor Spain proved *enough* of a home: "For another year I remained in Britain, and the more I became part of the Labour movement the more I came to realize that my home should be in America." Back in Harlem, in the 1950s, he rejoiced in "the press of all that is around me where I live, at home among my people"—even though he then moved back again to London.

Underlying the restlessness and nostalgia of Robeson's political journey was another question implicitly addressed by the Albert Hall speech: *where do I belong?* His insatiable, and repeatedly disappointed, need for "home" would on occasion cloud his judgment, as when the Korda brothers had played on his dream of an African homeland to convince him to star in *Sanders of the River*. More profoundly, it was Robeson's sense of dislocation and his fear of deracination that made him vulnerable to the lure of the Soviet Union and allowed him, unknowingly at first, to be scripted into a carefully stage-managed political drama.

In the early 1930s, Robeson had been targeted as a sympathetic high-profile foreigner by the Anglo-American Sector of VOKS, the All-Union Society for Cultural Relations with Foreign Countries. Although the official function of VOKS was to handle the Soviet Union's external cultural relations, one of its primary tasks—with the personal support of foreign minister Maxim Litvinov—was to cultivate such international sympathizers into active advocates for the regime. Robeson's first visit to Moscow, in December 1934, was at the invitation of Sergei Eisenstein, to discuss the possibility of a film about Toussaint L'Ouverture. When he arrived, VOKS officials were among the welcoming party at the station.

VOKS's most effective technique for winning over sophisticated visitors was to construct an experience in the Soviet Union that would play on their aspirations and vulnerabilities, mixing flattering public recognition with trips of real interest and social events that encouraged conversation and friendship. So it was that, within days of their arrival, Paul and Essie Robeson and their traveling companion, Marie Seton, were being entertained at an informal Christmas Eve dinner put on by Litvinov and his English wife, Ivy, along with Eisenstein, some Red Army generals, and the conductor Albert Coates. After a generous dinner and many glasses of vodka, according to Marie Seton's account, the guests danced. Even Robeson "abandoned his usual decorum and competed with Eisenstein who had learned the most intricate steps and Negro rhythms at the Savoy Ballroom in Harlem." Then Robeson sang, "Go down, Moses," with its plea to "Let my people go." Litvinov "laid his small, plump hand on Robeson's sleeve." "We are very glad you have come to our country," Seton records him saying. "All of us here know the position of the Negroes. We are one with your people—and you have remained one with your people." Later in the evening, Robeson told Eisenstein that he had been hesitant about the visit, as he had doubted that the Soviet Union would really be different from anywhere else. "But—maybe you'll understand—I feel like a human being for the first time since I grew up," he confided. "Here I am not a Negro but a human being. Before I came I could hardly believe that such a thing could be. In a few days I've straightened myself out. Here, for the first time in my life I walk in full human dignity. You cannot imagine what that means to me as a Negro."

However contrived the *mise en scène* of this event may have been, there is no reason to doubt Eisenstein's good faith or Litvinov's bonhomie. VOKS followed up on these new friendships by arranging an itinerary designed to convince Robeson that, in contrast to the dismal record of the United States, the Soviet Union really had dealt constructively with the question of ethnic minorities. In making that journey, he was following in the tracks of three friends from Harlem days: W. E. B. Du Bois, Langston Hughes, and Claude McKay. They too had been persuaded, to a greater or lesser degree, that Soviet internationalism might offer an alternative to Western paradigms of racially exclusive national identity. The Soviet Union was promising to lead an alliance of peoples, united by culture and marginalized by their colonial rulers or host states, in a quest for self-determination. Robeson was also attracted by Stalin's policy of *narodnost*, which fostered folk-based nationalism alongside technological modernization as a means to economic development. "Tractors chugged across the ancient fields," rhapsodized Marie Seton, "modern machines clattered in the factories but—Robeson's heart throbbed—the people still danced their ancient dances and sang their haunting songs born of the Asiatic steppes and a thousand generations."

VOKS played shrewdly on Robeson's passions: human dignity, folk identity, racial justice, and the idea of home. His yearning for a good society and the anger that made him so restless were both evident in an interview during that first visit to the USSR in 1934. What comes as a shock is less his endorsement of the Soviet regime than the juxtaposition of his desire to feel "in place" against an apparent acceptance of political violence. "From what I have already seen of the workings of the Soviet Government, I can only say that anybody who lifts his hand against it ought to be shot!" Robeson told the *Daily Worker*. Then, without missing a beat and as if to justify the brutality of that answer, he added: "I already regard myself at home here. I feel more kinship to the Russian people under their new society than I ever felt anywhere else."

That equation between violence and nostalgia suggests a revisionist interpretation of Robeson's Albert Hall performance and his subsequent political career. However apparently self-affirming the rhetoric of "*I have made my choice*" and "*I had no alternative*," the consequence of giving himself over to this particular moral-political vision was to find himself trapped within a compromised language and an unforgiving historical narrative. "No alternative" presupposes a Manichean vision of politics: *Are you with us, or against us?* "Us" triumphing over "them" tells history as teleology and subjugates an appreciation of historical open-endedness to the needs of state or party. Robeson's will to certainty, even at the cost of violence and self-destruction, reveals a bleaker side to his commitment than the critical consensus allows. His later life suggests that the political decision he had made by 1937 curtailed his scope for maneuver and agency, and it provides little evidence that his new political-existential script exorcised his inner demons or brought him much in the way of spiritual peace. Sublimating himself in the public cause turned out to be a way of acting out the painful complexity of his inner life, without working it through.

Paul Robeson's Tragedy

In Hegel's aesthetics, the epic hero had the capacity to transform the commonplace, by embodying, artistically, the unity between individual actions and universal principles. Hegel took it as axiomatic that such a conflation had been possible only in mythical or violent times, and he foreshadowed the modernists in believing that the world had become, with rare exceptions, too prosaically unheroic to allow that ideal to become a reality. In contrast, the tragic hero embodied a different transformative principle, one that shakes the "old world" and becomes universally valid only through the individual's death. It is this that makes the tragic principle *penetrate*, "albeit in another guise, undermining that which existed previously." In this Hegelian tradition, C. L. R. James believed that a "sense of the tragic" results, even in modernity, from "a sense of the inability of man in society to overcome the evil which seems inseparable from social and political organisation." Acknowledging this, in James's view, a tragic sensibility judges humanity "by the degree to which man is able to struggle against this overriding doom; to establish moral and psychological domination over the feeling of impotence and futility which it would otherwise impose."

To talk about Paul Robeson's life in terms of tragedy is not uncontroversial. Here, however, the issue is less whether the story of Robeson's life should be told as that of a resilient epic hero or as that of a heroic figure brought low by a tragic flaw, than, more narrowly, to find a framework for making sense of his political performances. The inspiration for using tragedy as that explanatory paradigm is the anthropologist David Scott's reading of *The Black Jacobins*, C. L. R. James's study of Toussaint L'Ouverture and the Haitian Revolution of 1791–1804. Scott's key argument is that when James revised the book in 1963, twenty-five years after its first publication, he refashioned it as a tragedy rather than as an epic or a romance. In doing so, he wrested his anticolonial narrative away from the conventional structure of past oppression, present struggles, and future triumphs. Instead, he recast it as "a dramatic confrontation between contingency and freedom, between human will and its conditioning limits." In contrast to "the epic revolutionary narrative," which "charts a steadily rising curve in which the end is already foreclosed by a horizon available through an act of rational, self-transparent will," Scott sees the tragic version as less teleological, more skeptical, and more interrogatory: "the rhythm is more tentative, its direction less determinative, more recursive, and its meaning less transparent."

This tragic sensibility adds a further critical edge to a reading of the heroic certainties of Paul Robeson's Albert Hall performance. In ancient Greek tragedy, any heroic action has two aspects. One is a rational, calculative balancing of pros and cons and the reflection on hoped-for ends and the planned means of achieving them. The other, according to Jean-Pierre Vernant and Pierre Vidal-Naquet, is an existential wager: "placing one's stake on what is unknown and incomprehensible, risking oneself on a terrain that remains impenetrable, entering into a game with supernatural forces, not knowing whether, as they join with one, they will bring success or doom." In such circumstances, even the most carefully planned action can be no more than "a chancy appeal to the gods and only by their reply, and usually to one's cost, will one learn what it really involved and meant." This was the type of wager Robeson was making when he declared, "*I have made my choice. I had no alternative.*" A tragic perspective undercuts any certainty about eventual success. It is only in retrospect, once the drama is over, that "actions take on their true significance and agents, through what they have in reality accomplished without realizing it, discover their true identity." The possibility then arises that it was Robeson's very disavowal of ambiguity and unpredictability that made it difficult to understand either himself or the events that would befall him: "human affairs remain enigmas that are the more obscure the more the actors believe themselves sure of what they are doing and what they are."

The paradox and indeterminacy that characterized the clash between Robeson's heroic pursuit of justice and the implacable hostility of "the old order" he challenged are evident in one of his most memorable political performances: his appearance before the House Committee on Un-American Activities (HUAC) on June 12, 1956. This was a very different occasion from the Albert Hall rallies in 1937. Then, Robeson's charismatic presence had enabled him to mobilize the audience within and beyond the Hall as a public. In cold-war Washington, he was subjected to a cynically staged ritual of humiliation. In contrast to the benign hugeness of the Albert Hall, the HUAC hearings took place in the Caucus Room of the Old Senate Office Building. Within that space, a dramatic arena had been created that accentuated face-to-face confrontation. Members of the committee sat in the central section of a raised three-sided bench, looking down on the table where witnesses and their lawyers sat, with clerks and other HUAC support staff crammed in around them. Whereas the Albert Hall rallies had been broadcast around the world on radio, the HUAC hearings were staged for the new medium of television. Newsreel cameras and glaring Klieg lights were positioned behind the wings of the raised bench, with press photographers crouched in front of it. There was some room left for members of the public to squeeze in, but not much.

HUAC in action

   Robeson's lawyers and family were nervous about how he would perform
at the hearing. A delay to the original appearance date of May 29 had been
granted on the grounds that he was too ill to travel, although his troubles
were as much psychological as physical. The mid-1950s marked a low ebb in
Robeson's life. The initial warmth of his welcome home to the United States
in 1939, and the huge success of the Popular Front radio *Ballad for Americans*,
had chilled, at least officially, as he continued to support the Soviet Union, to
criticize American foreign policy, and to denounce American racism. Things
turned especially ugly after he was reported to have said, at a Peace Congress
in Paris in 1949, that "American Negroes would never fight the Soviet Union."
A concert planned for August that year at Peekskill, a suburban area about
forty miles north of New York, where he had appeared successfully over the
previous three years, was disrupted by riots and threats of lynching. In 1950,
the State Department confiscated his passport and repeated attempts to have
it returned had been denied. Not being able to tour overseas made it hard to
earn a living. In 1955, two projects to which he had devoted much time and
energy collapsed. *Freedom* magazine, which represented his commitment to
African American rights, folded and the Council on African Affairs, through
which he waged the intellectual battle against colonialism, disbanded. In
March 1956, the *New York Times* published the first news of Khrushchev's

denunciation of Stalin's crimes and cult of personality. Apart from these distressing events, Robeson was physically unwell in 1955 and 1956, suffering from a recurrent urinary-tract infection and undergoing surgery for prostate cancer. He was also slipping into a phase of the recurrent depression that haunted him, when the subpoena to appear before the HUAC arrived.

Chairing Robeson's interrogation on June 12 was the Democrat Francis E. Walter of Pennsylvania, sitting with three similarly anti-Communist congressmen. Leading the questioning was HUAC's staff director, Richard Arens. As he arrived for the hearing, Robeson appeared so listless that his lawyers and family feared he might collapse. In the event, however, Robeson seized the initiative early. "Just a minute," he interrupted Arens after his interrogator's opening questions. "Do I have the privilege of asking whom I am addressing and who is addressing me?" After some discussion about passports—the ostensible topic of the hearing—Arens sprang his stock question. "Are you now a member of the Communist Party?" Robeson was imperious in his disdain: "Oh please, please, please." Pressed for a direct answer, Robeson quibbled about definitions of the Communist Party and asked whether Arens wanted to follow him into the polling booth to see how he had voted. When the chairman again demanded a response, Robeson (after a dramatic pause to consult his lawyer) invoked the Fifth Amendment—the right to protection against self-incrimination. For many witnesses summoned before HUAC, this move was interpreted as a sign of having something to hide and could lead to blacklisting or worse. Robeson felt that the State Department had already done its worst. Professionally, at least, he had little more to lose, and the tactic gave him the advantage of deciding which questions he would or would not answer.

Robeson's tricksiest subversion came when, drawing on his legal training and political apprenticeship as well as his years of acting experience, he challenged Francis Walter's authority.

"To whom am I talking?" asked Robeson. Walter identified himself as "the Chairman of this Committee."

"Mr. Walter?" responded Robeson.

Yes.

"The Pennsylvania Walter?"

"That is right."

Robeson asked about his contribution to the McCarran-Walter Act, which was designed to control the immigration of "dangerous aliens" and the emigration of "undesirables."

"You are the author of all of the bills that are going to keep all kinds of decent people out of the country?"

Walter took the bait: "No, only your kind."

"Colored people like myself… ?"

"We are trying to make it easier to get rid of your kind, too."

"You do not want any colored people to come in?" Robeson had shifted the terms of the interrogation away from his involvement with Soviet Communism, instead turning the spotlight on race relations in the United States and exposing the paranoid fantasies that underpinned them. When asked why he did not stay in Russia, Robeson thundered: "Because my father was a slave, and my people died to build this country, and I am going to stay here, and have a part of it just like you. And no Fascist-minded people will drive me from it. Is that clear?"

At some moments, Robeson openly mocked the careful scripting of the proceedings. When Arens demanded that he "confirm or deny the fact, that your Communist Party name was 'John Thomas'," Robeson guffawed: "This is really ridiculous."

"This is not a laughing matter," whined one Committee member.

"It is a laughing matter to me," responded Robeson, "this is complete nonsense."

At other times, in a Brechtian move, Robeson deflated the proceedings by exposing their confected theatricality. When his lawyer complained that the snapping of the press photographers was "nerve-wracking," Walter instructed them to take their pictures and then stop. "I am used to it and have been in moving pictures," teased Robeson. "Do you want me to pose for it good? Do you want me to smile? I cannot smile when I am talking to him." To a complaint that he could not be heard, Robeson shot back: "I am an actor, and I have medals for diction."

In only one passage of the interrogation did Robeson appear ill at ease. With Khrushchev's denunciation in mind, Arens repeatedly pressed him about his admiration for Stalin. Robeson's answers were evasive: "I do not know," "I cannot remember," "I do not remember." Picking up on current rumors, Arens asked whether he had changed his mind about Stalin. Stalin was a matter for the Soviet Union, said Robeson, and tried to switch the focus back to American politicians, present and past, who had been responsible "for sixty million to one hundred million black people dying in the slave ships and on the plantations, and don't ask me about anything, please." Arens used this answer to launch a series of questions about Soviet slave camps, with Walter egging him on. Again, Robeson equivocated—"I am interested in the place I am in, the country where I can do something about it"—but then became so enraged that he smashed his fist onto the table so hard that his lawyer feared he would break it. When the questioning turned to his family and friends, Robeson's studied politeness gave way to a more demotic register: "I have told you, mister," "Now you are making it up, brother." Genuinely angry, Robeson denounced the committee as the true "un-Americans, and you ought to be ashamed of yourselves." Apoplectic, Walter adjourned the hearing. Even so, Robeson got in the last word: "You should adjourn this forever, that is what I say."

At first glance, Robeson's interrogation—part courtroom drama, part battle of wits and part sinister farce—hardly comes across as tragic. Intellectually, he wiped the floor with his tormentors, displaying an informed understanding of global politics, of American race relations, and of the connections between the two that exposed their blinkered and vicious parochialism. Read as one episode in Robeson's longer biographical narrative, however, tragic undertones become apparent. For one thing, the HUAC hearing was a brutal enactment of the confrontation between the political challenge represented by Robeson and a ferociously self-defensive establishment. Robeson's bravura improvisation displayed passion, integrity, and wit, but that does not diminish what was at stake in the drama. These men were his enemies and they were out to destroy him, or at least to make it clear that there was no place for him in their America. ("The world had prepared no place for you, and if the world had its way, no place would ever exist," wrote James Baldwin in 1961. "Now, this is true for everyone, but, in the case of a Negro, this truth is absolutely naked: if he deludes himself about it, he will die.")

In that context, what is striking about the HUAC interrogation is the way that it worried at the uncertainties that had motivated Robeson's Albert Hall speech: *Who is Paul Robeson?* and, *Where—if anywhere—does Paul Robeson belong?* "The artist must elect to fight for Freedom or Slavery," Robeson had declared in 1937. By the mid-1950s, the moral choice was no longer so clear-cut. Robeson found himself caught between two repugnant options, two versions of "freedom," each of which entailed its own versions of "slavery." Must he bend to the paranoia and bigotry of his HUAC inquisitors? Or should he continue to act the Soviet fellow traveler, even though—as his evasions around Stalin and the gulags suggested—he was not unaware of the regime's crimes? This dilemma defined Robeson's tragedy: a good and exceptional man having to make an impossible choice between bad alternatives and therefore losing hope in the possibility of the future he had dreamed of and struggled for.

The extent of his knowledge about what was happening in the Soviet Union, and the depth of his unease about it, go to the heart of this tragedy. Signs of Robeson's doubts were evident as early as 1938, in a confrontation with his ten-year-old son. In 1936, Paul and Essie had sent Pauli to the Soviet Model School in Moscow, where his classmates included Stalin's daughter and Molotov's son. Even in that elite company, he sensed his fellow-pupils' anxiety about the "great purges." By 1938, Pauli had been transferred to a school in London for children of Soviet diplomats. One day, only months after the Albert Hall rallies, one of his schoolmates became distraught at the news of her parents being recalled to Moscow. Pauli mentioned to his father that he had recognized the name of a Russian family friend among a list of people shot during the current purge, and asked "whether something major had gone wrong under Stalin's rule." Robeson would not engage. "We all knew he was innocent," young Paul remembers yelling, "and you never said a word."

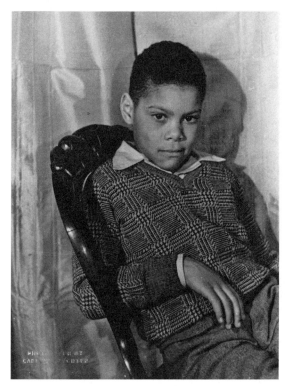

Paul Robeson Jr. ("Pauli"), 1935 (Carl Van Vechten)

Without meeting his son's eye, Robeson told him to keep quiet, "his voice a barely audible low rumble." Pauli was about to argue, when his father looked up: "The look in his eyes—an intense rage mixed with hurt—stopped me cold. I got up and left." A few days later, Robeson dispassionately justified Stalin's executions to his son, on the grounds that "great injustices may be inflicted on the minority when the majority is in the pursuit of a great and just cause." What is compelling here is less Robeson's expediency, than the way that the incident captures his combination of anger and psychological vulnerability. The look of "*intense rage mixed with hurt*," which young Paul saw in his father's eyes, uncannily echoes Aristotle's account of thymotic anger as a proper response to injustice, insofar as that anger represents "an impulse accompanied by distress, to a conspicuous slight directed without justification towards what concerns oneself or towards what concerns one's friends."

In June 1949, a few months after the Paris Peace Congress, Paul Robeson traveled to Moscow to take part in celebrations of the 150th anniversary of Pushkin's birth. By this time, the incipient xenophobia of Stalin's *narodnost* was becoming manifest. Soviet newspapers had launched a campaign against "cosmopolitanism and Zionism." Robeson's Jewish accompanist on the tour was denied an entry visa for the Soviet Union, and he would have known about the "mysterious" murder, early the previous year, of one of his closest Russian friends, the Jewish actor and director Solomon Mikhoels. Robeson and Essie had entertained Mikhoels when he made a fund-raising trip to the United States in 1943, in his capacity as chairman of the Soviet Jewish Anti-Fascist Committee. Accompanying Mikhoels on that visit had been the Yiddish writer Itzik Feffer, whom Robeson expected to meet in Moscow but who had disappeared from public view. When Robeson asked about Feffer's whereabouts, he was met by official prevarication. He continued to insist on a meeting, and Feffer was eventually allowed to see him alone in his hotel. Using gestures, Feffer let him know that his room was bugged. Turning up the music on the radio, the two men used mime and scribbled notes to converse. Feffer indicated that the KGB had been holding him in custody in the Lubyanka prison since the previous December, and that Mikhoels had been murdered on Stalin's orders. Drawing a finger across his throat, Feffer predicted his own fate. (Even though, unlike Robeson at the HUAC, Feffer did name names to the KGB, he was still executed in 1952.)

That evening, Robeson fulfilled the final public engagement of his visit, a concert broadcast nationally from the Tchaikovsky Hall. Many people in the audience, whether the elite of Jewish intellectuals or non-Jewish party members, had reason to be anxious about their own futures and all would have been uncomfortably aware of KGB agents planted around the auditorium. On stage, Robeson introduced his songs in impeccable Russian. He sang sixteen, each in its original language—English, French, Mandarin, and Italian. The audience response was enthusiastic. After he had sung "Ol' Man River," with which he would normally close his recital, he announced that he would give just one encore. He then spoke of the cultural affinities between the Jewish people of the United States and the Soviet Union, of his friendship with Mikhoels and Feffer, and of his joy at meeting Feffer earlier in the day. Having first recited its words in Russian, Robeson switched to Yiddish to sing "Zog Nit Keynmol," the anthem associated with the Warsaw Ghetto Rebellion: "For sure the hour for which we yearn will yet arrive, / And our marching steps will thunder: we survive!" The immediate reaction to this audacious rebuke to Stalin's anti-Semitic campaign was stunned silence, followed by a mixture of boos, shouts of disapproval, and a crescendo of applause.

Soviet censors edited out the remarks about Mikhoels and Feffer before the concert was broadcast, and Robeson himself remained doggedly silent about his awareness of Soviet anti-Semitism when he returned to the United States. He had decided that fighting for freedom, and against slavery, meant loyalty to the Soviet Union, no matter what—no matter even the danger that his disavowals might be perceived as acts of bad faith. In his 1967 novel *The Bass Saxophone*, for example, Josef Škvorecký looks back to that postwar moment in Czech history. There, as it had in the 1920s, jazz expressed a spirit of rebellion, whereas Robeson had come to epitomize conformism, collaboration,

Paul Robeson at a Soviet Embassy reception, Washington, 1950

and inauthenticity. When Škvorecký's young radicals demanded to hear progressive American musicians like Stan Kenton, the authorities "pushed Paul Robeson at us." As a result, "we hated that black apostle," who "of his own free will" agreed to perform at open-air concerts in Prague while dissident politicians were hanged and poets were locked up in prison: "Well, maybe it was wrong to hold it against Paul Robeson. No doubt he was acting in good faith, convinced he was fighting for a good cause. But they kept holding him up to us as an exemplary 'progressive jazzman,' and we hated him. May God rest his—one hopes—innocent soul."

When the novelist Doris Lessing met Paul and Essie at a Soviet embassy reception in London in the late 1950s—his passport had been returned in 1958, and they were again based in England—they struck her as "stupid," because they spoke entirely in "communist jargon". "Not one word was said in normal speech," recalled Lessing, citing phrases she was coming to despise: "capitalist lies, fascist imperialists, running dogs, democratic socialism (the Soviet Union), peace-loving peoples." It is a harsh judgment, explicable in part by the fact that Lessing was losing her own Communist faith at the time. She has admitted that she had not grasped the extent to which such doublespeak was used as a shield or camouflage: "When politics and public life become as

Paul Robeson in the dressing room after his concert at the Free Trade Hall, Manchester, England, 1958 (Neil Libbert)

polarized as they were then, then people may seem stupid." Robeson parroted the lines of a fellow traveler because, beset by enemies at home and dependent on the goodwill of his Soviet hosts, he really did feel that he had no alternative. He no longer *embodied* a commitment to universal aspirations, as he had once done. Instead, holding desperately to that commitment, he could only go through the motions of a compromised role.

Having to go on giving that performance, in the face of the dispiriting reality of the Soviet Union, increasingly took its toll. In March 1961, Robeson was visiting Moscow alone, after a row with Essie. One evening, although he announced that he was going to bed early, a noisy party was heard in his hotel suite late into the night. The next morning, his translator found Robeson on his bathroom floor with his wrists slashed, albeit superficially. Essie flew out, and Paul Jr. joined her a few days later. He immediately suspected that American agents had drugged his father—a view from which he never wavered. In any event, Robeson was in a distressed and paranoid state when he was admitted to hospital. A few months later, he confided to Paul Jr. that guests at the party had been cajoling him either to get a relative released from prison or to help them emigrate. When Paul Jr. cross-questioned the translator, she told him that, although his father was incoherent and disoriented when she found him, he had been muttering something about being "unworthy." Whether or not the CIA had drugged him, whether or not his action was prompted by political disillusionment, and whatever the state of his mental health, that mumbled "unworthy" suggests that Robeson was in the grip of shame. In the classical taxonomy of passions, shame was seen as a manifestation of the distress that Aristotle linked with anger: a man's reaction when he became aware of the impact his anger had on others, and his anxiety that he had been diminished by surrendering to that anger. In Robeson's case, the episode confirms the unbearable inner relationship between Robeson's "heroic" or performative self and the self that judged his compromises, bad faith, and guilty secrets.

Only a couple of days after Essie and he had returned to London in September 1961, Robeson suffered a catastrophic collapse at their flat in Connaught Square. He lay huddled on his bed, "positively cowering" in fear, and showing symptoms of agonizing despair. It was agreed that he should be moved to the Priory, a private psychiatric hospital in the suburb of Roehampton. The Priory sent a car for him, and he was gently coaxed into the back seat, with Essie on one side and their New York friend Helen Rosen on the other. Their route took them past the Soviet Embassy in Kensington. As the car approached it, Robeson became distressed. "You don't know what you're doing," he muttered, "you don't know what you're doing." Apparently convinced that "great danger was at hand," he signaled Essie and Helen to "get down!!" He pushed Helen onto the seat, and covered her with his body. "He was frightened," Helen later recounted, "cowering himself and trying to protect me." She had not realized what this building was, until Essie told her.

At the Priory, Robeson was subjected to an appallingly aggressive regime of electric shock treatment and mind-altering drugs, with no psychotherapy to complement or mitigate them. He remained there for more than two years, until Essie and some friends "rescued" him, in a cloak-and-dagger operation that involved stashed luggage, getaway cars, and decoys to draw off the press, and flew him to the Buch Clinic in East Berlin. That was in the fourth week of August 1963. In mid-December, Robeson and Essie returned to the United States for the last time. This was hardly the homecoming that had been foreshadowed in Robeson's rhetoric about his role in the struggle for freedom at the Albert Hall nearly forty years earlier. It might be seen as a tragic return, however, at least in Heidegger's austere sense that what makes a tragic hero tragic is a willed and violent drive for truth that leads to his "ruin and disaster." Robeson's "intense rage mixed with hurt," his shame in Moscow, his panic as he drove past the Soviet Embassy in London, and his final, exhausted withdrawal into comparative isolation from society all suggest how exorbitant a price Robeson paid for his attempt to overcome the world's injustices and for wagering everything on achieving subjective authenticity by committing to that struggle—by facing up to his fate in what Heidegger called "being-towards-death."

Josephine Baker, the Lincoln Memorial, August 1963

The fourth week of August 1963, during which Paul Robeson, abused and near mad, was making his flight from London to East Berlin, was a momentous one in the long African American struggle for freedom. On August 27, Robeson's old ally W. E. B. Du Bois died in Ghana at the age of 95. The following day, in a sweltering Washington, DC, Roy Wilkins, the executive secretary of the NAACP, who had succeeded Du Bois as editor of *The Crisis* in 1934, announced the news from the steps of the Lincoln Memorial to the crowd of over two hundred thousand people who had gathered for the March for Jobs and Freedom. No doubt through gritted teeth, given his bitter disagreements and many battles with Du Bois, Wilkins called for a minute's silence to honor his rebarbative predecessor's memory.

Four decades on from the Harlem Renaissance, the struggle had taken new forms. By the early 1960s, the focus was on political campaigns for civil and economic rights, with cultural and aesthetic issues taking a back seat. Nevertheless, the idea for a March for Jobs and Freedom came from a veteran of the renaissance, A. Philip Randolph, who had arrived in New York with aspirations to succeed as an actor before he became editor of Harlem's socialist *Messenger* in the 1920s. By 1963, Randolph had become president of the Negro American Labor Council, and vice-president of the most powerful federation of trades unions in the United States, the AFL-CIO. (He was also savagely critical of Paul Robeson's claims to "speak as the voice of the Negro people of America," given that he was—in Randolph's view—a "Johnny-come-lately to the cause of the Negro.") Randolph had first conceived of a march on Washington in 1941, as part of his campaign against racially discriminatory employment practices in the military and in the defense industries. On that occasion, there had been no march. Even the credible threat of one was enough to prompt President Franklin Roosevelt to respond to Randolph's demands and establish a Committee on Fair Employment Practice.

The politics behind the 1963 march were complex and fractious. Randolph, along with Martin Luther King and Bayard Rustin, who had worked with Randolph in the 1940s movement and was the main organizer of the march, wanted the emphasis to be on economic issues, including housing, employment, training, and a higher minimum wage. Roy Wilkins and the Urban League's Whitney Young saw the march more as a support for their advocacy. Their key aim was to help the passage of President Kennedy's civil rights bill through the Congress, and they therefore refused to countenance any hint of civil disobedience. More radical figures like John Lewis of the Student Nonviolent Coordinating Committee (SNCC) and James Farmer from the Congress of Racial Equality (CORE) agreed with the focus on economic demands, but they wanted to expose the limits of the politics of influence represented by Wilkins and Young. For them, the purpose of the march

Organizers of the March on Washington, Lincoln Memorial, August 1963.
Standing from left, Matthew Ahmann, Rabbi Joachim Prinz, John Lewis, the
Reverend Eugene Carson Blake, Floyd McKissick, Walter Reuther; sitting from
left, Whitney Young, Cleveland Robinson, A. Philip Randolph, Dr. Reverend
Martin Luther King Jr., Roy Wilkins

should be to protest against the inadequacies of Kennedy's legislation and to challenge his inactivity on civil rights and his continued collaboration with Southern segregationists. The disputes continued in the weeks leading up to the march, as a broader coalition was recruited, as the Kennedy administration attempted to exert some control, and as Rustin oversaw the extraordinary logistics that delivered the peaceful crowds on August 28.

The plan for the event was to have seven-minute speeches by representatives of the ten sponsoring organizations—Bayard Rustin threatened to haul them off the podium if they overran—plus the national anthem, an invocation by the Catholic archbishop of Washington, Patrick O'Doyle, a prayer, a brief tribute to women to placate protests against the exclusively male list of official speakers, and two sets of songs. The march was an early example of a truly global media event. CBS Television provided an outside broadcast nationally throughout the day, and the launch of the communication satellite Telstar enabled overseas broadcasters to provide live coverage in several countries around the world. (Paul and Essie Robeson watched the march live in London on the BBC.)

On the day, even though people knew that they were present at a significant historical event, the mood among the crowd was ambivalent and somewhat listless. Many were wilting in the heat. Too much waiting and milling about left people already tired from their journeys to Washington deflated. For most, speakers and celebrities on the steps of the Lincoln Memorial were no more than distant specks. Something was needed to bring the event into focus. The Gospel singer Mahalia Jackson touched a nerve with her electrifying rendition of "I've Been 'Buked, and I've Been Scorned." But it was Martin Luther King's closing address that transformed the day. To begin with, he stuck to his carefully timed script, avoiding his stump-speech line about "I have a dream" as advisers had warned him it was becoming a cliché. As he drew toward his conclusion, King knew that he had not managed to express the gravity and energy of the march. At that moment, behind him, Mahalia Jackson, who had already heard the dream refrain, called out, "Tell 'em about the dream, Martin." King put aside his script and shifted his stance at the podium from that of a lecturer to that of a preacher. "So even though we face the difficulties of today and tomorrow, I still have a dream," he intoned, and launched into his famous peroration. What King articulated was not a set of political demands around economic reforms and the amelioration of social inequalities, nor a reasoned evaluation of the president's civil rights bill. Instead, improvising on familiar themes and phrases, King gave voice to the passion and the yearning for change that drove the Freedom Movement. The emotional intensity was heightened as his performance took on the Gospel cadences of call-and-response, with interjections of "My Lord! My Lord!" from Mahalia Jackson and others urging him on to his thrilling conclusion: "Free at last, free at last. Thank God Almighty, free at last." (Five years later, Mahalia Jackson would sing King's favourite Gospel song at his funeral: Thomas S. Dorsey's "Take My Hand, Precious Lord.")

The performance made Martin Luther King a global celebrity and gave the Freedom Movement its telegenic public face. It also transformed the March on Washington from a political rally, conventional in form if unprecedented in scale, into something akin to a mythical festival. That festive atmosphere had already been established earlier in the day, serendipitously, as political bickering delayed the start of the official march from the Washington Monument to the Lincoln Memorial. Archbishop O'Doyle was threatening not to deliver the opening invocation unless the "inflammatory" language in John Lewis's draft speech was watered down. Furious last-minute negotiations and rewrites continued in a janitor's office below the Memorial. Above, organizers played for time, encouraging musicians—Odetta, Joan Baez, Bob Dylan, Peter, Paul and Mary and others—to string out their performances. In addition, a couple of guests not included in the official program were invited to speak. The first was

Fred Shuttlesworth, a blood-and-thunder preacher from Birmingham and a cofounder, with Martin Luther King, of the Southern Christian Leadership Conference. The second was Josephine Baker, who had flown in from Paris the night before.

As so often in Josephine Baker's life, separating reality from myth about her performance in Washington is not straightforward. By her own account, her speech lasted for twenty minutes. One biography quotes a text that would make that claim plausible. In this long version, Baker offers a familiar, fairy-tale version of her life: the little girl burned out of her house, who ran away to a "fairyland place" called France where she found fame and "walked into the palaces of kings and queens and into the houses of presidents."

> But I could not walk into a hotel in America and get a cup of coffee, and that made me mad. And when I get mad, you know that I open my big mouth. And then look out, 'cause when Josephine opens her mouth, they hear it all over the world.
>
> So I did open my mouth, and you know I did scream, and when I demanded what I was supposed to have and what I was entitled to, they still would not give it to me.

Despite being smeared as a Communist, the speech continues, Josephine "screamed loud enough" so that "they started to open that door just a little bit." Although "not a young woman now"—she claimed to be sixty, although she was actually fifty-seven—Baker explains that she always took the "rocky path" and tried to make it smoother for those who would follow. "I want you to have a chance at what I had. But I do not want you to have to run away to get it." The speech ends with Baker saying that she has just been handed a note inviting her "to visit the President of the United States in his home, the White House."

Although Josephine Baker's fabulous reworking of her biography as a tale of racial injustices, skin-of-her-teeth escapes, triumphs over adversity, and magical success would provide a telling contrast to the epic and very masculine heroism of Paul Robeson at the Albert Hall, it is hardly credible that she would have been permitted to deliver a twenty-minute speech. That would have made it longer than Martin Luther King's, which itself well exceeded its allotted time. Audio recordings of the march indicate that Baker actually made remarks lasting less than three minutes. The explanation for the discrepancy appears to be that, the day after the march, she phoned her friend Stephen Papich and gave him an account of the speech that, in retrospect, she felt she should have given. Papich in turn wrote down his recollection of what she had told him—possibly with his own embellishments—and included it in the memoir *Remembering Josephine Baker*, which he published in 1976.

On the day of the march, Josephine Baker actually came to the podium just as John Lewis bowed to Philip Randolph's emotional plea not to derail a day he had dreamt of for over twenty years, a compromise text was agreed, and Archbishop O'Doyle headed for the Lincoln Memorial. "I want you to know that this is the happiest day of my entire life," Baker told the crowd. "You're together as salt and pepper, just as you should be, just as I've always wanted you to be." Bayard Rustin nudged her and whispered, "Madam, you will have to stop now. We are beginning the march." "I'm going to finish this," responded Baker, and told the crowd, "I am glad that in my homeland this day has come to pass . . . You are on the eve of complete victory." Despite Rustin trying to hustle her off the podium, this was a genuinely emotional homecoming: "I'm glad that you have accepted me to come. I didn't ask you, I didn't have to. I just came, because it was my duty." To Rustin, she hissed, "Do you know who I am?" He was unmoved: "Madam, I do not care who you are. You are going to have to stop *now*. I am beginning the march." "Continue on," Baker managed to conclude, to warm applause. "You can't go wrong. The world is behind you."

Unlike Paul Robeson at the Albert Hall, Josephine Baker was not the star turn at the March on Washington. Nor did the event mark the beginning of a radical new commitment. Baker's politics did not define her life, as Robeson's did his. Although she was wholly sincere and serious about her antiracist campaigns, her beliefs and actions remained a projection of her feelings and experiences. Even so, her performance at the Lincoln Memorial was politically significant in a number of ways. Like Philip Randolph, she embodied the continuity of the black struggle and yet, at the same time, she too had witnessed the profound changes that separated the 1960s from the 1920s. She also served as a reminder of the global appropriation of black American culture and the geographical reach of the black diaspora. The actor Ossie Davis underlined this point, when he introduced Baker by declaring that her presence would "show the international character of the struggle in which we are currently engaged."

As with Robeson's speech, Baker's political performance in Washington was shaped by a mixture of historical forces and biographical events—most spectacularly in her decision to wear the uniform of the Women's Auxiliary of the French Air Force. Care in selecting costumes had always been a feature of Baker's performances. From the nakedness of her debut in Paris and the sly primitivism of her banana skirt, to the glamorous fashions of her years as a *vedette*, and to the increasingly self-parodying outfits in her later shows, Baker used costume to evoke, mock, and subvert ideas about race, sexuality, and gender, about primitivism and modernity, and about authenticity and artifice. So why this incongruous French Air Force uniform?

The costume had at least three sets of connotation. Most obviously, it signified Baker's dual loyalty to France and to the United States. She was proud of the role she had played in De Gaulle's counterintelligence during the war, which, as president, he honored by awarding her the Légion d'honneur and

Josephine Baker at the March on Washington, August 1963

Croix de Guerre with Palm. Second, Baker's wartime experience had brought into focus her opposition to any form of racism, fascism, or xenophobia. When she toured the United States in 1951, this heightened consciousness led her to insist that all her audiences and backstage crews should be integrated. With Bessie Buchanan, an old friend from the *Shuffle Along* chorus line and now an aspiring New York politician, she performed a citizens' arrest on an obstreperous drunk in the up-market Biltmore Hotel in Los Angeles. Later in the tour, she went to New York's Stork Club for dinner with Buchanan and other friends. Their meal never arrived. The incident was witnessed by the newspaper columnist Walter Winchell. When the NAACP took up the case, Walter White tried to persuade him to speak out. Winchell reacted by launching a vitriolic attack on Baker as an anti-American Communist sympathizer and denouncing her to the FBI. Her costume in Washington reflected the militancy provoked by those experiences. In her role as social activist, freedom fighter, and campaigner for multiculturalism, she was dressing for battle. Thirdly, however, Baker's uniform also hinted at the contradictory nature of her politics and her ambivalent relationship to the fantasy of the benign despot. General De Gaulle remained her great hero; five years after the march, she would march with him down the Champs-Élysées as he stared down the student uprisings of May 1968. In the mid-1930s, Baker had been dazzled, briefly, by the glamour of Mussolini, but she learned a political lesson from the backlash against her apparent support for his invasion of Ethiopia. In 1952, feeling rejected by the United States after the Stork Club incident, she visited Argentina not long after the death of Eva Perón. There she campaigned energetically on behalf of the dictator Juan Perón—again until she became disillusioned, and again provoking adverse comment in both the mainstream press and in the black community. This susceptibility to authoritarian figures was part of the fairy-tale paradigm through which Baker saw politics: the fantasy of the patriarch who can overcome all dangers and problems. Baker acted out this fantasy in the way that she made herself into an extravagantly benign but dictatorial matriarch. In 1947, she bought Les Milandes, a fifteenth-century château in the Dordogne, where over the next couple of decades she raised her Rainbow Tribe of twelve children adopted from around the world. This was Josephine Baker's own little kingdom. Apart from anything else, the military uniform in Washington signified, to her at least, that she was its absolute and, it would seem, often autocratic ruler.

Baker felt differently about America after her performance at the Lincoln Memorial. "Until the March on Washington, I had always had this little feeling in my stomach," she said. "I was always afraid. I couldn't meet white American people. I didn't want to be around them. But now that little feeling is gone. For the first time in my life I feel free. I know that everything is right now." Despite that new optimism, and despite her surely far-fetched claim that Coretta King asked her "to assume leadership of the movement" after Martin Luther King was assassinated in 1968, Baker did not remain actively engaged in the civil rights movement. She was unsympathetic to the separatism implicit in the emerging principle of "black power." "I think they must mix blood, otherwise the human race will degenerate," Baker said in 1970. "Mixing blood is marvellous. It makes strong and intelligent men." She remained committed to integration and assimilation, she continued to live in France, and she poured her political passion (as well as her money) into the Rainbow Tribe, her idiosyncratic experiment in domestic utopianism. ("We are dying to see the children," Essie Robeson wrote to her, "and we think it is all a marvellous human experiment.")

Only the Trying

In no sense was Josephine Baker a conventional politician. Paul Robeson campaigned energetically for Henry Wallace's Progressive Party, he actively supported the Council on African Affairs, he tirelessly addressed union meetings and antinuclear rallies, and he quietly acted as a political mentor to younger performers, including Dizzy Gillespie, Harry Belafonte, Sidney Poitier, and Ossie Davis. Even in Robeson's case, however, the interest of his political performances lies less in their programmatic intent than in what they reveal about that borderline where the political abuts the cultural and the two interact. Robeson's performances may have produced little in the way of political outcomes, but then neither, as many critics have complained, did the Harlem Renaissance or the March on Washington. Those too were symbolic events. And none the less important for it. Symbolic events are decisive in creating the affective prepolitical infrastructure of passion and affiliation that determines what is politically thinkable and imaginable, and so motivates and sustains belief and action. As performers and celebrities, Baker and Robeson enacted the possibility, rather than the content, of as yet unimagined alternative futures. The lines of Baker's dancing body and the timbre of Robeson's voice gave sensuous life to that "elsewhere" and "otherwise." They complicated the delusively simple temporality of political programs and promises by performing in the time of the "yet-to-come."

The cultural narratives that inform political imaginaries likewise exist on the cultural-political borderline. Different modes of 'emplotting' actions and events embody alternative patterns of desire and time. The epic or romantic narrative of suffering, struggle, redemption, and the emergence of a new people is built around a myth of origins (the *nostos*) and a teleological understanding of destiny, fate, or history. Paul Robeson's ethical vision of African American emancipation, postcolonial freedom, and international socialism took this eschatological form, and its psychological urgency for him was manifest in his yearning for "home." Robeson did live to see the civil rights movement of the 1960s, the end of the European empires in India, Africa, and Asia, and the beginnings of their postcolonial traumas. For good or ill, he had died by the time the Soviet empire imploded in 1989. What is clear, in any case, is that, whether or not the revolutionary narrative Robeson lived by was any good at predicting the future path of history, it was becoming anachronistic in a rapidly changing postwar world. It certainly lacked critical purchase in trying to engage with the complex reality of post–Cold War and postcolonial politics.

David Scott suggests that tragedy provides a better paradigm for understanding the contemporary world than the "critical languages" of "black emancipation and postcolonial critique." That is because our times are "out of joint." The challenge in "critically thinking through this postcolonial present," for Scott, is "not simply the naming of yet another horizon, and the fixing of the teleological plot that takes us there from here." Rather, "what is at stake is something like a refusal to be seduced and immobilized by the facile normalization of the present." The value of a "tragic sensibility" lies, not least, in the way that it "recasts our historical temporalities in significant ways" by being more attentive the contingent and recursive nature of historical change. This is the temporality that the older T.S. Eliot evoked in *East Coker*:

> There is only the fight to recover what has been lost
> And found and lost again and again: and now, under conditions
> That seem unpropitious. But perhaps neither gain nor loss.
> For us, there is only the trying. The rest is not our business.

For Scott, a tragic political vision is less overweening than the epic or the romantic, less impatient with paradox, and more respectful of "the contingencies of the past in the present." He has less to say about its subjective costs, however; the sort of cost exemplified by Paul Robeson's self-sacrifice. For the philosopher Simon Critchley, that is the trouble with tragedy. It requires the subject to be "too *heroic*," in the sense that the tragic hero achieves authenticity, or "becomes who they truly are," only in "the relation between action and desire in the experience of being-towards-death." Did the achievements of Paul Robeson's political performances justify the price of his destruction? Was his self-sacrifice even necessary? If not, a question follows. Is there a less lethal, more life-affirming way of narrating and enacting the political relation between desire and action?

Josephine Baker's idiosyncratic performance at the March on Washington suggests that there may be. What she did there demonstrated an as yet unmentioned form of political emplotment: *comedy*. Although it may not deliver the catharsis of tragedy, comedy does allow, in its own way, for the possibility of some partial liberation from humanity's fallen, finite, and fractured state. The action of comedy typically involves misunderstanding, disguise, misrecognition, deception, and metamorphosis—the to and fro of everyday life, in other words. The optimism inherent in the genre is made manifest when these elements are formally resolved and ideologically reconciled in the festive occasions that conventionally conclude a comic drama. Politically, such festivals symbolize the possibility of reconciliation between antagonistic social forces, and so offer the prospect of evanescent human triumphs over a perpetually dangerous world. The March on Washington might be seen as one such festival of reconciliation. Although only a vignette in that larger drama, the appearance of a nightclub dancer of a certain age, implausibly bewigged and dressed as a French airwoman, movingly addressing a huge crowd from the steps of a great national monument, while political big shots squabbled in a janitor's pokey hideaway in the bowels of the building, was irrefutably, beguilingly, and triumphantly comic. And not apolitical.

Comedy shares with tragedy an awareness of the paradoxical, contingent, and recursive nature of a history that repeats itself the first time as tragic, and the second time as farcical. Comedy may lack tragedy's sense of cataclysmic change, but it offers hope and resilience. To paraphrase Gramsci: tragedy of the intellect, but comedy of the will—a will guided less by hubris or self-sublimation than by *humor*, which, as Simon Critchley observes, "recalls us to the modesty and limitedness of the human condition, a limitedness that calls not for tragic-heroic affirmation but comic *acknowledgement*, not Promethean authenticity but laughable inauthenticity." As a principle and a paradigm, then, comedy has the serious virtue of uncoupling politics from fatuous notions of heroism, nostalgia, and human perfectibility.

To the extent that it is not just about the administration of things and people, or the management of competing forces and interests, politics involves critical reflection on the present and the imagining of possible futures. In their future orientation, politics and culture then coincide in their concern with a question famously posed by Salman Rushdie, which was alluded to in the introductory chapter to this book. That is, how does newness enter the world? Rushdie raised the issue when defending his novel *The Satanic Verses* (1988) and justifying the use of comedy in his assault on inward-looking communitarianism. For the Rushdie of the 1980s, "newness" was the antithesis of any cultural authoritarianism. He saw it as a celebration of "hybridity, impurity, intermingling, the transformation that comes of a new and unexpected combinations of human beings, cultures, ideas, politics, movies, songs" and that "rejoices in mongrelization and fears the absolutism of the Pure."

Rushdie also believed that this comic sensibility was "the great possibility that mass migration gives the world." In the language of political philosophy, it was his articulation of a cosmopolitan disposition. The notion of a lived cosmopolitanism helps to make sense of the careers, the travels, and the politics of both Josephine Baker and Paul Robeson. Certainly, Rushdie's enthusiasm for newness and "mongrelization" chimes with many of Baker's views, as well as with her migrant's eye view of the contingent claims of place and belonging. Her theme song was, after all, "J'ai deux amours, Mon pays et Paris." For Robeson, however, the embrace or even recognition of cosmopolitanism was not a political option. When he proclaimed, "I have made my choice," at the Albert Hall in 1937, he could articulate that choice using only the vocabulary available to him. Under Stalinism, the term "cosmopolitanism" had, quite literally, been banished from the Soviet political lexicon as "a reactionary theory that preaches indifference to the fatherland, to national traditions and to national culture" and a threat to "proletarian internationalism." If one looks at the way that Robeson lived his life, however, rather than at the way he articulated his politics, then a more cosmopolitan figure emerges.

In the interests of toeing the party line and maintaining his publicly constructed persona (his "dignity"), Robeson disavowed important aspects of himself: his ambition, his impatience with convention, his unapologetic erotic life, his sense of fun, his ruthlessness and, for all the talk of home, his choice of the nomadism, that Édouard Glissant named "errantry." The premise of cosmopolitanism is that there *are* always alternatives, existentially as well as politically, and it is the principle of uncertainty at the heart of cosmopolitanism that holds open the possibility that things can become otherwise and be better. Cosmopolitanism embraces experimentation, inauthenticity, and principled homelessness. That was not an image of himself that Robeson would have wanted to see in the mirror, but in many ways that is who he was. The tragedy of his later life might then be understood as an instance—or a performance—of thwarted cosmopolitanism.

Pee Wee Russell, Muggsy Spanier, Miff Mole, and Joe Grauso outside Nick's Tavern, New York City, c. June 1946 (William P. Gottlieb)

Coda

NICK'S BAR, NEW YORK CITY

Home is where one starts from. As we grow older
The world becomes stranger, the pattern more complicated
Of dead and living.

—T. S. ELIOT, *EAST COKER*

Jean-Paul Sartre first visited the United States in 1945, as the war was ending, when he was invited to join a delegation of journalists sponsored by the State Department. While there, he learned to love the "massive blocks" and "grand vistas" of New York, but the experience laid to rest any youthful fantasies about America being the scene of freedom or a source of creativity. In the old days, American cinema had promised to become "the art of the future" and jazz "the music of the future." Now disenchantment had set in. The talkies had "not fulfilled the promise of silent cinema." Jazz was "in slow decline," and had "more of the past in it than of the future." Returning to New York two years later, in 1947, Sartre found himself sitting in one of the city's dives. This time, listening to jazz in Nick's Bar felt like the real thing. Here, present at the moment of its creation, the music made sense: "Jazz, like bananas, has to be consumed on the spot." So much for those student evenings in Paris around the gramophone with Simone de Beauvoir: records were "just a pretext for shedding a few tears in good company." Jazz at Nick's Bar was visceral and immediate, a noise that drowned out fantasy. "Everybody listens. No one dreams."

When Siegfried Kracauer had arrived in New York as an unknown refugee in 1941, after eight precarious years in Paris, he too experienced a disjunction between new reality and old dreams. For him, it was not that the former swamped the latter. Rather, the two merged disconcertingly into one composite, layered experience. Exile felt like an uncanny homecoming. Sailing into New York harbor, Kracauer recognized sights, sounds, and characters that had previously always been mediated through Hollywood movies, and the "strange feeling of having already seen all this began to grow upon me." At this moment of arrival, the "European observer" was still able, one last time, to make a judgment about "the validity of the image of American life he had received in European theatres." The image of "America" faded as Kracauer adapted to the here-and-now actuality of New York: "As soon as the former European acquires an opinion of American reality, he loses the possibility of using it to confirm or reject his old impressions." Even so, he could still acknowledge their affective reality on the other side of the Atlantic. He may no longer be able to believe them, "but that says nothing against their validity in Europe."

In Nick's Bar, it wasn't a question of images or impressions, but of gut-level impact. The jazz was speaking to "the best part" of Sartre, "the most unfeeling and most free, the part which doesn't want sad songs or sprightly ones but a moment of deafening explosion." Sartre does not say who was playing or what they were playing. That is a pity. What was and what was not "real" jazz had again become a controversial question in the mid-1940s and, just as in the debates about spirituals and jazz during the Harlem Renaissance twenty years earlier, the schism turned on attitudes toward modernity and modernism. The hegemony of swing was challenged first by New Orleans revivalists. These white and often Marxist enthusiasts insisted that Dixieland was the only authentic jazz, a "folk" expression of an oppressed black American identity. Its supposed authenticity exposed the standardization, commodification, and commercialization of swing—its culture-industry *modernity*. A second critical challenge to the jazz tradition was explicitly *modernist*. Musicians like Dizzy Gillespie, Charlie Parker, Bud Powell, and Max Roach set out to remake jazz by creating music that was avant-garde, self-reflexive and confrontingly difficult. Bebop was emerging as the most visible and influential manifestation of this jazz modernism at the very moment Sartre was sweating in Nick's Bar. (There were other experiments, such as the progressive jazz of Stan Kenton that Josef Škvorecký and his radical young friends in Czechoslovakia so admired.)

Sartre was not hearing bebop. Nick's Bar was a revivalist haunt. The guitarist Eddie Condon had played there, before he opened his own club nearby. Around the time of Sartre's visit, Nick's featured the cornet player Muggsy Spanier, the trombonist Miff Mole, and the clarinetist Pee Wee Russell. None of them fits the description Sartre gives of the musicians he saw. Very likely, they would have been a pick-up band. Whoever they were, what matters was the effect they had on him. "You have to yell: the combo has become an immense spinning top, and if you don't keep yelling it will tumble down. . . . A whole crowd of people is yelling in rhythm. You don't hear the jazz anymore, you see people on the stand sweating in rhythm, you feel like whirling around and around, howling at death, hitting the girl next to you in the face." But the type of jazz also matters. Sartre was being moved by revivalist Dixieland, and that truly was a music that smacked of the past rather than the future. Although he would later get to know Charlie Parker and Miles Davis and appreciate their music, his violent response at Nick's Bar harks back to the orgiastic embrace of jazz that Michel Leiris remembered from Paris after the First World War, rather than looking forward to its more modernist manifestations.

During the twenty-five years he lived in the United States, Kracauer wrote two classic studies on cinema, *From Caligari to Hitler* and *Theory of Film*. Toward the end of his life, he also developed an idiosyncratic approach to historiography based on the concept—and the experience, no doubt—of exile. In some ways, the perspective of the exile-historian is a reworking of Kracauer's earlier ideas about *distraction* as a characteristic orientation of urban modernity. In Weimar, he had used mass-cultural phenomena like movies and the Tiller Girls to expose the mediation, or virtualization, of experience: a process he described then as determining the "provisional status of all given configurations." Now, in postwar New York, it was the inside/outside view of the refugee that he used to establish the critical distance necessary to encompass the defining "provisionality" of modernity. The exile is an observer who is both at home and not at home, a chronicler who lives in "the near-vacuum of extraterritoriality, the very no-man's-land which Marcel entered when he first caught sight of his grandmother." The exile has become a stranger to "the culture which was his own," but remains "sufficiently uncommitted" to his new home to be able "to get inside the minds of the foreign people in whose midst he is living." Kracauer found the aesthetic analogue to the critical distance of this historical vision in cinema. Film offered a mediated eye that can "redeem" physical reality, just as history seeks to redeem events and mentalities.

For Kracauer, both the camera and historiography operate in the sphere of what he called "anteroom thinking"; that is, an attitude that engages with the distinctive reality of modernity through a suspicious openness to its concrete details, an aesthetic attention to its cultural texture, and an attenuated optimism about its existential potential. Anteroom thinking grasps the world in its perennial state of emergence, rather than deductively as the determinate manifestation of a structure of sociological categories or of philosophical certainties. It embraces ways of seeing, modes of explanation, and attempts at understanding that "share their *inherently provisional character* with the material they record, explore and penetrate." At the same time, the "anteroom" denotes the modern experience of contingency and becoming. It is itself one aspect of the object of study: "it is this 'anteroom' in which we breathe, move, and live." Kracauer's approach shifts a historical understanding of modernity away from great events and abstract social forces to the diurnal "life-world" of sense-impressions, imagination, and affect. Insofar as it is responsive to the phenomenological immediacy of the world and yet aware of its ineluctably "provisional" actuality, an example of this type of "anteroom thinking" might be cited from Ralph Ellison's *Invisible Man* (1952). On a hot Harlem afternoon, the novel's protagonist has just broken with his Marxist mentors, not least because he could not stomach their "scientific" version of history. Walking the streets, he hears a languid blues played by a jazz band being pumped out through a record-store loudspeaker. "Was this all that would be recorded?" he wonders. "Was this the only true history of the times, a mood blared by trumpets, trombones, saxophones and drums, a song with turgid, inadequate words?" *Mood* is the crucial word. It captures how that unique moment felt, but it also conveys how that past feeling was determined by the intuition of an alternative future sensed through the music.

In the late 1970s, Simone de Beauvoir conducted a series of farewell conversations with Jean-Paul Sartre. At one moment, apparently out of nowhere, Beauvoir is struck by the memory of how important jazz had been to them. "There was jazz too," she reminds him. "Why, we didn't mention it when we were talking about your love for music. Jazz meant a great deal to you." "A great deal," he concedes, and then drifts off into complaints about his first visits to the United States. Fifty years on, in the midst of the Cold War and at the height of the Vietnam War, Sartre—now alcoholic, effectively blind, and close to death—no longer seemed able to recall how the timbre and rhythm of jazz had given him an aesthetic premonition of a different way of being-in-the-world, which then translated into an image of "America" as the promise of vitality, sensuality, and rebellion.

In *Old Age*, written a decade before those sad, final interviews, Simone de Beauvoir had already confronted the reality that the experience of freedom is constrained in old age by the finitude of our embodied humanity, as well as by the way that old people are perceived and treated in modern Western societies. She quotes Sainte-Beuve: "We harden in some places and rot in others: we never ripen." She describes old age in terms that foreshadow Sartre's fate. Of Michel Leiris, she writes that he faced a "limited future and a frozen past," and of Freud, that the "hardening of his mind was largely due to the shrinking of his future." Sartre's inability, or disinclination, to remember the affective significance of jazz and America is another iteration of that hardening and shrinking. The fact that he could no longer *feel* what jazz had meant to him underlines Beauvoir's point that we never experience the future, in and as the present, in the same way that we formerly inhabited it, as expectation. The present cannot deliver what we hoped for from the future, which is "that fullness of being at which life so vainly aims." "No man," she insists, "can say, 'I have had a fine life' because a life is something that one does not *have*, that one does not possess."

Lives

Josephine Baker died in Paris, at the age of sixty-nine, on April 12, 1975. In her last years, she remained as capricious, complex, willful, and self-mythologizing as ever. Her obsession with the Rainbow Tribe and her spending on Les Milandes, including the creation of the Jorama, a wax museum memorializing her life, led to the break-up of her (fourth) marriage to the bandleader Jo Bouillon, to bankruptcy, and, in 1969, to eviction. Photographs show her sitting pathetically on the steps of the château, wearing nightgown and a crocheted cap, as she embarked on a hunger strike. It is a distressing image, but one knowingly staged for media consumption. It succeeded to the extent that Brigitte Bardot issued an appeal on television, which in turn provoked a press debate about whether the state should be supporting the Rainbow Tribe. In keeping with her fairy-tale self-authoring, Baker was rescued by Grace Kelly, once a Hollywood star and now Princess Grace of the louche statelet of Monaco. She provided Baker with a villa for herself and her adopted children.

Even if she could not "possess" her life, in Simone de Beauvoir's sense, Baker did everything she could to turn it into a marketable commodity. In the 1970s, she sounded out Langston Hughes, James Baldwin, and several other writers about new biographies to add to the pile of "lives" she had sponsored over the years. Despite increasing ill-health, she continued to perform and tour relentlessly in a series of comeback shows that were built around scenes from her childhood, her early career, and her later travails—the future now behind her. Her last and most spectacular comeback was in *Joséphine*, at the Théâtre Bobino in Paris. It was after just two performances of *Joséphine* that Baker died quietly in bed, from a stroke, surrounded by adulatory newspaper reviews. There were two funerals. The first was a nationally televised media spectacle, staged in the presence of the great and good from the French establishment, which drew a crowd of twenty thousand people to the church of La Madeleine in the heart of Paris. As a decorated French war hero, Baker was accorded a military farewell, including a flag-draped coffin and a twenty-one-gun salute. Six months later, after a small private ceremony organized by Princess Grace, she was buried in Monaco on the fiftieth anniversary of her opening in *La Revue nègre*.

After Paul Robeson's ordeal at the Priory and his treatment in East Berlin, he and Essie returned to the United States for the last time at the end of December 1963. His career as a public performer was over. Although he held firm to his beliefs and welcomed the public tributes periodically offered to him, he effectively withdrew from public life. Cancer killed Essie, painfully, in 1965. Robeson spent the final eight years of his life sequestered in his sister Marian's house, in Philadelphia. He died quietly, after a series of strokes, on January 23, 1976, just nine months after Josephine Baker. He was seventy-seven. His funeral was held in Harlem. Paul Jr. chose his epitaph: "The artist must elect to fight for freedom or slavery. I have made my choice. I had no alternative."

Robeson would sometimes refer to his past to explain or justify his convictions. He also tried to "own" his life, in the sense that he wanted to be the only person to define who he was, and he resented claims by others who told him what his life meant. Unlike Baker, he never mined his biography for raw material to make a public entertainment. Far from it. Although he welcomed the affirmation of others, he seems to have experienced celebrity for the most part as an irksome side effect of his chosen career. He would no doubt have been angry and despairing that *Paul Robeson*, a two-act play written by Phillip Hayes Dean and starring James Earl Jones, was sent out on the road around the United States in 1977, only a year after his death. In his place, and not surprisingly, Paul Robeson Jr. railed against the production and made sure that it was denied access to his father's recordings or to any materials controlled by the Robeson estate. Shortly before the show was due to open on Broadway, in January 1978, a group of Robeson's friends, admirers, and supporters—including Paul Jr., the writers Maya Angelou and James Baldwin, the dancer Alvin Ailey, Martin Luther King's widow, Coretta King, and a number of politicians and academics—published an "open letter to the entertainment industry" in *Variety*. The statement denounced the play as "a pernicious perversion of the essence of Paul Robeson" and "a rewriting of history" that effaced his uncompromising socialist militancy and substituted familiar, more digestible psychological explanations for political agency: an "effort to create 'acceptable' motivation to soften the genuine ones." Whatever the play implied, Robeson had "believed that his art and his being were inseparable from his race and his politics, and he adamantly insisted on using his great gifts as a revolutionary instrument in the cause of the liberation of the Blacks of America and of Africa, and the oppressed of all nations."

In an article for *Village Voice*, James Baldwin rejected Phillip Hayes Dean's accusation that the statement's sponsors were acting as an "un-black activities committee." They did not want to censor the play, they just could not condone "the trivialization of Robeson" and "the debasement of his legacy." Those who knew him had a responsibility to challenge the way that the play usurped and simplified his life. "The man the play presents is not Paul Robeson." Despite that limited ambition, Baldwin granted that there was "much, much more than this to say, for this controversy raises enormous questions, questions within questions: of life versus entertainment, life versus art, of awaking or sleeping, of warring responsibilities with which we will be struggling until we die."

The questions that Baldwin raises about the ethics of biographical writing bring into focus some of the reasons why there may be historical value in studying the careers of Josephine Baker and Paul Robeson, as well as some of the challenges. Baldwin's reference to life, at least if "life" is understood in light of Simone de Beauvoir's assertion that "a life is something that one does not *have*, that one does not possess," serves as a warning against the biographical fallacy of treating the lives of others as political allegories. In a broader sociological sense, one question raised by the lives of Josephine Baker and Paul Robeson is the way that subjective or lived experience ("life") was transformed in the twentieth century. "Modernity" represents the attempt to describe, explain, and understand that process of transformation, to which both "entertainment" and "art" contributed. At the same time, however, "entertainment" and "art" also attempted to *record* the affective reality of modernization, and they both provided imaginative resources with which to *negotiate* its consequences—for example, through the primitivist fantasy that the blackness of Baker and Robeson equated with an authenticity of being (or "hyperpresence") that might compensate for the "hollowing out" of modern experience. A conventional distinction would see "entertainment" providing a balm that soothed the transition to this brave new world by inducing a form of mass cultural "sleeping," whereas "art" was supposed to "awaken" the critical faculties that could oppose it. In that context, "modernism" might be understood, in some of its manifestations at least, as a search for artistic forms and practices that could enunciate the changed nature of human nature in modern times. Whether those attempts celebrated or contested the transformation—Baldwin's "warring responsibilities," perhaps—they at least promised the anguished consolation of understanding it.

The careers of Josephine Baker and Paul Robeson, like the international appropriation of jazz, illustrate why the contribution of twentieth-century "entertainment" to understanding these changes in the experience of being human should not be dismissed too quickly. To take a more detailed piece of evidence, recall Ralph Ellison's sentence: "Was this the only true history of the times, a mood blared by trumpets, trombones, saxophones and drums, a song with turgid, inadequate words?" The implicit claim in the question is that the sound of a particular popular song in a particular place on a particular day might be seen as a singular instance of the abstract-sounding process of "how modernity was lived." The intensity of the sound gestured toward a "fullness of being" that the cynical banality of the song revealed was not to be found in the here and now. ("Some of these days, You're going to miss me, honey.") "Fullness of being" is always elusively and tantalizingly elsewhere, always sensed aesthetically and affectively rather than achieved in consciousness or in art. In Ellison's rendering, a man hearing a song on a New York street enacts a characteristic *form* of experience (or a "structure of feeling," if you like, or a "habitus") that may be inferred from the gossipy mass of incidents, relationships, and performances recalled and recounted in these pages. These events may appear little more than anecdotes, but anecdotal thinking (like anteroom thinking) has its own methodological power. The narration of a singular, microcosmic event poses the question of how the world had to be for that event to take place and for it to make sense.

The threads of anecdote about Josephine Baker and Paul Robeson, about the roles they played in art and in life, and about their travels and the people that they met, weave into shifting patterns that can be seen, in retrospect, to have constituted the texture of twentieth-century modernity: motifs of belonging and dislocation, home and migration, America and Europe, black and white, purity and mongrelization, authenticity and hybridity, futures past and nostalgias present. It is against the ground of these patterns that Josephine Baker and Paul Robeson emerge as figures of their time and, still, as compromised signs of freedom.

{ ACKNOWLEDGMENTS }

Some of the research for *Some of These Days* was funded by a Discovery Project Grant (DP0664990) from the Australian Research Council. Under its Publication Subsidy Scheme, the Australian Academy of the Humanities contributed to the cost of the images in the book. I am grateful to both organizations.

The seeds of the project were sown when, in the early 1990s, I worked alongside Ali Rattansi on a course at the Open University in the United Kingdom entitled 'Race', Education and Society. I started work on what has become *Some of These Days* while a senior research fellow at the International Research Centre for Cultural Studies (IFK) in Vienna in the first half of 2003. I thank the IFK for that invitation, especially Lutz Musner, and I am grateful to the scholars and visitors in and around the center who commented on my earliest, tentative explorations. Later, I also worked on the project during a two-week visit to Nottingham University in 2007: thanks to Peter Brooker and Nick Hewitt for the invitation. Much of the research and some of the writing were carried out at the British Library in London, where my sister Fiona Fowler was generous in her hospitality. I enjoyed an all-too-brief research visit to the Beinecke Library at Yale University.

One of the reasons that it took me longer to finish the book than it should have done is that, having joined the University of New South Wales (UNSW Australia) on my return from Vienna, I became first Associate Dean (2005) and then Dean of Arts & Social Sciences (2007) there. Taking a leadership role in an ambitious and self-reforming institution has proved a sometimes bumpy but, in the end, rewarding adventure, and I have benefited from working with very talented colleagues. Anthony Lambert was a diligent assistant in the first phase of research. Jane Mills read what was in effect a quasi-final draft, and offered insightful editorial comments. George Kouvaros, Julian Murphet, James Phillips, and Ian Tyrrell made very helpful suggestions on individual chapters. I am also grateful to my Vice Chancellor, Fred Hilmer, for allowing me to take three months for writing between my first and second terms as Dean.

Earlier iterations of some parts of the book have appeared in books and journals, although all have been substantially reworked and transformed: "Kracauer and the Dancing Girls," in *New Formations* 61 (Spring 2007); "As it Happened . . . : *Borderline*, the Uncanny and the Cosmopolitan," in *Uncanny Modernity: Cultural Theories, Modern Anxieties*, ed. Jo Collins and

John Jervis (Houndmills: Palgrave Macmillan, 2008); "Jazz Modernism and Film Art: Dudley Murphy and *Ballet mécanique*," in *Modernism/Modernity* 16, no. 1 (2009), 25–49; "Robeson Agonistes," in *Modernism and Masculinity*, ed. Natalya Lusty and Julian Murphet, 141–158 (Cambridge: Cambridge University Press, 2014). Along the way, I have discussed the ideas in the book at various conferences. Among them were the Screen Studies conferences in Glasgow, 2004 and 2013; the Society for Cinema and Media Studies conference in London and the "Sites of Cosmopolitanism" conference run by the Centre for Public Culture and Ideas, Griffith University, in Brisbane, both in 2005; the "Branding Cities and Urban Borders" symposium held at Australia House in London, 2006 (thanks to Stephanie Hemelryk Donald for the invitation); the Film and History Association of Australia and New Zealand conference, "Cinema, Modernity and Modernism," at UNSW in 2010; "Alain Locke in the 21st Century," University of Oxford, 2012 (thanks to Laura Marcus); the Australasian Association of Literature/Centre for Modernism Studies in Australia conference "Modern Soundscapes," 2013 (thanks to Helen Groth and Julian Murphet); and the International Association for the Study of the Culture of Cities, "Affective Cities: Scenes of Innovation II," York University, Toronto, 2014 (thanks to Alan Blum).

I am grateful to Laura Marcus not only for looking at an early draft but also for introducing me to Brendan O'Neill at Oxford University Press. I thank Brendan for his support, and also Oxford's three anonymous readers for their helpful and provocative insights. Jo Chipperfield provided much needed expertise in picture research, and Stefan Solomon came to the rescue on last-minute editorial matters. Sophie Jeffery has been a loyal, tireless, and cheerful assistant for a number of years, and has quietly helped to keep this project on the rails. Josh Annesley and Justin Harris deserve a mention for helping to keep body and soul together.

Above all, I want to express profound gratitude to three very special people. My daughters, Morag and Ellen, were girls when I started writing, mature and independent young women by the time the book was finished. I thank them for putting up with their father's strange obsessions and apologize if sometimes I became more distracted than I should have been. The same goes, many times over, for Stephi Hemelryk Donald, who has been with me lovingly through thick and thin. *Some of These Days*: "just for you only."

{ LIST OF ILLUSTRATIONS }

{ LIST OF PLATES }

1. Paul Robeson by Winold Reiss, 1924. © The Reiss Archives / Manuscripts, Archives and Rare Books Division, Schomburg Center for Research in Black Culture, The New York Public Library, Astor, Lenox and Tilden Foundations.
2. *Survey Graphic*, featuring Winold Reiss's portrait of Roland Hayes, 1925. Schomburg Center, New York Public Library. © Manuscripts, Archives and Rare Books Division, Schomburg Center for Research in Black Culture, The New York Public Library, Astor, Lenox and Tilden Foundations.
3. Poster for *La Revue négre*, Paul Colin, 1925.
4. Josephine Baker, Paul Colin, *Le Tumulte noir*, 1927. Coloured lithograph. Bibliothèque nationale de France. © Paul Colin/ADAGP. Licensed by Viscopy, 2014.
5. Josephine Baker, Paul Colin, *Le Tumulte noir*, 1927. Coloured lithograph. Bibliothèque nationale de France. © Paul Colin/ADAGP. Licensed by Viscopy, 2014.
6. Fernand Léger, *Élement méchanique (Mechanical Element)*, 1924. Oil on Canvas, 146 x 97cm. © Fernand Léger/ADAGP. Licensed by Viscopy, 2014.
7. Fernand Léger, *Jazz (Variente)*, c. 1930. Ink on paper, 31.2 x 23 cm. © Fernand Léger/ADAGP. Licensed by Viscopy, 2014.
8. Le Corbusier, *Josephine Baker and Le Corbusier in front of the Sugar Loaf*, Rio de Janeiro, 1929. Pencil on paper, 12 x 13.8cm. © Le Corbusier/ADAGP. Licensed by Viscopy, 2014.

{ NOTES }

Introduction: A Migration of Stars

Page 1 *Simone de Beauvoir recalls her student days*: Simone de Beauvoir, *Memoirs of a Dutiful Daughter*, trans. James Kirkup (London: André Deutsch; Weidenfeld and Nicolson, 1959), 338; Beauvoir, *The Prime of Life*, trans. Peter Green (London: André Deutsch and Weidenfeld and Nicolson, 1962), 114–115.

Page 1 *a dreamworld "America"*: Beauvoir, *Adieux: A Farewell to Sartre*, trans. Patrick O'Brian (New York: Pantheon, 1984), 397, 234.

Page 2 *political aestheticism*: Beauvoir, *Prime of Life*, 115–116.

Page 2 *rebellion through ventriloquism*: Michael North, *The Dialect of Modernism: Race, Language, and Twentieth-Century Literature* (New York: Oxford University Press, 1994), 9.

Page 2 *La Nausée*: Jean-Paul Sartre, *Nausea*, trans. Lloyd Alexander, intro. Richard Howard (New York: New Directions, 2007), 176–178. See also Carole Seymour Jones, *A Dangerous Liaison: Simone de Beauvoir and Jean-Paul Sartre* (London: Century, 2008), 138–139.

Page 4 *like Al Jolson's Jew blacking up*: On the significance of Jolson and *The Jazz Singer*, see Michael Rogin, *Blackface, White Noise: Jewish Immigrants in the Hollywood Melting Pot* (Berkeley: University of California Press, 1996); North, *Dialect of Modernism*; and Linda Williams, "Posing as Black, Passing as White: The Melos of Black and White Melodrama in the Jazz Age," in *Playing the Race Card: Melodramas of Black and White from Uncle Tom to O. J. Simpson*, 136–186 (Princeton, NJ: Princeton University Press, 2002).

Page 4 *The creation of newness*: Salman Rushdie, *Imaginary Homelands: Essays and Criticism, 1981–1991* (London: Granta, 1992), 394.

Page 4 *The white imagination*: Josephine Baker and Jo Bouillon, *Josephine*, trans. Mariana Fitzpatrick (New York: Harper and Row, 1977), 54. For biographical and critical studies of Josephine Baker, see Baker and Bouillon, *Josephine*; Lynn Haney, *Naked at the Feast: A Biography of Josephine Baker* (New York: Dodd, Mead, 1981); Bryan Hammond and Patrick O'Connor, *Josephine Baker* (London: Jonathan Cape, 1988); Phyllis Rose, *Jazz Cleopatra: Josephine Baker in Her Time* (New York: Vintage, 1989); Jean-Claude Baker and Chris Chase, *Josephine: The Hungry Heart* (New York: Random House, 1993); Ean Wood, *The Josephine Baker Story* (London: Sanctuary, 2000); Bennetta Jules-Rosette, *Josephine Baker in Art and Life: The Icon and the Image* (Urbana: University of Illinois Press, 2007); Anne Anlin Cheng, *Second Skin: Josephine Baker and the Modern Surface* (New York: Oxford University Press, 2011).

Page 5 *The Negroes are conquering Paris*: Ivan Goll, "The Negroes Are Conquering Europe," ["Die Neger eroben Europa," *Die literarische Welt*, 2, {January 15, 1926}, 3–4], in *The Weimar Republic Sourcebook*, ed. Anton Kaes, Martin Jay, and Edward Dimendberg, 559–560 (Berkeley: University of California Press, 1994).

Page 5 *Negro art*: Paul Guillaume quoted in Jean-Louis Paudrat, "From Africa," in *"Primitivism" in 20th Century Art: Affinity of the Tribal and the Modern*, ed. William Rubin, 1:125–178 (New York: Museum of Modern Art, 1984), 158–159; quoted in Bernard Gendron, *Between Montmartre and the Mudd Club: Popular Music and the Avant-Garde* (Chicago: University of Chicago Press, 2002), 106; James Clifford, "Negrophilia," in *A New History of French Literature*, ed. Denis Hollier, 901–907 (Cambridge, MA: Harvard University Press, 1994), 901–902; Colin Nettlebeck, *Dancing with de Beauvoir: Jazz and the French* (Melbourne: Melbourne University Press, 2004), 28ff. See also Jody Blake, *Le Tumulte noir: Modernist Art and Popular Entertainment in Jazz-Age Paris, 1900–1930* (University Park: Pennsylvania State University Press, 1996).

Page 5 *Jazz became part of this mélange*: William A. Shack, *Harlem in Montmartre: A Paris Jazz Story between the Great Wars* (Berkeley: University of California Press, 2001); Gendron, *Between Montmartre and the Mudd Club*, 108; Nettlebeck, *Dancing with de Beauvoir*, 106.

Page 6 *In his autobiography*: Michel Leiris, *Manhood: A Journey from Childhood into the Fierce Order of Virility* [1939], trans. Richard Howard (San Francisco: North Point, 1985), 109. See also Jeremy F. Lane, *"Rythme de Travail, Rythme de Jazz*: Jazz, Primitivism, and *Machinisme* in Inter-War France," *Atlantic Studies* 4, no. 1 (April 2007), 103–116, at 106.

Page 7 *This was a dance*: Goll, "Negroes Are Conquering Europe," 559–560; also Blake *Tumulte noir*, 5.

Page 7 *Pfitzner*: quoted in Peter Jelavich, *Berlin Cabaret* (Cambridge MA: Harvard University Press, 1996), 170.

Page 7 *What remains*: Alice Gerstel, "Jazz Band," *Die Aktion* 12, nos. 4–5 (February 4, 1922), 90–91, in Kaes, Jay, and Dimendberg, *Weimar Republic Sourcebook*, 555.

Page 8 *Leiris disavowed the "foolishness"*: Leiris's 1981 afterword to *L'Afrique fantôme* (Paris: Gallimard, 1981); cited and translated by Marie-Denise Shelton, "Primitive Self: Colonial Impulses in Michel Leiris's *L'Afrique fantôme*," in *Prehistories of the Future: The Primitivist Project and the Culture of Modernism*, ed. Elazar Barkan and Ronald Bush, 326–338 (Stanford, CA: Stanford University Press, 1995), 328. Leiris, "Civilization" (1929), in *Brisées: Broken Branches*, trans. Lydia Davis (San Francisco: North Point, 1989), 20; quoted in Sieglinde Lemke, *Primitivist Modernism: Black Culture and the Origins of Transatlantic Modernism.*(Oxford: Oxford University Press, 1998), 27.

Page 8 *Simmel's premise*: Georg Simmel, "The Metropolis and Mental Life" (1903), in *Simmel on Culture*, ed. David Frisby and Mike Featherstone, 174–186 (London: Sage, 1988), 174–175, 184.

Page 9 *the sensory foundations of psychic life*: Simmel, "Metropolis and Mental Life," 175, emphasis added. For the discussion of the "sensorium," see Miriam Bratu Hansen, *Cinema and Experience: Siegfried Kracauer, Walter Benjamin, and Theodor W. Adorno* (Berkeley: University of California Press, 2012), 4; Sarah Danius, *The Senses of Modernism: Technology, Perception and Aesthetics* (Ithaca, NY: Cornell University Press, 2002), 23.

Page 9 *a phantom as impalpable*: Marcel Proust, *Remembrance of Things Past*, vol. 2, trans. C. K. Scott Moncrieff and Terence Kilmartin (London: Chatto and Windus, 1968), 135, 137. For an insightful discussion, see Danius, *Senses of Modernism*, 14–15.

Page 10 *Benjamin saw a medium*: Hansen, *Cinema and Experience*, 79. Walter Benjamin, "The Work of Art in the Age of its Technological Reproducibility," in *Selected Writings*, vol. 3, *1935–1938*, ed. Howard Eiland and Michael W. Jennings, 101–133 (Cambridge, MA: Belknap Press of Harvard University Press, 2002), 117.

Page 10 *Then a new serpent*: Ilya Ehrenburg, *The Life of the Automobile* [1929], trans. Joachim Neugroschel (New York: Urizen, 1976), 2.

Page 10 *Simmel had observed*: Simmel, "Metropolis and Mental Life," 182.

Page 10 *radio and television were bringing*: Brian Massumi, *Parables for the Virtual: Movement, Affect, Sensation* (Durham, NC: Duke University Press, 2002), 85.

Page 10 *technology simultaneously enhanced*: Julian Murphet, *Multimedia Modernism: Literature and the Anglo-American Avant-Garde* (Cambridge: Cambridge University Press, 2009), 3.

Page 10 *Novelists attempted to convey*: John Cournos, *Babel* (London: Heinemann, 1923), 73–74; Robert Musil, *The Man without Qualities*, trans. Sophie Wilkins (New York: Alfred A. Knopf, 1995), 4.

Page 11 *the philosopher Martin Heidegger*: Martin Heidegger, "The Age of the World Picture" (1938), in *The Heidegger Reader*, ed. Günter Figal, trans. Jerome Veith, 207–223 (Bloomington: Indiana University Press, 2009), 222–223.

Page 11 *it seemed natural*: Beauvoir, *Prime of Life*, 115. "*Hallelujah*" is a reference to King Vidor's 1929 film *Hallelujah!*.

Page 11 *the continual never-having-been-here-before*: Heidegger, "Age of the World Picture," 222.

Page 12 *Genuine film drama*: cited in Hansen, *Cinema and Experience*, 12, 26. Siegfried Kracauer, *The Mass Ornament: Weimar Essays*, ed. and trans. Thomas Y. Levin (Cambridge, MA: Harvard University Press, 1995), 326–328, 292.

Page 13 *"vernacular modernism"*: Miriam Bratu Hansen, "Fallen Women, Rising Stars, New Horizons: Shanghai Silent Film as Vernacular Modernism," *Film Quarterly*, 54, no. 1 (Autumn 2000), 10–22, at 10–11; also Hansen, "America, Paris, the Alps: Kracauer (and Benjamin) on Cinema and Modernity," in *Cinema and the Invention of Modern Life*, ed. Leo Charney and Vanessa Schwartz, 362–402 (Berkeley: University of California Press, 1995), 365–366.

Page 13 *Do sing again*: Margot Peters, *Mrs. Pat: A Biography of Mrs Patrick Campbell* (London: Bodley Head, 1984), 382.

Page 13 *Robeson had been born*: For biographical details, see Martin Duberman, *Paul Robeson: A Biography* (New York: New Press, 1995); Sheila Tully Boyle and Andrew Bunie, *Paul Robeson: The Years of Promise and Achievement* (Amherst: University of Massachusetts Press, 2001); Paul Robeson, Jr., *The Undiscovered Paul Robeson: An Artist's Journey, 1898–1939* (New York: Wiley, 2001), and *The Undiscovered Paul Robeson: Quest for Freedom, 1939–1976* (New York: Wiley, 2010); Jordan Goodman, *Paul Robeson: A Watched Man* (London: Verso, 2013). Also Paul Robeson, *Here I Stand* (London: Dennis Dobson, 1958). For an excellent biography that gives Essie Robeson her due, see Barbara Ransby, *Eslanda: The Large and Unconventional Life of Mrs. Paul Robeson* (New Haven, CT: Yale University Press, 2013).

Page 14 *the intelligentsia and the society people*: Duberman, *Paul Robeson*, 90.

Page 14 *In postwar London*: On the impact of jazz in London, see Eric Hobsbawm, "Jazz Comes to Europe," in *Uncommon People: Resistance, Rebellion and Jazz* (London: Abacus, 1999), 356; and David Horn, "The Identity of Jazz," in *The Cambridge Companion to Jazz*, ed. Mervyn Cooke and David Horn, 9–32 (Cambridge: Cambridge University Press, 2002), 11.

Page 15 *Jack Hylton*: Nettlebeck, *Dancing with de Beauvoir*, 42.

Page 15 *the first group to "discover" Robeson*: Marie Seton, *Paul Robeson* (London: Dennis Dobson, 1958), 42.

Page 16 *the novelist Evelyn Waugh*: Evelyn Waugh, *The Diaries of Evelyn Waugh* [1976], ed. Michael Davie (London: Phoenix, 1995), 233, 300.

Page 16 *the animus evident in these references*: Douglas Lane Patey, *The Life of Evelyn Waugh: A Critical Biography* (Oxford: Blackwell, 2001), 17. Waugh, *Diaries*, 296–297. In this book, the word "nigger" is used only in historical quotations. Even though its use was widespread in this period, it would be disingenuous to claim that those who used it were unaware of the offense it caused.

Page 17 *When I saw the cathedrals*: Evelyn Waugh, *Decline and Fall: An Illustrated Novelette* [1927] (Boston: Little, Brown, 1956), 103.

Page 17 *the American imagist poet*: H.D. [Hilda Doolittle], "Two Americans," with "The Usual Star," (London: privately printed, 1928), 102.

Page 18 *the figure of Paul Robeson*: Bill Schwarz, "Black Metropolis, White England," in *Modern Times: Reflections on a Century of English Modernity*, ed. Mica Nava and Alan O'Shea, 176–207 (London: Routledge, 1996), 187.

Page 18 *to argue about jazz*: Kathy J. Ogren, *The Jazz Revolution: Twenties America and the Meaning of Jazz* (New York: Oxford University Press, 1989), 7.

Page 18 *The word jazz*: F. Scott Fitzgerald, *My Lost City: Personal Essays, 1920–1940* (Cambridge: Cambridge University Press, 2005), 132.

Page 18 *His head on the pillow*: Cournos, *Babel*, 321.

Page 18 *"jazz modernism"*: Alfred Appel Jr. *Jazz Modernism: From Ellington and Armstrong to Matisse and Joyce* (New York: Alfred A. Knopf, 2002), 13. See also Gendron, *Between Montmartre and the Mudd Club*.

Page 19 *the Bloomsbury art critic*: Clive Bell, *Since Cézanne* (London: Chatto and Windus, 1922), 213–230.

Page 21 *In a debate at Oxford*: *The Letters of T. S. Eliot*, ed. Valerie Eliot, vol. 1, *1898–1922* (London: Faber and Faber, 1988), 70; quoted in David Trotter, *Cinema and Modernism* (Oxford: Blackwell, 2007), 138.

Page 21 *a letter in 1919*: Eliot, *Letters*, 228; quoted in David Chinitz, *T. S. Eliot and the Cultural Divide* (Chicago: University of Chicago Press, 2003), 21.

Page 22 *The strange, the surprising*: Eliot, London Letter, July 1921, *Dial* 71, no. 2 (August 1921), 213–217, quoted in Lawrence Rainey, *Revisiting "The Waste Land"* (New Haven, CT: Yale University Press, 2007), 50.

Page 22 *the novelist Ralph Ellison*: quoted in Michael North, ed., *The Waste Land: Authoritative Text, Contexts, Criticism* (London: W. W. Norton, 2001), 166.

Page 22 *the budding poet Louis MacNiece*: quoted in Trotter, *Cinema and Modernism*, 2.

Page 23 *the minstrel shows of Eliot's St. Louis childhood*: On Eliot, St. Louis, and the art of mélange, see Ann Douglas, *Terrible Honesty: Mongrel Manhattan in the 1920s* (London: Picador, 1996), 114–115; Chinitz, *T. S. Eliot*, 45. Quotations from "The Waste Land" are taken from T. S. Eliot, *Collected Poems, 1909–1962* (London: Faber and Faber, 1963), 53–76.

Page 23 *a consciously anthropological understanding of culture*: See Marc Manganaro, *Culture, 1922: The Emergence of a Concept* (Princeton, NJ: Princeton University Press, 2002), chap. 1; Rainey, *Revisiting*, 113; Chinitz, *T. S. Eliot*, 6.

Page 24 *Among Negroes*: Gertrude Stein, *Useful Knowledge* (London: John Lane, Bodley Head, 1928), 60.

Page 25 *modernism's propensity*: Douglas Mao and Rebecca L. Walkowitz, eds., *Bad Modernisms* (Durham, NC: Duke University Press, 2006), 2.

Page 25 *"transatlantic modernism" and the "black Atlantic"*: See, for example, Paul Gilroy, *The Black Atlantic: Modernity and Double Consciousness* (Cambridge MA: Harvard University Press, 1993); and Brent Hayes Edwards, *The Practice of Diaspora: Literature, Translation, and the Rise of Black Internationalism* (Cambridge, MA: Harvard University Press, 2003).

Page 26 *the idea of being modern*: Peter Brooker, "Afterword: 'Newness' in Modernism, Early and Late," in *Oxford Handbook of Modernisms*, ed. Peter Brooker, Andrzej Gasiorek, Deborah Longworth, and Andrew Thacker (Oxford: Oxford University Press, 2010), 1026.

Page 26 *oscillation between belonging and dislocation*: Gianni Vattimo, *The Transparent Society* (Cambridge: Polity, 1992), 10.

Chapter 1: New Negro

Page 29 *C. L. R. James*: C. L. R. James, "Paul Robeson: Black Star," in James, *Spheres of Experience: Selected Writings*, 256–264 (London: Allison and Busby, 1980), 256, 261. C. L. R. James, "Black Intellectuals in Britain," in *Colour, Culture and Consciousness: Immigrant Intellectuals in Britain*, ed. Bhikhu Parekh, 154–163 (London: George Allen and Unwin, 1974), 154.

Page 29 *Harlem Renaissance*: "Harlem Renaissance" is a retrospective term, conflating what was known in the 1920s as the Negro Renaissance with the "vogue" for Harlem in white Manhattan. Although the renaissance, as such, was in the first instance a literary movement, with the publication of James Weldon Johnson's *Book of American Negro Poetry* in 1922 representing just one of many imputed starting points, the broader movement was associated with the "New Negro" campaigns for black recognition, black self-defense, and black rights, that dated back to the 1890s. Alain Locke's 1925 anthology *The New Negro* established Harlem as locus and symbol of the renaissance, and broadened its concerns beyond literature and the arts to the social sciences, philosophy, and politics: Alain Locke, ed., *The New Negro* (New York: Albert and Charles Boni, 1925).

Page 31 *great Mecca*: James Weldon Johnson, in Locke, *New Negro*, 301, 310.

Page 31 *growing proportion of black Americans*: On the demography, Clare Corbould, *Becoming African Americans: Public Life in Harlem, 1919–1939* (Cambridge, MA: Harvard University Press, 2009), 7. On the historical context, George Hutchinson, *The Harlem Renaissance in Black and White* (Cambridge, MA: Belknap Press of Harvard University Press, 1995).

Page 31 *Alain Locke*: See Leonard Harris and Charles Molesworth, *Alain L. Locke: The Biography of a Philosopher* (Chicago: University of Chicago Press, 2008).

Page 31 *philosophical mid-wife*: Leonard Harris, ed., *The Philosophy of Alain Locke: Harlem Renaissance and Beyond* (Philadelphia, PA: Temple University Press, 1989), 16–17.

Page 31 *cultural cosmopolitan*: Locke, "The New Negro," in *New Negro*, 11–12.

Page 32 *Paul Robeson was a hero*: Eslanda Goode Robeson, *Paul Robeson: Negro* (London: Victor Gollancz, 1930), 67–68.

Page 33 *Elizabeth Shepley Sergeant*: "The Man with His Home in a Rock," *New Republic* (March 3, 1926); quoted in Hazel V. Carby, *Race Men* (Cambridge, MA: Harvard University Press, 1998), 48.

Page 33 *This narrative was a "romance"*: Hayden White, *Metahistory: The Historical Imagination in Nineteenth-Century Europe* (Baltimore, MD: Johns Hopkins University Press, 1973), 8–9.

Page 34 *a generation of artists*: Locke, "Negro Youth Speaks," in *New Negro*, 50. See Carby, *Race Men*.

Page 35 *Locke understood the Great Migration*: Locke, *New Negro*, 6. See also Jonathan W. Gray, "Harlem Modernism," in *Oxford Handbook of Modernisms*, ed. Brooker et al., 235–248.

Page 35 *Arthur Schomburg*: Schomburg, in Locke, *New Negro*, 231.

Page 35 *The outcome of this remaking*: Harris and Molesworth, *Alain L. Locke*, 93–94. Corbould, *Becoming African Americans*. "Diasporic" and "ethnographic" are taken from Joel Kahn, *Culture, Multiculture, Postculture* (London: Sage, 1995), 114–115. See also Harris, *Philosophy of Alain Locke*, 6.

Page 36 *Harlem's cabaret culture*: Shane Vogel, *The Scene of Harlem Cabaret: Race, Sexuality, Performance* (Chicago: University of Chicago Press, 2009), and Douglas, *Terrible Honesty*. For Langston Hughes on the origins of the Harlem Renaissance, see Hughes, *The Big Sea: An Autobiography* (New York: Knopf, 1940), 223, 224. On sexuality, see also Isaac Julien's 1989 film *Looking for Langston*, released on DVD through the British Film Institute.

Page 36 *their pragmatism, their pluralism, and their modernism*: This is the thesis brilliantly developed in Part 1 of Hutchinson, *Harlem Renaissance in Black and White*.

Page 36 *Locke reflected*: Alain Locke, "Beauty Instead of Ashes," *Nation* 126 (April 18, 1928), 433; reprinted in *The Critical Temper of Alain Locke*, ed. Jeffrey C. Stewart (New York: Garland, 1983), 24. For discussion, see North, *Dialect of Modernism*, 128; Harris and Molesworth, *Alain L. Locke*, 214–215.

Page 36 *two competing journals*: Hutchinson, *Harlem Renaissance in Black and White*, 39, 142, 145, 173.

Page 37 *Du Bois was never wholly at ease*: Arnold Rampersad, *The Art and Imagination of W. E. B. Du Bois* (Cambridge, MA: Harvard University Press, 1976), 184–185.

Page 37 *the portrayal of the truth*: Du Bois, "Negro Art," *Crisis* 22 (June 1921), 55–56; quoted in Rampersad, *Art and Imagination*, 191.

Page 37 *All art is propaganda*: Du Bois, "Criteria of Negro Art," *Crisis* 32 (October 1926), 290–297; quoted in Manning Marable, *W. E. B. Du Bois: Black Radical Democrat* (Boston: Twayne, 1986), 132.

Page 37 *Charles Johnson's sociological training*: Hutchinson, *Harlem Renaissance in Black and White*, 172–177.

Page 38 *Van Vechten's novel*: On Van Vechten's Harlem as a social microcosm, see Kahn, *Culture, Multiculture, Postculture*, 110. Hughes, *Big Sea*, 270. Robeson to Van Vechten, Duberman, *Paul Robeson*, 100. James Weldon Johnson, "Romance and Tragedy in Harlem: A Review," *Opportunity* 4 (1926), 316–317. Locke, "Beauty Instead of Ashes," 433; in Stewart, *Critical Temper of Alain Locke*, 24.

Page 38 *Negrotarian*: Emily Bernard, "The Renaissance and the Vogue," in *The Cambridge Companion to the Harlem Renaissance*, ed. George Hutchinson, 28–40 (Cambridge: Cambridge University Press, 2007), 36. Essie Robeson, quoted in Douglas, *Terrible Honesty*, 288. Michael Gold, "Notes of the Month," *New Masses* 5 (February 1930), 3; quoted in Hutchinson, *Harlem Renaissance in Black and White*, 272.

Page 38 *a blow in the face*: *The Crisis*, December 1926, 81–82. "Decadence," quoted in Hutchinson, *Harlem Renaissance in Black and White*, 166.

Page 39 *only good Negroes*: Hughes, *Big Sea*, 266–267.

Page 39 *double consciousness*: W. E. B. Du Bois, *The Souls of Black Folk* [1903], ed. Brent Hayes Edwards (Oxford: Oxford University Press, 2007), 8, 9.

Page 39 *As soon as another person*: Gertrude Stein, *The Autobiography of Alice B. Toklas* (New York: Harcourt, Brace, 1933), 292; quoted in Werner Sollors, *Ethnic Modernism* (Cambridge, MA: Harvard University Press, 2008), 31.

Page 39 *most "Negro performers"*: Robeson, *Here I Stand*, 39.

Page 41 *Gilpin took exception*: Louis Sheaffer, *O'Neill: Son and Artist* (London: Paul Elek, 1974), 35.

Page 41 *O'Neill complained*: Travis Bogard and Jackson R. Bryer, eds., *Selected Letters of Eugene O'Neill* (New Haven, CT: Yale University Press, 1988), 177.

Page 42 *doubtful formula of hereditary cultural reversion*: William Stanley Braithwaite, "The Negro in American Literature," in Locke, *New Negro*, 35.

Page 42 *I am still being damned*: *Opportunity*, December 1924, quoted in Robeson Jr., *Undiscovered Paul Robeson: An Artist's Journey*, 78. On Robeson's defense of *Emperor Jones*, see Shannon Steen, "Melancholy Bodies: Racial Subjectivity and Whiteness in O'Neill's *The Emperor Jones*," *Theatre Journal* 52, no. 3 (2000), 346, quoting Robeson in *Opportunity* (December 1924), 58; also Carby, *Race Men*, 68, 79.

Page 42 *social anxieties and tensions of modernity*: Carby, *Race Men*, 68, 79.

Page 42 *That Irishman*: Sheaffer *O'Neill*, 37.

Page 42 *melancholic and corrosive sense*: Steen, "Melancholy Bodies," 357, 359.

Page 44 *Oscar Micheaux's* Body and Soul: Jane M. Gaines, *Fire and Desire: Mixed-Race Movies in the Silent Era* (Chicago: University of Chicago Press, 2001), 6–7.

Page 44 *a controversial reading*: Charles Musser, "To Redream the Dreams of White Playwrights: Reappropriation and Resistance in Oscar Micheaux's *Body and Soul*," in *Oscar Micheaux and his Circle: African-American Filmmaking and Race Cinema of the Silent Era*, ed. Pearl Bowser, Jane Gaines, and Charles Musser, 97–131 (Bloomington: Indiana University Press, 2001). Musser credits Hazel Carby with first establishing the link between *Roseanne* and *Body and Soul*, 102.

Page 45 *The scandalous insinuation*: Musser, "To Redream the Dreams of White Playwrights," 113.

Page 46 *first public recital of spirituals*: Paul Allen Anderson, *Deep River: Music and Memory in Harlem Renaissance Thought* (Durham, NC: Duke University Press, 2001), 96. Boyle and Bunie, *Paul Robeson*, 143. Lawrence Brown, *Spirituals: Five Negro Songs* (London: Schott, 1923).

Page 46 *Brown bumped into Robeson*: Seton, *Paul Robeson*, 34–35.

Page 46 *Carl was amazed*: Eslanda Robeson's diary, March 29, 1925, quoted in Robeson, *Artist's Journey*, 87.

Page 47 *It pleased me to believe*: MacKinley Helm, *Angel Mo' and Her Son, Roland Hayes* (Boston: Little, Brown, 1942), 189; quoted in Anderson, *Deep River*, 7.

Page 47 *an admission of equal value*: Locke, "Roland Hayes: An Appreciation," *Opportunity* (December 1923), 356–358.

Page 47 *I will never sing spirituals*: Anderson, *Deep River*, 97.

Page 47 *very high class*: Eslanda Robeson's diary, April 19, 1925, quoted in Robeson, *Artist's Journey*, 87.

Page 47 *Robeson and Brown entered*: Shepley Sergeant, "The Man with His Home in a Rock," quoted in Boyle and Bunie, *Paul Robeson*, 146. Seton, *Paul Robeson*, 36; Boyle and Bunie, *Paul Robeson*, 146–147. *New York Times*, April 20, 1925, quoted in Seton, *Paul Robeson*, 37.

Page 48 *an* Opportunity *editorial*: "Lyrus Africanus." *Opportunity* (November 1925); quoted in Anderson, *Deep River*, 62.

Page 48 *In* The Book of American Negro Spirituals: James Weldon Johnson, J. Rosamond Johnson, and Lawrence Brown, eds., *The Book of American Negro Spirituals* (London: Chapman and Hill, 1926), 29, 48.

Page 48 *The poet Carl Sandburg*: Duberman, *Paul Robeson*, 81; Anderson, *Deep River*, 97.

Page 48 *In a program note*: Carl Van Vechten, *"Keep A-Inchin' Along": Selected Writings of Carl van Vechten about Black Art and Letters*, ed. Bruce Kellner (Westport, CT: Greenwood, 1979), 158.

Page 48 *Johnson also believed*: Johnson, Johnson, and Brown, *American Negro Spirituals*, 14, 29.

Page 48 *Van Vechten was well aware*: Van Vechten, *Keep A-Inchin' Along*, 157.

Page 48 *modernized this tradition*: Boyle and Bunie, *Paul Robson*, 138–139.

Page 49 *I'm afraid we shall never agree*: Anderson, *Deep River*, 93.

Page 49 *Locke had accepted*: Alain Locke, "The Negro Spirituals," in *New Negro*, 207–208.

Page 49 *an opportunity for rehabilitation*: Duberman, *Paul Robeson*, 81; Edgar G. Brown, *New York News*, April 25, 1925; Duberman, *Paul Robeson*, 80; *Detroit Evening Times*, January 20, 1926; Robeson Jr., *Undiscovered Robeson: An Artist's Journey*, 87.

Page 49 *a third, dissenting view*: Hurston in Nancy Cunard, *Negro: Anthology made by N. Cunard, 1931–1933* (London: Nancy Cunard at Wishart, 1934), 359–360. Stein, quoted in Sollors, *Ethnic Modernism*, 31–32.

Page 50 *his famous 1926 polemic*: Langston Hughes, "The Negro Artist and the racial Mountain," *The Nation* (June 1926), 693–694.

Page 52 *jazz was a worry*: Duberman, *Paul Robeson*, 176–177.

Page 52 *Rogers tried to redeem jazz*: J. A. Rogers, "Jazz at Home," in Locke, *New Negro*, 221–224.

Page 52 *Fletcher Henderson*: Jeffrey Magee, *The Uncrowned King of Swing: Fletcher Henderson and Big Band Jazz* (Oxford and New York: Oxford University Press, 2005), 5.

Page 53 *Ethel Waters*: Quoted in Magee, *Uncrowned King*, 21.

Page 54 *the creation of a new music*: Magee, *Uncrowned King*, 26.

Page 54 *the principle of jazz*: Unsigned editorial, "Jazz," *Opportunity* 3 (1925), 132–133; Hutchinson, *Harlem Renaissance in Black and White*, 182.

Page 54 *his music was accepted*: See Magee, *Uncrowned King*, 27–28.

Page 55 *many harsh things*: Rogers, quoted in Duberman, *Paul Robeson*, 114.

Page 55 *This new gospel music*: Arthur Kempton, *Boogaloo: The Quintessence of American Popular Music* (Ann Arbor: University of Michigan Press, 2005), 39. Langston Hughes, "Jazz as Communication," seminar at 1956 Newport Jazz Festival; http://www.poetryfoundation.org/learning/essay/237856, accessed October 22, 2014. Kahn, *Culture, Multiculture, Postculture*.

Page 55 *Langston Hughes reflected wryly*: Hughes, *Big Sea*, 225.

Chapter 2: Between the Jungle and the Skyscraper

Page 59 *Janet Flanner had just started*: Janet Flanner, *Paris Was Yesterday* (New York: Viking, 1972), xx–xxi.

Page 60 *The premiere of* La Revue nègre: The discussion of *La Revue nègre* as event and performance follows a methodology outlined in Francis Sparshott, *A Measured Pace: Towards a Philosophical Understanding of the Arts of Dance* (Toronto: University of Toronto Press, 1995), 266.

Page 60 *energetic, rhythmic, boldly new entertainers*: Karen C. C. Dalton and Henry Louis Gates Jr., "Josephine Baker and Paul Colin: African American Dance Seen through Parisian Eyes," *Critical Inquiry* 24, no. 4 (Summer 1998), 921–922.

Page 60 *The campaign was a success*: Rose, *Jazz Cleopatra*, 7–9.

Page 61 *The music was composed*: Shack, *Harlem in Montmartre*, 35; Rose, *Jazz Cleopatra*, 63; Blake, *Tumulte noire*, 93.

Page 62 *Rolf de Maré was a wealthy Swedish enthusiast*: On de Maré and the Ballets Suèdois, see Ramsay Burt, *Alien Bodies: Representations of Modernity, "Race" and Nation in Early Modern Dance* (London: Routledge, 1998), chaps. 2 and 3.

Page 63 *Josephine Baker still recalled the sting*: Baker and Bouillon, *Josephine*, 50.

Page 64 *Driven by dark forces*: Baker and Bouillon, *Josephine*, 54, 51–52.

Page 64 *she stood out*: *Dance Magazine*, quoted in Hammond and O'Connor, *Josephine Baker*, 9–10.

Page 64 *Sissle reflected*: Noble Sissle, "How Jo Baker Got Started," *Negro Digest*, November 17, 1951, quoted in Rose, *Jazz Cleopatra*, 60.

Page 65 *She could dance and she could clown joy into you*: Ethel Waters, quoted in Burt, *Alien Bodies*, 66.

Page 65 *the bad boy of American music*: On the Antheil concert, see Rose, *Jazz Cleopatra*, 17–18, 22; and Emily Thompson, *The Soundscape of Modernity: Architectural Acoustics and the Culture of Listening in America, 1900–1933* (Cambridge MA: MIT Press, 1988), 142.

Page 66 *Celestial harpists reacted in visible horror*: Colin quoted in Dalton and Gates, "Josephine Baker and Paul Colin," 920.

Page 66 *lamentable transatlantic exhibitionism*: De Flers, quoted in Rose, *Jazz Cleopatra*, 32. Divoire, introduction to Marcel Sauvage's *Voyages et aventures de Joséphine Baker* (1931), quoted in Haney, *Naked at the Feast*.

Page 66 *He grasped the dynamic*: Joan Acocella and Lynn Garafola, eds., *André Levinson on Dance: Writings from Paris in the Twenties* (Hanover, PA: Wesleyan University Press, 1991), 74.

Page 67 *compared Baker unfavorably*: Arnold Haskell, "Further Studies in Ballet: Negro Dancing," *Dancing Times*, January 1930, 455–456, quoted in Burt, *Alien Bodies*, 62. Eslanda Robeson on *La Revue nègre*, in Boyle and Bunie, *Paul Robeson*, 187. Cook quoted in Rose, *Jazz Cleopatra*, 79–80. On the judgment of jazz musicians, see Shack, *Harlem in Montmartre*, 37; Haney, *Naked at the Feast*, 125; Chris Goddard, *Jazz Away from Home* (London: Paddington, 1979), 83.

Page 68 *The city had a jewel-like sparkle*: Baker and Bouillon, *Josephine*, 58.

Page 68 *the wildness of her forefathers*: *Berliner Tageblatt* quoted in Nancy Nenno, "Femininity, the Primitive and Modern Urban Space: Josephine Baker in Berlin," in *Women in the Metropolis: Gender and Modernity in Weimar Culture*, edited by Katharina von Ankum, 145–161 (Berkeley: University of California Press, 1997). Max Reinhardt quoted in Rose, *Jazz Cleopatra*, 85.

Page 69 *Kessler tried to unscramble*: Harry Kessler, *Berlin in Lights: The Diaries of Count Harry Kessler* (New York: Grove, 2000), 282.

Page 70 *At the Folies-Bergère on opening night*: cummings quoted in Hammond and O'Connor, *Josephine Baker*, 41–42, emphasis added. For discussion see Burt, *Alien Bodies*, 67–71; Dalton and Gates, "Josephine Baker and Paul Colin," 917–918.

Page 70 *Covering the event for* Vogue: Nancy Cunard, "Letter from Paris," quoted in Rose, *Jazz Cleopatra*, 100.

Page 70 *Trained to "sink their personalities into the line"*: Doremy Vernon, *Tiller's Girls* (London: Robson, 1988), 78, quoted in Burt, *Alien Bodies*, 84.

Page 71 *the popularity of the dance troupes*: Kracauer, *Mass Ornament*, 75. See also Jelavich, *Berlin Cabaret*, 177.

Page 72 *products of American distraction factories*: Kracauer, *Mass Ornament*, 75. On Haller and his rivals, see Jelavich, *Berlin Cabaret*, 165–166, 176ff.

Page 73 *The human figure enlisted in the mass ornament*: Kracauer, *Mass Ornament*, 77 (translation modified), 83.

Page 73 *Modernization and the instrumental reason of capitalism*: See D. N. Rodowick, *Reading the Figural, or, Philosophy after the New Media* (Durham, NC: Duke University Press, 2001), 145ff.

Page 73 *Four years later*: Kracauer, "Girls and Crisis," in Kaes, Jay, and Dimendberg, *Weimar Republic Sourcebook*, 565–566.

Page 74 *In Vienna*: On Baker's reception in Vienna in 1928, see Roman Horak, "Josepine Baker in Wien—oder doch nicht? Über die Wirksamkeit des 'zeitlos Popularen'," in *Metropole Wien: Texturen der Moderne*, ed. Roman Horak, Wolfgangf Maderthaner, Siegfried Mattl, Gerhard Meissel, Lutz Musner, and Alfred Pfoser, vol. 1 (Vienna: WUV-Universitätsverlag, 2000), 169–213.

Page 75 *the cultural mood and the political climate had changed*: Nenno, "Femininity, the Primitive, and Modern Urban Space," 157–158.

Page 75 *prompted Siegfried Kracauer to rethink*: Kracauer, *The Salaried Masses*, trans. Quintin Hoare, intro. Inka Mülder-Bach (London: Verso, 1998), 13. Kracauer, "Girls and Crisis," in Kaes, Jay, and Dimendberg, *Weimar Republic Sourcebook*, 565–566.

Page 75 *covered herself in ridicule*: Soupault, quoted in Blake, *Tumulte noire*, 133.

Page 76 *Baker rehearsed intensively*: On the US tour, see Rose, *Jazz Cleopatra*, 169ff.

Page 76 *The hard work of the company*: Colette, quoted Hammond and O'Connor, *Josephine Baker*, 142–143; Burt, *Alien Bodies*, 77–78.

Page 77 *a kind of muscular sympathy*: Jonathan Rée, *I See a Voice: A Philosophical History of Language, Deafness and the Senses* (London: HarperCollins, 1999), 358–359.

Chapter 3: Ballet mécanique

Page 80 *O'Neill's judgment of the film*: Quoted in Jennie Saxena, Ken Weissman and James Cozart, "Preserving African-American Cinema: The Case of *Emperor Jones* (1933)," *The Moving Image* 3, no. 1 (2003), 43.

Page 82 *Her movie career petered out*: Some of Washington's critical writings are republished in Antonia Lant, ed., *The Red Velvet Seat* (London: Verso, 2006).

Page 82 *One story*: Thomas R. Cripps, *Slow Fade to Black: The Negro in American Film, 1900–1942* (Oxford: Oxford University Press, 1993), 205; Krin Gabbard, *Jammin' at the Margins: Jazz and the American Cinema* (Chicago: University of Chicago Press, 1996), 161.

Page 82 *he made his first films*: *The Song of the Cypress* and *Danse Macabre* are both available on *Unseen Cinema: Early American Avant-Garde Film, 1894–1941*, vol. 7, *Viva la Dance: The Beginnings of Ciné-Dance* (Image Entertainment, 2005).

Page 83 *fantastic speed and rhythm*: Quoted in Susan Delson, *Dudley Murphy: Hollywood Wild Card* (Minneapolis: University of Minnesota Press, 2006), 95.

Page 84 *it embodies jazz modernism's alchemy*: Appel, *Jazz Modernism*, 13.

Page 84 *wrote Pound in a letter*: Pound quoted in Delson, *Dudley Murphy*, 52, 53.

Page 84 *Murphy's recollection*: Murphy, quoted in Judi Freeman, "Bridging Purism and Surrealism: The Origins and Production of Fernand Léger's *Ballet mécanique*," in *Dada and Surrealist Film*, ed. Rudolf E. Kuenzli, 28–45 (New York: Willis Locker and Owens, 1987), 31. The misspellings are Murphy's.

Page 85 *Evening of the Bearded Heart*: Other films screened at the "Evening of the Bearded Heart" included one of Hans Richter's abstract films and a version of Charles Sheeler's and Paul Strand's *Manahatta*; Delson, *Dudley Murphy*, 47.

Page 85 *They also planned*: On the pornographic images and a particular perspective on the production of *Ballet mécanique*, see William Moritz, "Americans in Paris: Man Ray and Dudley Murphy," in *Lovers of Cinema: The First American Film Avant-Garde, 1919–1945*, ed. Jan-Christopher Horak, 118–136 (Madison: University of Wisconsin Press, 1995).

Page 85 *At Ezra Pound's prompting*: Delson, *Dudley Murphy*, 54.

Page 85 *Antheil claims that he alone*: Delson, *Dudley Murphy*, 54.

Page 85 *a motion-picture accompaniment*: Quoted in Freeman, "Bridging Purism and Surrealism," 33.

Page 85 *a dream*: Quoted in David Savran, *Highbrow/Lowdown: Theater, Jazz, and the Making of the New Middle Class* (Ann Arbor: University of Michigan Press, 2009), 209.

Page 85 *separate lives*: A print of the film with Antheil's score adapted to fit in is in the *Unseen Cinema* collection.

Page 86 *a new plastic contribution*: Fernand Léger, "A Critical Essay on the Plastic Quality of Abel Gance's Film *The Wheel*" (1922), in *Functions of Painting*, trans. Alexandra Anderson (New York: Viking, 1973), 20.

Page 86 *his war experience*: Léger quoted in James Clifford, *The Predicament of Culture: Twentieth-Century Ethnography, Literature, and Art* (Cambridge, MA: Harvard University Press, 1988), 120. Léger, "Notes on Contemporary Plastic Life" (1923), in *Functions of Painting*, 24–25.

Page 87 *a geometric world*: Léger, "Notes on the Mechanical Element" (1923), in *Functions of Painting*, 29–30. Film-making ambitions quoted in Standish D. Lawder, *The Cubist Cinema* (New York: New York University Press, 1975), 89.

Page 87 *the essence of that machine-age Beauty*: Léger, "The Machine Aesthetic: The Manufactured Object, the Artisan and the Artist" (1924), in *Functions of Painting*, 52–54; see also Malcolm Turvey, "The Avant-Garde and the 'New Spirit': The Case of *Ballet mécanique*," *October* 102 (2002), 35–58, 50.

Page 88 *The particular interest of the film*: Léger's notes quoted in Freeman, "Bridging Purism and Surrealism," 38–39. Murphy on the mannequin's legs, quoted in Delson, *Dudley Murphy*, 46; Freeman, "Bridging Purism and Surrealism," 31, 42.

Page 89 *The provocative dadaist voice*: Quoted in Kuenzli, *Dada and Surrealist Film*, 3.

Page 91 *in with the mechanical eye of the camera*: This reading differs from Standish Lawder's in many ways magisterial account. Of Katherine on the swing, he asserts the "the content of the image is of little importance" and he suggests that Léger and Murphy appear only "somewhat inadvertently"; Lawder, *Cubist Cinema*, 136, 137.

Page 91 *the account of jazz*: Leiris, *Manhood*, 109.

Page 93 *music has had two giant blood infusions*: George Antheil, "The Negro on the Spiral; or A Method of Negro Music," in Cunard, *Negro*, 348, 350, 346.

Page 94 *tempered a primitivist aesthetic*: Léger, "The Machine Aesthetic: Geometric Order and Truth" (1925), in *Functions of Painting*, 63. See also Blake, *Tumulte noir*, 148–149, 85.

Page 95 *Léger referred to the way*: Léger, "Notes on the Mechanical Element," 28.

Page 95 *the washerwoman climbing the steps*: Murphy and Léger quoted in Freeman, "Bridging Purism and Surrealism," 31, 38–39; Léger, "*Ballet Mécanique*" (c. 1924), in *Functions of Painting*, 51.

Page 96 *the treatment of the spoof headline*: See Lawder, *Cubist Cinema*, 153–154.

Page 97 *a certain cinematic rhythm*: Léger, "The Spectacle" (1924), in *Functions of Painting*, 36–37. Murphy, quoted in Delson, *Dudley Murphy*, 62. "Dramatis Personae," *Criterion* 1 (1922–1923), 303–306; quoted in Trotter, *Cinema and Modernism*, 142.

Page 98 *the second iteration of the Charlot/Katherine juxtaposition*: The placing of Charlot's second appearance varies in the different available versions of the film.

Page 99 *each came up with his own solution*: Delson, *Dudley Murphy*, 61.

Page 100 *The film combines*: Léger, "Notes on the Mechanical Element," 30; "*Ballet Mécanique*," 50.

Page 100 *Comparing Gertrude Stein's style*: Eliot, quoted in Chinitz, *T. S. Eliot*, 50. Milhaud in Blake, *Tumulte noir*, 148–149, 85. Antheil, "The Negro on the Spiral," 348.

Page 104 *his fellow experimentalist*: Herman G. Weinberg, review of *Emperor Jones*, *Close Up* (December 1933), 351–352.

Page 106 *locomotive rhythms*: See Joel Dinerstein, *Swinging the Machine: Modernity, Technology, and African American Culture between the World Wars* (Amherst: University of Massachusetts Press, 2003).

Page 106 *One intellectual who did not recant*: Jeanneret, quoted in Blake, *Tumulte noir*, 142, 137, 158. See also Dinerstein, *Swinging the Machine*, 4–5.

Page 107 *inventing new ways of dancing*: I take the phrase "Cinema invents new ways of dancing" from Adrian Martin, with thanks.

Chapter 4: Jazz In Stone And Steel

Page 109 *he not only gave a lecture*: On the Berlin lecture, see Janet Stewart, *Fashioning Vienna: Adolf Loos's Cultural Criticism* (London: Routledge, 2000), 23.

Page 109 *the best house*: In Burkhardt Rukschcio and Roland Schachel, *Adolf Loos* (Vienna: Residenz Verlag, 1982), 323; quoted in Kim Tanzer, "Baker's Loos and Loos's Loss: Architecting the Body," in *Center 9: Regarding the Proper*, ed. Kevin Alter and Elizabeth Danze, 76–89 (Austin: University of Texas Center for American Architecture and Design, 1995), 88. Cheng, *Second Skin*, which covers some of the same ground as this chapter, appeared after it was written.

Page 109 *South America taught him*: Le Corbusier, *Precisions*, trans. Edith Schreiber Aujame (Cambridge, MA: MIT Press, 1991), 12–13. Mardges Bacon, *Le Corbusier in America: Travels in the Land of the Timid* (Cambridge, MA: MIT Press, 2001), 221–222.

Page 110 *She has a good little heart*: Rose, *Jazz Cleopatra*, 153.

Page 111 *The house Adolf Loos designed*: See Panayotis Tournikiotis, *Adolf Loos* (New York: Princeton Architectural Press, 1994), 95, 98; Karen Burns, "A House for Josephine Baker," in *Postcolonial Space(s)*, ed. Gülsüm Baydar Nalbantoğlu and Wong Chong Thai, 53–72 (New York: Princeton Architectural Press, 1997), 56.

Page 111 *Loos designed domestic interiors*: Loos on the architect's task, quoted in Beatriz Colomina, *Privacy and Publicity: Modern Architecture as Mass Media* (Cambridge, MA: MIT Press, 1994), 265. On dance, domestic interiors, and the "upward spiral of sequentially revealed volumes," see Tanzer, "Baker's Loos and Loos's Loss," 79, 81.

Page 112 *the arrangement of the large salon*: Ungers, quoted in Colomina, *Privacy and Publicity*, 260. See also Tanzer, "Baker's Loos and Loos's Loss," 81–82. Farès el-Dahdah, "The Josephine Baker House: For Loos's Pleasure," *Assemblage* 26 (1995), 72–87.

Page 113 *The house does not have to tell anything*: Loos on the work of art and the house, from his article "Architecture" (1910), quoted in Tanzer, "Baker's Loos and Loos's Loss," 80.

Page 113 *example after example of architectural criticism*: See Burns, "House for Josephine Baker," 54 and 55–58, where she quotes and discusses Ludwig Münz and Gustav Künstler, *Adolf Loos: Pioneer of Modern Architecture* (London: Thames and Hudson, 1966), 195; Benedetto Gravagnuolo, *Adolf Loos* (New York: Rizzoli, 1982), 191; Joseph Rykwert, *The Necessity of Artifice* (London: Academy Editions, 1982), 72; Paul Groenendijk and Piet Vollaard, *Adolf Loos House for Josephine Baker* (Rotterdam: Uitgeverij, 1985), 36; Tournikiotis, *Adolf Loos*, 95.

Page 113 *Loos's practical experience of empire*: This section is indebted to Stewart, "The Other: National Cultural Mythologies," in *Fashioning Vienna*, 42–70. On ornament and evolution, see "Ladies' fashion" (1898), in Adolf Loos, *Spoken into the Void: Collected Essays by Adolf Loos, 1897–1900*, trans. Jane O. Newman and John H. Smith, intro. Aldo Rossi (Cambridge, MA: MIT Press, 1987), 102. Loos on Red Indians and Papuans, quoted in Stewart, *Fashioning Vienna*, 42, 70, 63. On Loos's taxonomy of cultures, see Stewart, *Fashioning Vienna*, 44ff.

Page 115 *a modern "America"*: A conversation with Elana Shapira in Vienna, in 2003, reassured me that this American line of thought was worth pursuing. I am grateful to her for sharing her ideas. On Loos and America, see Stewart, *Fashioning Vienna*, 44–51.

Page 115 *The relevance to the Baker house*: See Tanzer, "Baker's Loos and Loos's Loss," 84.

Page 116 *Baker planned the interior*: On the house and family life, Colomina, *Privacy and Publicity*, 260. On Baker's civilized daily life, Baker and Bouillon, *Josephine*, 55.

Page 117 *Le Corbusier's dance sequence*: Le Corbusier's notes quoted in Petrine Archer-Shaw, *Negrophilia: Avant-garde Paris and Black Culture in the 1920s* (London: Thames and Hudson, 2000), 132. See also Blake, *Tumulte noir*, 149.

Page 117 *a Purist edge*: On Purism, Blake, *Tumulte noir*, 138. On whitewash, Le Corbusier (1925), *L'art décoratif d'aujourd'hui* (Paris: Éditions G. Grès, 1925), 188 (*The Decorative Art of Today*, trans. James Dunnett [Cambridge, MA: MIT Press, 1987]); quoted in Mark Wigley, *White Walls, Designer Dresses: The Fashioning of Modern Architecture* (Cambridge MA: MIT Press, 2001), 3. Albert Jeanneret, quoted in Blake, *Tumulte noir*, 158. Le Corbusier, *When the Cathedrals Were White: A Journey to the Country of Timid People*, trans. Francis Edwin Hyslop (New York: Reynal and Hitchcock, 1947), 164.

Page 118 *the aristocratic German aesthete*: See Laird M. Easton, *The Red Count: The Life and Times of Harry Kessler* (Berkeley: University of California Press, 2002), 212; and Kessler, *Berlin in Lights*.

Page 119 *My plot is how Solomon*: Easton, *Red Count*, 366–367.

Page 120 *the "Hot Voodoo" number*: See Patrice Petro, "The Hottentot and the Blonde Venus," in *Aftershocks of the New: Feminism and Film History* (New Brunswick, NJ: Rutgers University Press, 2002), 136–156; Sianne Ngai, "Black Venus, *Blonde Venus*," in *Bad Modernisms*, ed. Douglas Mao and Rebecca L. Walkowitz, 145–178 (Durham, NC: Duke University Press, 2006); Janet Staiger, *Perverse Spectators: The Practices of Film Reception* (New York: New York University Press, 2000), 83–86.

Page 122 *That German cow*: On "aping," see Ngai, "Black Venus, *Blonde Venus*." Baker on Dietrich, in Baker and Chase, *Josephine*, 456.

Page 122 *his sexual fascination with women of colour*: Le Corbusier, *Journey to the East* (Cambridge, MA: MIT Press, 1987), 94, 83.

Page 123 *play of light on white walls*: On sensuality and colour, Wigley, *White Walls, Designer Dresses*, 206. On the art of the peasant and annually painted houses, Le Corbusier, *Journey to the East*, 15.

Page 123 *the redevelopment of Algiers*: On Le Corbusier's plans for Algiers, see Zeynep Çelik, "Excerpts from 'Le Corbusier, Orientalism, Colonialism,'" in *Gender, Space, Architecture: An Interdisciplinary Introduction*, ed. Jane Rendell, Barbara Penner, and Iain Borden, 321–331 (London: Routledge, 2000), 326.

Page 124 *Vex not tradition*: Lyautey, quoted in Paul Rabinow, *French Modern: Norms and Forms of the Social Environment* (Cambridge, MA: MIT Press, 1989), 285; Çelik, "Le Corbusier, Orientalism, Colonialism," 322.

Page 124 *Yes, in Morocco*: Lyautey, quoted in Çelik, "Le Corbusier, Orientalism, Colonialism," 322–323.

Page 125 *In his reaction to the Casbah*: Le Corbusier, quoted in Çelik, "Le Corbusier, Orientalism, Colonialism," 324. On Algiers and its population, and for Fanon quote, see David Macey, *Frantz Fanon: A Life* (London: Granta, 2000), 471.

Page 125 *He visited the brothels*: See Çelik, "Le Corbusier, Orientalism, Colonialism," 327, and Beatriz Colomina, "Battle Lines: E.1027," in *Center 9: Regarding the Proper*, edited by Kevin Alter and Elizabeth Danze, 22–31 (Austin: University of Texas Center for American Architecture and Design, 1995).

Page 126 *Algiers drops out of sight*: Çelik, "Le Corbusier, Orientalism, Colonialism," 326, 327, 324.

Page 127 *Le Corbusier's relationship to Algiers*: Çelik, "Le Corbusier, Orientalism, Colonialism," 328.

Page 127 *the social and architectural optimism*: Le Corbusier, *When the Cathedrals Were White*, 4–6, 108, 105.

Page 127 *On Broadway*: Le Corbusier, *When the Cathedrals Were White*, 102, 157.

Page 128 *Manhattan is hot jazz*: Le Corbusier, *When the Cathedrals Were White*, 165, 158–159, 161.

Page 130 *My ears still full of hot jazz*: Le Corbusier, *When the Cathedrals Were White*, 163.

Chapter 5: Borderlines

Page 133 *Collectively styling themselves POOL*: See Susan Stanford Friedman, *Penelope's Web: Gender, Modernity, H.D.'s Fiction* (Cambridge: Cambridge University Press, 1990), 17. The rationale for the name POOL was given in their 1929 catalog of publications: "The expanding ripples from a stone dropped in a pool have become more a symbol for the growth of an idea than a simple matter of hydraulics. . ... As the stone will cause a spread of ripples to the water's edge, so ideas once started will go to their unknown boundary.... These concentric expansions are exemplified in POOL, which is the source simply—the stone—the idea."

Page 134 *"borderline" neuroses and perversion*: H.D., "Borderline," in (eds), *Close Up, 1927–1933: Cinema and Modernism*, ed. James Donald, Anne Friedberg, and Laura Marcus, 221–236 (Princeton: Princeton University Press, 1998), 221.

Page 134 *a reading of Freud's 1919 essay*: Sigmund Freud, "The 'Uncanny' (1919)," in *The Pelican Freud Library*, ed. James Strachey, vol. 14, *Art and Literature*, ed. Albert Dickson, 335–376 (Harmondsworth: Penguin, 1985), 339, 343.

Page 134 *"heimlich" is a word the meaning of which*: Freud, "Uncanny," 347, 345, 368.

Page 135 *Thinking about Angst*: Martin Heidegger, *Being and Time*, trans. John Macquarrie and Edward Robinson (Oxford: Blackwell, 1962), 233; quoted, in modified translation, in James Phillips, *Heidegger's "Volk": Between National Socialism and Poetry* (Stanford: Stanford University Press, 2005), 200.

Page 135 *drew the more radical inference*: Heidegger, *Being and Time*, 231; quoted in Phillips, *Heidegger's "Volk"*, 200.

Page 136 *We, who are homeless*: Friedrich Nietzsche, *The Gay Science*, ed. Bernard Williams (Cambridge: Cambridge University Press, 2001), 241–242. See Andrew Benjamin, *Style and Time: Essays on the Politics of Appearance* (Evanston, IL: Northwestern University Press, 2006), 120; Rodolphe Gasché, *Europe, or the Infinite Task: A Study of a Philosophical Concept* (Stanford, CA: Stanford University Press, 2009).

Page 137 *The "Negro in Film" issue*: *Close Up* 5, no. 3 (September 1929), 214; *Close Up* 5, no. 2 (August 1929), 108. Emphasis added.

Page 138 *the timbre of "negro" voices*: Alice Maurice, " 'Cinema at Its Source': Synchronizing Race and Sound in the Early Talkies," *Camera Obscura* 17, no. 1 (2002), 31–71, at 44–45. Elmer Carter, "Of Negro Motion Pictures," *Close Up* 5, no. 2 (August 1929), 119. Benchley, quoted in Maurice, "Cinema at Its Source," 32.

Page 138 *back to the uncanny*: Mladen Dolar, *A Voice and Nothing More* (Cambridge, MA: MIT Press, 2006), 7. On the "acousmatic," see Michel Chion, *Audio-Vision: Sound on Screen* (New York: Columbia University Press, 1994).

Page 139 *Two strategies for the use of black actors*: Again, see Maurice, "Cinema at Its Source."

Page 139 *It is this hyperpresence*: "Hyperpresence" is Alice Maurice's term; see Maurice, "Cinema at Its Source," 45. *Close Up* 5, no. 2 (August 1929), 90.

Page 139 *what Macpherson tried to express*: Macpherson, *Close Up* 5, no. 2 (August 1929), 85, 87–88.

Page 140 *eugenicism of the perspective*: Herring, *Close Up* 5, no. 2 (August 1929), 97, 101, 104.

Page 141 *potential authenticity of "Negro art"*: Potamkin, *Close Up* 5, no. 2 (August 1929), 109, reproduced in *Close Up 1927–1933*: Cinema and Modernism, pp. 65–73.

Page 141 *the POOL group's 1930 film*: A high-quality DVD transfer of *Borderline*, made by the British Film Institute, with a musical score by Courtney Pine, is available as part of the Criterion Collection's compilation *Paul Robeson: Portraits of the Artist* (2007). On H.D.'s abortion, see Donna Hollenberg, "Abortion, Identity Formation, and the Expatriate Woman Writer: H.D. and Kay Boyle in the Twenties," *Twentieth Century Literature* 40, no. 4 (Winter 1994), 499–517. Macpherson, *Close Up* 7, no.5, (November 1930), 381.

Page 144 *an enlightened film critic*: On Herring, Onlooker, in *To-Day's Cinema*, October 14, 1930.

Page 147 *to square the ledger*: I am grateful to James Phillips for drawing Heidegger's linking of the uncanny and conscience to my attention. Dated "1/3/31" (March 1, 1931), the "neuroses/nature" publicity handout was written for a Spanish tour of *Borderline*.

Page 147 *the pamphlet that H.D. wrote*: H.D., "Borderline," in Donald, Friedberg, and Marcus, *Close Up, 1927–1933*, 221, emphasis added.

Page 148 *the cosmic racial borderline*: Donald, Friedberg, and Marcus, *Close Up, 1927–1933*, 221.

Page 148 *critics have often lamented*: Richard Dyer, *Heavenly Bodies* (Houndmills: Macmillan, 1987), 131–132. Carby, *Race Men*, 67–68. Jean Walton, " 'Nightmare of the Uncoordinated White-Folk': Race, Psychoanalysis, and H.D.'s *Borderline*," in *The Psychoanalysis of Race*, ed. Christopher Lane, 395–416 (New York: Columbia University Press, 1998), 400–401.

Page 148 *Essie's own more light-hearted judgment*: Duberman, *Paul Robeson*, 130ff.

Page 149 *Anxiety is anxious*: Heidegger, *Being and Time*, 393. Macpherson in Cunard, *Negro*, 335–339. H.D. pamphlet in Donald, Friedberg, and Marcus, *Close Up, 1927–1933*, 221–236, at 224.

Page 150 *When is an African not an African?*: Donald, Friedberg, and Marcus, *Close Up, 1927–1933*, 111.

Page 151 *H.D.'s story*: H.D., "Two Americans," in *New Directions 51: An International Anthology of Prose and Poetry*, 58–68 (New York: New Directions, 1987)

Page 151 *Weather-worn marble*: H.D., "Two Americans," 59

Page 151 *Their faces remained faces*: H.D., "Two Americans," 58.

Page 151 *They met in a field of honour*: H.D., "Two Americans," 58.

Page 153 *The voice that spoke on everybody's wireless*: Dolar, *Voice and Nothing More*, 70. H.D., "Two Americans," 59–60.

Page 154 *modern being-in-the-world*: H.D., "Two Americans," 97–98, 101–102.

Page 154 *She said the four most likely young bucks*: H.D., "Two Americans," 64.

Page 155 *Mohammed and the mountain*: H.D., "Two Americans," 68.

Chapter 6: Down the River of Dreams

Page 157 Close Up *ceased publication*: Donald, Friedberg, and Marcus, *Close Up, 1927–1933*, 306.

Page 159 *Allégret travelled with him*: Sam Rohdie, *Promised Lands: Cinema, Geography, Modernism* (London: BFI, 2001), 220–225 (the telling phrase "cheaply bought" is his); also, Emily Apter, *Continental Drift: From National Characters to Virtual Subjects* (Chicago: Chicago University Press, 1999), 184. On Rim, see Archer-Shaw, *Negrophilia*, 103–105, 156.

Page 160 *I am proud*: *Tit-Bits*, May 27, 1933; *Daily Express*, August 4, 1933; quoted in Duberman, *Paul Robeson*, 169.

Page 161 *For the first time*: Robeson in *Observer*, Duberman, *Paul Robeson*, 179. To Davis's accusation, Robeson could only respond, "You're right." *Daily Worker*, December 27, 1935, and May 10, 1936, quoted in Gerald Hone, "Comrades and Friends: The Personal/Political World of Paul Robeson," in Jeffrey C. Stewart, ed., *Paul Robeson: Artist and Citizen* (New Brunswick, NJ: Rutgers University Press, 1998), 199–200. On *Sanders of the River* and its aftermath, Duberman, *Paul Robeson*, 178–182. *Daily Herald*, January 5, 1935, quoted in Schwarz, "Black Metropolis, White England," 184; also Stewart, *Paul Robeson*, 239.

Page 161 *Had I been born*: Stewart, *Paul Robeson*, 235; Duberman, *Paul Robeson*, 204.

Page 162 *press reviews*: Duberman, *Paul Robeson*, 636, 204.

Page 162 *the rise of the Popular Front*: Dudley Andrew and Steven Ungar, *Popular Front Aesthetics and the Poetics of Culture* (Cambridge, MA: Belknap Press of Harvard University Press, 2005).

Page 163 *its "poetic realist" style*: Ginette Vincendeau, *Pépé le Moko* (London: BFI, 1998), 62.

Page 163 *appealed to intellectuals*: Cocteau and Greene, quoted in Vincendeau, *Pépé le Moko*, 7. Italo Calvino, "A Cinema-Goer's Autobiography," in *The Road to San Giovanni* (London: Vintage, 1994), 49 (translation modified), 38 (emphasis added), 60. Beauvoir, quoted in Macey, *Frantz Fanon*, 345.

Page 165 *trajectories through different spaces*: The institutional geography of Zouzou and Baker's 1935 film *Princesse Tam Tam* are charted in Elizabeth Ezra, *The Colonial Unconscious: Race and Culture in Interwar France* (Ithaca, NY: Cornell University Press, 2000).

Page 168 *Zinga's search for home*: See Mark A. Reid, "Race, Working-Class Consciousness, and Dreaming in Africa," in Stewart, *Paul Robeson*, 165–176.

Page 169 *a space that is symbolic and political*: Vincendeau, *Pépé le Moko*, 11ff. See also Tom Conley, *Cartographic Cinema* (Minneapolis: University of Minnesota Press, 2007). On the perspective of the *dieu voyeur*, see Michel de Certeau, *The Practice of Everyday Life*, trans. Steven Rendall (Berkeley: University of California Press, 1984), 93–95. On Hannah Arendt's discussion of colonial bureaucracy and its taxonomy of race, see Kalpana Seshadri-Crooks, *Desiring Whiteness: A Lacanian Analysis of Race* (London: Routledge, 2000), 79–80. Lyautey quoted in Çelik, 'Le Corbusier, Orientalism, Colonialism," 322–323. Loti, quoted and discussed in Apter, *Continental Drift*, 136, 103, 106.

Page 172 *fantasy of spatial transparency*: On transparency and the fact of the city, see the chapter "Walking the Streets," in Certeau, *Everyday Life*.

Page 172 *shared love of Paris*: My account draws on Vincendeau's analysis in *Pépé le Moko*, 22, 51.

Page 172 *the ambivalence of his in-between status*: "In-betweeness," "mimicry," and "sly civility" are all terms deployed to understand colonial discourse in Homi Bhabha, *The Location of Culture* (London: Routledge, 1994).

Page 175 *process of transformation*: See Samuel Weber, *Return to Freud: Jacques Lacan's Dislocation of Psychoanalysis* (Cambridge: Cambridge University Press, 1991), 2–3.

Page 175 *the dream-space acts as more than just a setting*: see Richard Boothby, *Freud as Philosopher: Metapsychology after Lacan* (New York: Routledge, 2001), 114–115.

Page 175 *the analogy of a telescope*: Boothby, *Freud as Philosopher*, 114–115. Weber, *Return to Freud*, 67–68.

Page 176 *wildly indecent dance*: Colin quoted and discussed in Archer-Shaw, *Negrophilia*, 127–128.

Page 177 *the most condescending and dehumanizing*: Appel, *Jazz Modernism*, 38.

Page 177 *Sartre's account of looking*: Jean-Paul Sartre, *Being and Nothingness*, trans. Hazel Barnes (New York: Washington Square, 1993), 320ff. On Sartre and the look, see Joan Copjec, *Imagine There's No Woman: Ethics and Sublimation* (Cambridge, MA: MIT Press, 2002), 209ff.

Page 178 *the audience's familiarity with Fréhel*: See Vincendeau, *Pépé le Moko*, 24; also Vincendeau, "The *Mise-en-scene* of Suffering: French Realist Women Singers," *New Formations* 3 (Winter 1987), 107–128.

Page 178 *the eighteen-year-old Jadin*: Colette, *The Vagabond* [1910] (New York: Farrar, Strauss and Giroux, 2001), 16–17.

Page 180 *mourning a lost home*: On mourning: see Anne Anlin Cheng, *The Melancholy of Race: Psychoanalysis, Assimilation, and Hidden Grief* (New York: Oxford University Press, 2001), esp. 11–12. Freud, quoted in Robert B. Pippin, *Modernism as a Philosophical Problem*, 2nd ed. (Malden, MA: Blackwell, 1999), 150; translation modified by Pippin.

Page 181 *radical existential displacement*: See Copjec, *Imagine There's No Woman*, 97.

Page 181 *three anthropological functions for music*: Gilles Deleuze and Félix Guattari, *A Thousand Plateaus: Capitalism and Schizophrenia* (London: Athlone, 1988), 311. On "the way home," "the creation of a home," and "the home in our hearts," see also Ian Buchanan, *Deleuzism: A Metacommentary* (Durham, NC: Duke University Press, 2000).

Page 182 *glass harmonica*: Deleuze and Guattari, *Thousand Plateaus*, 323, 348.

Page 184 *complicated time*: John Rajchman, *The Deleuze Connections* (Cambridge, MA: MIT Press, 2000), 83.

Page 185 *affect proper to the natal*: Deleuze and Guattari, *Thousand Plateaus*, 332, 349–350.

Page 185 *melancholic nothingness of the modern self*: See Copjec, *Imagine There's No Woman*, 105; also Seshadri-Crooks, *Desiring Whiteness*.

Page 186 *claims of racial or ethnic identity*: "Ethnic absolutism" and "conviviality" are Paul Gilroy's terms: see Gilroy, *Postcolonial Melancholia* (New York: Columbia University Press, 2005), 98ff.

Chapter 7: Here I Stand

Page 189 *backing into politics*: Jules-Rosette, *Josephine Baker in Art and Life*, 214.

Page 189 *performed politics*: Similar approaches (sometimes leading to different conclusions) have been adopted in two path-breaking studies: Jules-Rosette's *Josephine Baker in Art and Life* and Tony Perucci, *Paul Robeson and the Cold War Performance Complex: Race, Madness, Activism* (Ann Arbor: University of Michigan Press, 2012).

Page 190 *Like every true artist*: Robeson, *Here I Stand*, 60.

Page 190 *The artist must elect*: Robeson, *Here I Stand*, 60, emphasis added. The report in the *Sunday Worker*, on November 14, introduced its own gloss: "The history of this era" becomes the "history of the capitalist era," and the latter part of the sentence reads: "despoiled of their lands, their culture destroyed, they are *in every country, save one,* denied equal protection of the law" ("Paul Robeson Speaks for His People and All Humanity," *Sunday Worker,* November 14, 1937; quoted in Carby, *Race Men,* 83.

Page 191 *Many recent scholars*: Jeffrey C. Stewart, "Paul Robeson and the Problem of Modernism," in *Rhapsodies in Black: Art of the Harlem Renaissance,* ed. Joanna Skipwith, 90–101 (London: Hayward Gallery, 1997), 99–100, and "The New Negro as Citizen," in Hutchinson, *Cambridge Companion to the Harlem Renaissance,* 21–22; Carby, *Race Men,* 83; Boyle and Bunie, *Paul Robeson,* 377–378.

Page 192 *socialist and anticolonialist ideas*: Robeson, *Here I Stand,* 40, 41. *Reynolds News* and HUAC quotes are in Goodman, *Paul Robeson,* 27, 241.

Page 192 *James lamented*: Interviewed and quoted in Boyle and Bunie, *Paul Robeson,* 299.

Page 192 *a pampered, aristocratic life*: Robeson Jr., *Artist's Journey,* 163.

Page 192 *a chance meeting in Bloomsbury*: This is the version of the anecdote published in *Black World* 20 (November 1970), quoted in Boyle and Bunie, *Paul Robeson,* 261. A later, more guarded, version records Robeson saying, "Well, maybe there is something in what you say, but you know who it is." "Yes, I know who it is, and I know it isn't you, Paul," James replies, "but nevertheless it is very funny." James, *Spheres of Existence,* 263–264.

Page 194 *stripped to the waist*: *Daily Graphic,* May 23, 1931, quoted in Duberman, *Paul Robeson,* 148. James Baldwin, "The Black Boy Looks at the White Boy," in *The Price of the Ticket: Collected Nonfiction, 1948–1985* (London: Michael Joseph, 1985), 290. On Robeson's erotic history, see Martin Duberman, "Writing Robeson," *The Nation,* December 28, 1998.

Page 194 *Essie had published her biography*: Eslanda to Van Vechten, quoted in Boyle and Bunie, *Paul Robeson,* 230; Eslanda Goode Robeson, *Paul Robeson,* 69.

Page 195 *At a press conference*: Duberman, *Paul Robeson,* 140, 160.

Page 195 *His son suggests*: Robeson Jr., *Artist's Journey,* 173.

Page 195 *sword of Damocles*: *Manchester Guardian,* December 14, 1934, quoted in Boyle and Bunie, *Paul Robeson,* 300–301.

Page 197 *well suited to play the hero*: On thymos and its associated passions, see Josef Früchtl, *The Impertinent Self: A Heroic History of Modernity* (Stanford: Stanford University Press, 2009), 156, 157; Robert Pippin, *Hollywood Westerns and American Myth* (New Haven: Yale University Press, 2010), 47–48; Philip Fisher, *The Vehement Passions* (Princeton: Princeton University Press, 2002), 228.

Page 197 *He fantasized about setting up home*: Robeson, *Here I Stand,* 40–41; Boyle and Bunie, *Paul Robeson,* 385, quoting *Daily Worker* July 24, 1938; Seton, *Paul Robeson,* 94; Robeson, *Here I Stand,* 53–54.

Page 198 *VOKS*: Ludmila Stern, *Western Intellectuals and the Soviet Union, 1920–40: From Red Square to the Left Bank* (London: Routledge, 2007); Boyle and Bunie, *Paul Robeson,* 302–303.

Page 198 *After a generous dinner*: Seton, *Paul Robeson,* 95.

Page 199 *In making that journey*: See Kate Baldwin, *Beyond the Color Line and the Iron Curtain: Reading Encounters between Black and Red, 1922–1963* (Durham, NC: Duke University Press, 2008).

Page 199 *Tractors chugged*: Seton, *Paul Robeson,* 109–110.

Page 199 *an interview during that first visit*: "'I Am at Home' Says Robeson at Reception in Soviet Union," Interview by Vern Smith, *Daily Worker,* January 15, 1935.

Page 200 *In Hegel's aesthetics*: Früchtl, *Impertinent Self*, 26, 156, 41, 36, 156. C. L. R. James, letter to Maxwell Geismar, April 11, 1961, in Ann Grimshaw, ed., *The C. L. R. James Reader* (Oxford: Blackwell, 1992), 278; discussed in David Scott, *Conscripts of Modernity: The Tragedy of Colonial Enlightenment* (Durham, NC: Duke University Press, 2004), 209–221.

Page 200 *in terms of tragedy*: Paul Robeson Jr. objected fiercely to the way that Martin Duberman's biography told his father's story as a tragedy, in which Robeson's flaw—his "uncompromising anger, a dogged refusal to bow"—unleashed the fear and hostility of forces that were out to destroy him. There is also good evidence that, as part of Robeson's hounding in the 1950s, there were systematic attempts, by mainstream African American activists as well as the United States Government, to portray him as a tragic hero. In February 1951, Robeson's erstwhile friend, the NAACP leader Walter White, published "The Strange Case of Paul Robeson" in *Ebony*, mourning the way that "this wonderfully talented man" had been "derailed" and gone "careening into the Communist camp," escaping into a "dream world" Russia, in which racism was supposed not to exist. Robeson had become a "neurotic" and "bewildered" man, wrote White, "more to be pitied than damned." In the same year, a Public Affairs Officer in the US consulate in Accra, in what was then the Gold Coast, complained to the State Department about the ease with which "the Communists" exploited "the U.S. Negro problem in general and the Robeson case in particular," and proposed "a thorough-going, sympathetic and regretful but straight talking treatment of the whole Robeson episode," "preferably by an American Negro." As if on cue, the November 1951 issue of the NAACP journal, *The Crisis*, duly carried an article, written under the pen name "Robert Allen," entitled "Paul Robeson: The Lost Shepherd," which was widely distributed throughout Africa.

Page 200 *The inspiration for using tragedy*: Scott, *Conscripts of Modernity*, 135.

Page 201 *any heroic action has two aspects*: Jean-Pierre Vernant and Pierre Vidal-Naquet, *Myth and Tragedy in Ancient Greece*, trans. Janet Lloyd (New York: Zone, 1990), 45.

Page 201 *his appearance before the House Committee on Un-American Activities*: Many commentators have noted the inherent theatricality of the HUAC hearings: the critic and playwright Eric Bentley described them as "a rite of purification that would put the fear of God (HUAC's man in heaven) in the as yet unpurified." Eric Bentley, ed., *Thirty Years of Treason: Excerpts from the Hearings before the House Committee on Un-American Activities, 1938–1968* [1971] (New York: Thunder's Mouth Press, Nation, 2002), 947. Bentley also wrote a docudrama based on the hearings the following year: *Are You Now Or Have You Ever Been?* See Duberman, *Paul Robeson*, 437–443; Robeson Jr., *Quest for Freedom*, 249, 255; Perucci, chap. 1, "Black performances and the Stagecraft of Statecraft," in *Paul Robeson and the Cold War Performance Complex*, 33–61; Goodman, *Paul Robeson*, 229–242.

Page 205 *The world had prepared no place for you*: Baldwin, 'The Black Boy," *Price of the Ticket*, 298.

Page 205 *Pauli mentioned to his father*: Robeson, Jr., *Artist's Journey*, 305–306.

Page 206 *Aristotle's account of thymotic anger*: Aristotle, *Rhetoric* 2.2, quoted in Paul Rabinow, *Marking Time: On the Anthropology of the Contemporary* (Princeton: Princeton University Press, 2008), 93.

Page 207 *That evening, Robeson fulfilled the final public engagement*: David Levering Lewis "Paul Robeson and the U.S.S.R.," in *Paul Robeson: Artist and Citizen*, ed. Jeffrey C. Stewart, (New Brunswick: Rutgers University Press, 1998), 225–226; Duberman, *Paul Robeson*, 352–353; Robeson Jr., *Quest for Freedom*, 150.

Page 207 *In his 1967 novel*: Josef Škvorecký, *The Bass Saxophone* (New York: Alfred A. Knopf, 1977), 19.

Page 208 *they struck her as "stupid"*: Doris Lessing, *Walking in the Shade, 1949–1962* (New York: Harper Perennial, 1998), 166.

Page 210 *in the grip of shame*: Fisher, *Vehement Passions*, 196–197. Robeson Jr., *Quest for Freedom*, 314, 312.

Page 210 *what makes a Tragic hero tragic*: On "being-towards-death" (*Sein-zum-Tode*), see Martin Heidegger, *Introduction to Metaphysics*, trans. by Ralph Mannheim (New Haven, CT: Yale University Press, 1959), 151; discussed in Simon Critchley, *Infinitely Demanding: Ethics of Commitment, Politics of Resistance* (London: Verso, 2007), 76–77. See also Früchtl, *Impertinent Self*, 41.

Page 211 *in a sweltering Washington, DC*: On the March on Washington, see Stephen Tuck, *We Ain't What We Ought to Be: The Black Freedom Struggle from Emancipation to Obama* (Cambridge, MA: Belknap Press of Harvard University Press, 2010), 316–320; Charles Euchner, *Nobody Turn Me Around: A People's History of the 1963 March on Washington* (Boston: Beacon Press, 2010); Jerald Podair, *Bayard Rustin: American Dreamer* (Lanham, MD: Rowman and Littlefield, 2009); Gary Younge, "Martin Luther King: The Story behind His 'I Have a Dream' Speech," *The Guardian*, August 9, 2013; Michael M. Phillips, "Civil-Rights Leader Rustin Gets His Due 50 Years Later," *Wall Street Journal*, August 26, 2013.

Page 211 *critical of Paul Robeson's claims*: Randolph quoted in Goodman, *Paul Robeson*, 145, 146.

Page 214 *fairy-tale version of her life*: Stephen Papich, *Remembering Josephine* (Indianapolis: Bobbs-Merrill, 1976), 210–213. See also Jules-Rosette, *Josephine Baker in Art and Life*, 235–237, and Matthew Pratt Guterl, *Josephine Baker and the Rainbow Tribe* (Harvard: Harvard University Press, 2014), 139–140.

Page 217 *she raised her Rainbow Tribe*: see Jules-Rosette, *Josephine Baker in Art and Life*, and Guterl, *Josephine Baker and the Rainbow Tribe*.

Page 217 *Until the March on Washington*: "Josephine Baker: A Lion Abroad, But More Like a Lamb at Home," *National Observer*, April 6, 1964, 16; John Vinocur, "Josephine Baker and Black Power," *Washington Post*, October 4, 1970; both quoted Rose, *Jazz Cleopatra*, 242–243.

Page 217 *We are dying to see the children*: Essie Robeson, quoted in Guterl, *Josephine Baker and the Rainbow Tribe*, 100.

Page 217 *acted as a political mentor*: Richard Iton, *In Search of the Black Fantastic: Politics and Popular Culture in the Post-Civil Rights Era* (New York: Oxford, 2008), 57–58.

Page 218 *tragedy provides a better paradigm*: Scott, *Conscripts of Modernity*, 2, 210.

Page 218 *There is only the fight*: Eliot, *Collected Poems*, 182.

Page 219 *the trouble with tragedy*: Critchley, *Infinitely Demanding*, 77–78.

Page 219 *Comedy of the will*: Critchley, *Infinitely Demanding*, 82.

Page 220 *how does newness enter the world?*: Rushdie, *Imaginary Homelands*, 393.

Page 220 *banished from the Soviet political lexicon*: See Robert Fine and Robin Cohen, "Four Cosmopolitan Moments," in *Conceiving Cosmopolitanism: Theory, Context and Practice*, ed. Steven Vertovec and Robin Cohen, 137–164 (Oxford: Oxford University Press, 2002), 146.

Page 220 *his choice of the nomadism*: Édouard Glissant, *Poetics of Relation*, trans. Betsy Wing (Ann Arbor, University of Michigan Press, 1997), 11–22.

Coda: Nick's Bar, New York City

Page 223 *Home is where one starts from*: Eliot, *Collected Poems*, 182.

Page 223 *massive blocks*: Jean-Paul Sartre, "New York: Colonial City," in *Modern Times: Selected Non-Fiction*, ed. Geoffrey Wall, trans. Robin Buss (London: Penguin, 2000), 3–9, 7, 9.

Page 223 *This time, listening to jazz*: Sartre, "Nick's Bar, New York City," in *We Have Only This Life to Live: The Selected Essays of Jean-Paul Sartre, 1939–1975*, ed. Ronald Aronson and Adrian van den Hoven (New York: New York Review Books, 2013), 126–128; 126, 127.

Page 223 *When Siegfried Kracauer had arrived*: Kracauer, "Why France Liked Our Films" (1942), in *Siegfried Kracauer's American Writings: Essays on Film and Popular Culture*, ed. Johannes von Moltke and Kristy Rawson (Berkeley: University of California Press, 2012), 39–40.

Page 224 *In Nick's Bar*: Sartre, "Nick's Bar," 127.

Page 224 *a controversial question*: Gendron, *Between Monmartre and the Mudd Club*: chap. 6, "Moldy Figs and Modernists," 121–142, and chap. 7, "Bebop under Fire," 143–157.

Page 224 *You have to yell*: Sartre, "Nick's Bar," 128.

Page 225 *two classic studies on cinema*: Kracauer, *From Caligari to Hitler: A Psychological History of the German Film* (Princeton, NJ: Princeton University Press, 1947); Kracauer, *Theory of Film: The Redemption of Physical Reality* (Oxford: Oxford University Press, 1960; Princeton, NJ: Princeton University Press, 1997).

Page 225 *idiosyncratic approach to historiography*: Kracauer, *History: The Last Things before the Last* (New York: Oxford University Press, 1969), 83–84.

Page 225 *provisional status*: quoted in Hansen, *Cinema and Experience*, 26.

Page 225 *anteroom thinking*: Kracauer, *History*, 191 (emphasis added), 195. Gertrud Koch makes the equation between the anteroom and the life-world in *Siegfried Kracauer: An Introduction* (Princeton, NJ: Princeton University Press, 2000), 117.

Page 226 *On a hot Harlem afternoon*: Ralph Ellison, *Invisible Man* [1952] (Harmondsworth: Penguin, 1965), 357.

Page 226 *There was jazz too*: Beauvoir, *Adieux*, 234.

Page 226 *In Old Age*: Simone de Beauvoir, *Old Age*, trans. Patrick O'Brian (London: André Deutsch; Weidenfeld and Nicolson, 1972), 380, 378, 524, 368.

Page 228 *a group of Robeson's friends*: Iton, *In Search of the Black Fantastic*, 75–80. See also the New York Times obituaries of Paul Robeson Jr. (April 27, 2014), and Phillip Hayes Dean (April 22, 2014).

{ BIBLIOGRAPHY }

Acocella, Joan, and Lynn Garafola, eds. *André Levinson on Dance: Writings from Paris in the Twenties*. Hanover, PA: Wesleyan University Press, 1991.

Alter, Kevin, and Elizabeth Danze, eds. *Center 9: Regarding the Proper*. Austin: University of Texas Center for American Architecture and Design, 1995.

Anderson, Paul Allen. *Deep River: Music and Memory in Harlem Renaissance Thought*. Durham, NC: Duke University Press, 2001.

Andrew, Dudley, and Steven Ungar. *Popular Front Aesthetics and the Poetics of Culture*. Cambridge, MA: Belknap Press of Harvard University Press, 2008.

Ankum, Katharina von, ed. *Women in the Metropolis: Gender and Modernity in Weimar Culture*. Berkeley: University of California Press, 1997.

Appel, Alfred, Jr. *Jazz Modernism: From Ellington and Armstrong to Matisse and Joyce*. New York: Alfred A. Knopf, 2002.

Apter, Emily. *Continental Drift: From National Characters to Virtual Subjects*. Chicago: Chicago University Press, 1999.

Archer-Shaw, Petrine. *Negrophilia: Avant-garde Paris and Black Culture in the 1920s*. London: Thames and Hudson, 2000.

Bacon, Mardges. *Le Corbusier in America: Travels in the Land of the Timid*. Cambridge, MA: MIT Press, 2001.

Baker, Jean-Claude, and Chris Chase. *Josephine: The Hungry Heart*. New York: Random House, 1993.

Baker, Josephine, and Jo Bouillon. *Josephine*. Translated by Mariana Fitzpatrick. New York: Harper and Row, 1977.

Baldwin, James. *The Price of the Ticket: Collected Nonfiction, 1948–1985*. London: Michael Joseph, 1985.

Baldwin, Kate. *Beyond the Color Line and the Iron Curtain: Reading Encounters between Black and Red, 1922–1963*. Durham, NC: Duke University Press, 2008.

Barkan, Elazar, and Ronald Bush, eds. *Prehistories of the Future: The Primitivist Project and the Culture of Modernism*. Stanford, CA: Stanford University Press, 1995.

Beauvoir, Simone de. *Memoirs of a Dutiful Daughter*. Translated by James Kirkup. London: André Deutsch and Weidenfeld and Nicolson, 1959.

———. *The Prime of Life*. Translated by Peter Green. London: André Deutsch and Weidenfeld and Nicolson, 1962.

———. *Old Age*. Translated by Patrick O'Brian. London: André Deutsch and Weidenfeld and Nicolson, 1972.

———. *Adieux: A Farewell to Sartre*. Translated by Patrick O'Brian. New York: Pantheon, 1984.

Bell, Clive. *Since Cézanne*. London: Chatto and Windus, 1922.

Benjamin, Andrew. *Style and Time: Essays on the Politics of Appearance*. Evanston, IL: Northwestern University Press, 2006.

Benjamin, Walter. *Selected Writings*, vol. 3, *1935–1938*, edited by Howard Eiland and Michael W. Jennings. Cambridge, MA: Belknap Press of Harvard University Press, 2002.

Bentley, Eric, ed. *Thirty Years of Treason: Excerpts from the Hearings before the House Committee on Un-American Activities, 1938–1968.* New York: Thunder's Mouth, Nation, 2002.

Bhabha, Homi. *The Location of Culture.* London: Routledge, 1994.

Blake, Jody. *Le Tumulte noir: Modernist Art and Popular Entertainment in Jazz-Age Paris, 1900–1930.* University Park: Pennsylvania State University Press, 1996.

Bogard, Travis, and Jackson R. Bryer, eds., *Selected Letters of Eugene O'Neill.* New Haven, CT: Yale University Press, 1988.

Boothby, Richard. *Freud as Philosopher: Metapsychology after Lacan.* New York: Routledge, 2001.

Bowser, Pearl, Jane Gaines and Charles Musser, eds. *Oscar Micheaux and his Circle: African-American Filmmaking and Race Cinema of the Silent Era.* Bloomington: Indiana University Press, 2001.

Boyle, Sheila Tully, and Andrew Bunie. *Paul Robeson: The Years of Promise and Achievement.* Amherst: University of Massachusetts Press, 2001.

Brooker, Peter, Andrzej Gasiorek, Deborah Longworth, and Andrew Thacker, eds. *Oxford Handbook of Modernisms.* Oxford: Oxford University Press, 2010.

Brown, Lawrence. *Spirituals: Five Negro Songs.* London: Schott, 1923.

Buchanan, Ian. *Deleuzism: A Metacommentary.* Durham, NC: Duke University Press, 2000.

Burns, Karen. "A House for Josephine Baker." In *Postcolonial Space(s)*, edited by Gülsüm Baydar Nalbantoğlu and Wong Chong Thai, 53–72. New York: Princeton Architectural Press, 1997.

Burt, Ramsay. *Alien Bodies: Representations of Modernity, "Race" and Nation in Early Modern Dance.* London: Routledge, 1998.

Calvino, Italo. *The Road to San Giovanni.* London: Vintage, 1994.

Carby, Hazel V. *Race Men.* Cambridge, MA: Harvard University Press, 1998.

Çelik, Zeynep. "Excerpts from 'Le Corbusier, Orientalism, Colonialism.'" In *Gender, Space, Architecture: An Interdisciplinary Introduction*, edited by Jane Rendell, Barbara Penner, and Iain Borden, 321–331. London: Routledge, 2000.

Certeau, Michel de. *The Practice of Everyday Life.* Translated by Steven Rendall. Berkeley: University of California Press, 1984.

Charney, Leo, and Vanessa Schwartz, eds. *Cinema and the Invention of Modern Life.* Berkeley: University of California Press, 1995.

Cheng, Anne Anlin. *The Melancholy of Race: Psychoanalysis, Assimilation, and Hidden Grief.* New York: Oxford University Press, 2001.

———. *Second Skin: Josephine Baker and the Modern Surface.* New York: Oxford University Press, 2011.

Chinitz, David. *T. S. Eliot and the Cultural Divide.* Chicago: University of Chicago Press, 2003.

Chion, Maurice. *Audio-Vision: Sound on Screen.* New York: Columbia University Press, 1994.

Clifford, James. *The Predicament of Culture: Twentieth-Century Ethnography, Literature, and Art.* Cambridge, MA: Harvard University Press, 1988.

———. "Negrophilia." In, *A New History of French Literature*, edited by Denis Hollier, 901–908. Cambridge, MA: Harvard University Press, 1994.

Colette. *The Vagabond* [1910]. New York: Farrar, Strauss and Giroux, 2001.

Colomina, Beatriz. *Privacy and Publicity: Modern Architecture as Mass Media*. Cambridge, MA: MIT Press, 1994.

———. "Battle Lines: E.1027." In *Center 9: Regarding the Proper*, edited by Kevin Alter and Elizabeth Danze, 22–31. Austin: University of Texas Center for American Architecture and Design, 1995.

Conley, Tom. *Cartographic Cinema*. Minneapolis: University of Minnesota Press, 2007.

Cooke, Mervyn, and David Horn, eds. *The Cambridge Companion to Jazz*. Cambridge: Cambridge University Press, 2003.

Copjec, Joan. *Imagine There's No Woman: Ethics and Sublimation*. Cambridge, MA: MIT Press, 2002.

Corbould, Clare. *Becoming African Americans: Public Life in Harlem, 1919–1939*. Cambridge, MA: Harvard University Press, 2009.

Cournos, John. *Babel*. London: Heinemann, 1923.

Cripps, Thomas R. *Slow Fade to Black: The Negro in American Film, 1900–1942*. Oxford: Oxford University Press, 1993.

Critchley, Simon. *Infinitely Demanding: Ethics of Commitment, Politics of Resistance*. London: Verso, 2007.

Cunard, Nancy, ed. *Negro: Anthology Made by Nancy Cunard, 1931–1933*. London: Nancy Cunard at Wishart, 1934.

Dalton, Karen C. C., and Henry Louis Gates Jr. "Josephine Baker and Paul Colin: African American Dance Seen through Parisian eyes." *Critical Inquiry* 24, no. 4, (Summer 1998), 903–934.

Danius, Sarah. *The Senses of Modernism: Technology, Perception and Aesthetics*. Ithaca, NY: Cornell University Press, 2002.

Deleuze, Gilles, and Félix Guattari. *A Thousand Plateaus: Capitalism and Schizophrenia*. London: Athlone, 1988.

Delson, Susan. *Dudley Murphy: Hollywood Wild Card*. Minneapolis: University of Minnesota Press, 2006.

Dinerstein, Joel. *Swinging the Machine: Modernity, Technology, and African American Culture between the World Wars*. Amherst: University of Massachusetts Press, 2003.

Dolar, Mladen. *A Voice and Nothing More*. Cambridge, MA: MIT Press, 2006.

Donald, James, Anne Friedberg, and Laura Marcus, eds. *Close Up, 1927–1933: Cinema and Modernism*. Princeton, NJ: Princeton University Press, 1998.

Douglas, Ann. *Terrible Honesty: Mongrel Manhattan in the 1920s*. London: Picador, 1996.

Duberman, Martin. *Paul Robeson: A Biography*. New York: New Press, 1995.

———. "Writing Robeson." *The Nation*, December 28, 1998.

Du Bois, W. E. B. *The Souls of Black Folk* [1903]. Edited by Brent Hayes Edwards. Oxford: Oxford University Press, 2007.

Dyer, Richard. *Heavenly Bodies: Film Stars and Society*. Houndmills: Macmillan, 1987.

Easton, Laird M. *The Red Count: The Life and Times of Harry Kessler*. Berkeley: University of California Press, 2002.

Edwards, Brent Hayes. *The Practice of Diaspora: Literature, Translation, and the Rise of Black Internationalism*. Cambridge, MA: Harvard University Press, 2003.

Ehrenburg, Ilya. *The Life of the Automobile* [1929]. Translated by Joachim Neugroschel. New York: Urizen, 1976.

el-Dahdah, Farès. "The Josephine Baker House: For Loos's Pleasure." *Assemblage* 26 (1995), 72–87.

Eliot, T. S. *Collected Poems, 1909–1962*. London: Faber and Faber, 1963.

———. *The Letters of T. S. Eliot*. Edited by Valerie Eliot. Vol. 1, *1898–1922*. London: Faber and Faber, 1988.

Ellison, Ralph. *Invisible Man* [1952]. Harmondsworth: Penguin, 1965.

Euchner, Charles. *Nobody Turn Me Around: A People's History of the 1963 March on Washington*. Boston: Beacon, 2010.

Ezra, Elizabeth. *The Colonial Unconscious: Race and Culture in Interwar France*. Ithaca, NY: Cornell University Press, 2000.

Fine, Robert, and Robin Cohen. "Four Cosmopolitan Moments." In *Conceiving Cosmopolitanism: Theory, Context, and Practice*, edited by Steven Vertovec and Robin Cohen, 137–164. Oxford: Oxford University Press, 2002.

Fisher, Philip. *The Vehement Passions*. Princeton, NJ: Princeton University Press, 2002.

Fitzgerald, F. Scott. *My Lost City: Personal Essays, 1920–1940*. Cambridge: Cambridge University Press, 2005.

Flanner, Janet. *Paris Was Yesterday*. New York: Viking, 1972.

Freeman, Judi. "Bridging Purism and Surrealism: The Origins and Production of Fernand Léger's *Ballet Mécanique*." In *Dada and Surrealist Film*, edited by Rudolf E. Kuenzli, 28–45. New York: Willis Locker and Owens, 1987.

Freud, Sigmund. "The 'Uncanny' (1919)." In *The Pelican Freud Library*. Edited by James Strachey. Vol. 14, *Art and Literature*, edited by Albert Dickson, 335–376. Harmondsworth: Penguin, 1985.

Friedman, Susan Stanford. *Penelope's Web: Gender, Modernity, H.D.'s Fiction*. Cambridge: Cambridge University Press, 1990.

Frisby, David, and Mike Featherstone, eds. *Simmel on Culture*. London: Sage, 1988.

Früchtl, Josef. *The Impertinent Self: A Heroic History of Modernity*. Stanford, CA: Stanford University Press, 2009.

Gabbard, Krin. *Jammin' at the Margins: Jazz and the American Cinema*. Chicago: University of Chicago Press, 1996.

Gaines, Jane M. *Fire and Desire: Mixed-Race Movies in the Silent Era*. Chicago: University of Chicago Press, 2001.

Gasché, Rodolphe. *Europe, or the Infinite Task: A Study of a Philosophical Concept*. Stanford, CA: Stanford University Press, 2009.

Gendron, Bernard. *Between Montmartre and the Mudd Club: Popular Music and the Avant-Garde*. Chicago: University of Chicago Press, 2002.

Gerstel, Alice. "Jazz Band." In *The Weimar Republic Sourcebook*, edited by Anton Kaes, Martin Jay, and Edward Dimendberg, 554–555. Berkeley: University of California Press, 1994.

Gilroy, Paul. *The Black Atlantic: Modernity and Double Consciousness*. Cambridge, MA: Harvard University Press, 1993.

———. *Postcolonial Melancholia*. New York: Columbia University Press, 2005.

Glissant, Édouard. *Poetics of Relation*. Translated by Betsy Wing. Ann Arbor: University of Michigan Press, 1997.

Goddard, Chris. *Jazz Away from Home*. London: Paddington, 1979.

Goodman, Jordan. *Paul Robeson: A Watched Man*. London: Verso, 2013.

Grimshaw, Ann, ed. *The C. L. R. James Reader*. Oxford: Blackwell, 1992.

Guterl, Matthew Pratt. *Josephine Baker and the Rainbow Tribe*. Cambridge, MA: Harvard University Press, 2014.

H.D. [Hilda Doolittle]. "Two Americans." In *New Directions 51: An International Anthology of Prose and Poetry*, 58–68. New York: New Directions, 1987.

Hammond, Bryan, and Patrick O'Connor. *Josephine Baker*. London: Jonathan Cape, 1988.

Haney, Lynn. *Naked at the Feast: A Biography of Josephine Baker*. New York: Dodd, Mead, 1981.

Hansen, Miriam Bratu. *Cinema and Experience: Siegfried Kracauer, Walter Benjamin, and Theodor W. Adorno*. Berkeley: University of California Press, 2012.

———. "Fallen Women, Rising Stars, New Horizons: Shanghai Silent Film as Vernacular Modernism." *Film Quarterly* 54, no. 1 (Autumn 2000), 10–22.

Harris, Leonard, ed. *The Philosophy of Alain Locke: Harlem Renaissance and Beyond*. Philadelphia, PA: Temple University Press, 1989.

Harris, Leonard, and Charles Molesworth. *Alain L. Locke: The Biography of a Philosopher*. Chicago: University of Chicago Press, 2008.

Heidegger, Martin. *Being and Time*. Translated by John Macquarrie and Edward Robinson. Oxford: Blackwell, 1962.

———. *An Introduction to Metaphysics*. Translated by Ralph Mannheim. New Haven, CT: Yale University Press, 1959.

———. "The Age of the World Picture" (1938). In *The Heidegger Reader*, edited by Günter Figal, translated by Jerome Veith, 207–223. Bloomington: Indiana University Press, 2009.

Helm, MacKinley. *Angel Mo' and Her Son, Roland Hayes*. Boston: Little, Brown, 1942.

Hobsbawm, Eric. "Jazz Comes to Europe." In *Uncommon People: Resistance, Rebellion and Jazz*. London: Abacus, 1999.

Hollenberg, Donna. "Abortion, Identity Formation, and the Expatriate Woman Writer: H.D. and Kay Boyle in the Twenties." *Twentieth Century Literature* 40, no. 4 (Winter 1994), 499–517.

Hollier, Denis, ed. *A New History of French Literature*. Cambridge, MA: Harvard University Press, 1994.

Horak, Jan-Christopher, ed. *Lovers of Cinema: The First American Film Avant-Garde, 1919–1945*. Madison: University of Wisconsin Press, 1995.

Horak, Roman. "Josepine Baker in Wien—oder doch nicht? Über die Wirksamkeit des 'zeitlos Popularen.'" In *Metropole Wien: Texturen der Moderne*, edited by Roman Horak, Wolfgangf Maderthaner, Siegfried Mattl, Gerhard Meissel, Lutz Musner, and Alfred Pfoser, vol. 1: 169–213. Vienna: WUV-Universitätsverlag, 2000.

Horn, David. "The Identity of Jazz." In *The Cambridge Companion to Jazz*, edited by Mervyn Cooke and David Horn, 9–32. Cambridge: Cambridge University Press, 2002.

Hughes, Langston. *The Big Sea: An Autobiography*. New York: Alfred A. Knopf, 1940.

Hutchinson, George. *The Harlem Renaissance in Black and White*. Cambridge, MA: Belknap Press of Harvard University Press, 1995.

———, ed. *The Cambridge Companion to the Harlem Renaissance*. Cambridge: Cambridge University Press, 2007.

Iton, Richard. *In Search of the Black Fantastic: Politics and Popular Culture in the Post-Civil Rights Era*. New York: Oxford University Press, 2008.

James, C. L. R. *Spheres of Experience: Selected Writings*. London: Allison and Busby, 1980.

Jelavich, Peter. *Berlin Cabaret*. Cambridge, MA: Harvard University Press, 1996.

Johnson, James Weldon, J. Rosamond Johnson, and Lawrence Brown, eds. *The Book of American Negro Spirituals*. London: Chapman and Hill, 1926.

Jones, Carole Seymour. *A Dangerous Liaison: Simone de Beauvoir and Jean-Paul Sartre*. London: Century, 2008.

Jules-Rosette, Bennetta. *Josephine Baker in Art and Life: The Icon and the Image*. Urbana: University of Illinois Press, 2007.

Kaes, Anton, Martin Jay, and Edward Dimendberg, eds. *The Weimar Republic Sourcebook*. Berkeley: University of California Press, 1994.

Kahn, Joel. *Culture, Multiculture, Postculture*. London: Sage, 1995.

Kempton, Arthur. *Boogaloo: The Quintessence of American Popular Music*. Ann Arbor: University of Michigan Press, 2005.

Kessler, Harry. *Berlin in Lights: The Diaries of Count Harry Kessler*. New York: Grove, 2000.

Koch, Gertrud. *Siegfried Kracauer: An Introduction*. Princeton, NJ: Princeton University Press, 2000.

Kracauer, Siegfried. *From Caligari to Hitler: A Psychological History of the German Film*. Princeton, NJ: Princeton University Press, 1947.

———. *Theory of Film: The Redemption of Physical Reality*. Oxford: Oxford University Press, 1960; Princeton, NJ: Princeton University Press, 1997.

———. *History: The Last Things before the Last*. New York: Oxford University Press, 1969.

———. *The Mass Ornament: Weimar Essays*. Edited and translated by Thomas Y. Levin. Cambridge, MA: Harvard University Press, 1995.

———. *The Salaried Masses*. Translated by Quintin Hoare, introduction by Inka Mülder-Bach. London: Verso, 1998.

———. *Siegfried Kracauer's American Writings: Essays on Film and Popular Culture*. Edited by Johannes von Moltke and Kristy Rawson. Berkeley: University of California Press, 2012.

Kuenzli, Rudolf E., ed. *Dada and Surrealist Film*. New York: Willis Locker and Owens, 1987.

Lane, Christopher, ed. *The Psychoanalysis of Race*. New York: Columbia University Press, 1998.

Lane, Jeremy F. "*Rythme de Travail, Rythme de Jazz*: Jazz, Primitivism, and *Machinisme* in Inter-War France." *Atlantic Studies* 4, no. 1 (April 2007), 103–116.

Lant, Antonia, ed. *The Red Velvet Seat*. London: Verso, 2006.

Lawder, Standish D. *The Cubist Cinema*. New York: New York University Press, 1975.

Le Corbusier [Charles-Édouard Jeanneret]. *L'art décoratif d'aujourd'hui*. Paris: Éditions G. Grès, 1925. Translated by James Dunnett as *The Decorative Art of Today*. Cambridge, MA: MIT Press, 1987.

———. *Journey to the East*. Cambridge, MA: MIT Press, 1987.

———. *Precisions*. Translated by Edith Schreiber Aujame. Cambridge, MA: MIT Press, 1991.

———. *When the Cathedrals Were White: A Journey to the Country of Timid People*. Translated by Francis Edwin Hyslop. New York: Reynal and Hitchcock, 1947.

Léger, Fernand. *Functions of Painting*. Translated by Alexandra Anderson. New York: Viking, 1973.

Leiris, Michel. *L'Afrique fantôme*. Paris: Gallimard, 1981.

———. *Manhood: A Journey from Childhood into the Fierce Order of Virility* [1939]. Translated by Richard Howard. San Francisco: North Point, 1985.

———. *Brisées: Broken Branches*. Translated by Lydia Davis. San Francisco: North Point, 1989.

Lemke, Sieglinde. *Primitivist Modernism: Black Culture and the Origins of Transatlantic Modernism*. Oxford: Oxford University Press, 1998.

Lessing, Doris. *Walking in the Shade, 1949–1962*. New York: Harper Perennial, 1998.

Lewis, David Levering. "Paul Robeson and the U.S.S.R." In *Paul Robeson: Artist and Citizen*, edited by Jeffrey C. Stewart, 217–233. New Brunswick, NJ: Rutgers University Press, 1998.

Locke, Alain, ed. *The New Negro*. New York: Albert and Charles Boni, 1925.

Loos, Adolf. *Spoken into the Void: Collected Essays by Adolf Loos, 1897–1900*. Translated by Jane O. Newman and John H. Smith, introduction by Aldo Rossi. Cambridge, MA: MIT Press, 1987.

Macey, David. *Frantz Fanon: A Life*. London: Granta, 2000.

Magee, Jeffrey. *The Uncrowned King of Swing: Fletcher Henderson and Big Band Jazz*. Oxford and New York: Oxford University Press, 2005.

Manganaro, Marc. *Culture, 1922: The Emergence of a Concept*. Princeton, NJ: Princeton University Press, 2002.

Mao, Douglas, and Rebecca L. Walkowitz, eds. *Bad Modernisms*. Durham, NC: Duke University Press, 2006.

Marable, Manning. *W. E. B. Du Bois: Black Radical Democrat*. Boston: Twayne, 1986.

Massumi, Brian. *Parables for the Virtual: Movement, Affect, Sensation*. Durham, NC: Duke University Press, 2002.

Maurice, Alice. "'Cinema at Its Source': Synchronizing Race and Sound in the Early Talkies." *Camera Obscura* 17, no. 1 (2002), 31–71.

Moritz, William. "Americans in Paris: Man Ray and Dudley Murphy." In *Lovers of Cinema: The First American Film Avant-Garde, 1919–1945*, edited by Jan-Christopher Horak, 118–136. Madison: University of Wisconsin Press, 1995.

Murphet, Julian. *Multimedia Modernism: Literature and the Anglo-American Avant-Garde*. Cambridge: Cambridge University Press, 2009.

Musil, Robert. *The Man without Qualities*. Translated by Sophie Wilkins. New York: Alfred A. Knopf, 1995.

Musser, Charles. "To Redream the Dreams of White Playwrights: Reappropriation and Resistance in Oscar Micheaux's *Body and Soul*." In *Oscar Micheaux and his Circle: African-American Filmmaking and Race Cinema of the Silent Era*, edited by Pearl Bowser, Jane Gaines, and Charles Musser, 97–131. Bloomington: Indiana University Press, 2001.

Nalbantoğlu, Gülsüm Baydar, and Wong Chong Thai, eds. *Postcolonial Space(s)*. New York: Princeton Architectural Press, 1997.

Nava, Mica, and Alan O'Shea, eds. *Modern Times: Reflections on a Century of English Modernity*. London: Routledge, 1996.

Nenno, Nancy. "Femininity, the Primitive, and Modern Urban Space: Josephine Baker in Berlin." In *Women in the Metropolis: Gender and Modernity in Weimar Culture*, edited by Katharina von Ankum, 145–161. Berkeley: University of California Press, 1997.

Nettlebeck, Colin. *Dancing with de Beauvoir: Jazz and the French*. Melbourne: Melbourne University Press, 2004.

Ngai, Sianne. "Black Venus, *Blonde Venus*." In *Bad Modernisms*, edited by Douglas Mao and Rebecca L. Walkowitz, 145–178. Durham, NC: Duke University Press, 2006.

Nietzsche, Friedrich. *The Gay Science*. Edited by Bernard Williams. Cambridge: Cambridge University Press, 2001.

North, Michael. *The Dialect of Modernism: Race, Language, and Twentieth-Century Literature*. New York: Oxford University Press, 1994.

———, ed. *The Waste Land: Authoritative Text, Contexts, Criticism*. London: W. W. Norton, 2001.

Ogren, Kathy J. *The Jazz Revolution: Twenties America and the Meaning of Jazz*. New York: Oxford University Press, 1989.

Papich, Stephen. *Remembering Josephine*. Indianapolis: Bobbs-Merrill, 1976.

Parekh, Bhikhu, ed. *Colour, Culture and Consciousness: Immigrant Intellectuals in Britain*. London: George Allen and Unwin, 1974.

Patey, Douglas Lane. *The Life of Evelyn Waugh: A Critical Biography*. Oxford: Blackwell, 2001.

Perucci, Tony. *Paul Robeson and the Cold War Performance Complex: Race, Madness, Activism*. Ann Arbor: University of Michigan Press, 2012.

Peters, Margot. *Mrs. Pat: A Biography of Mrs Patrick Campbell*. London: Bodley Head, 1984.

Petro, Patrice. *Aftershocks of the New: Feminism and Film History*. New Brunswick, NJ: Rutgers University Press, 2002.

Phillips, James. *Heidegger's "Volk": Between National Socialism and Poetry*. Stanford, CA: Stanford University Press, 2005.

Pippin, Robert B. *Modernism as a Philosophical Problem*. 2nd ed. Malden, MA: Blackwell, 1999.

———. *Hollywood Westerns and American Myth*. New Haven, CT: Yale University Press, 2010.

Podair, Jerald. *Bayard Rustin: American Dreamer*. Lanham, MD: Rowman and Littlefield, 2009.

Proust, Marcel. *Remembrance of Things Past*, vol. 2. Translated by C. K. Scott Moncrieff and Terence Kilmartin. London: Chatto and Windus, 1968.

Rabinow, Paul. *French Modern: Norms and Forms of the Social Environment*. Cambridge, MA: MIT Press, 1989.

———. *Marking Time: On the Anthropology of the Contemporary*. Princeton, NJ: Princeton University Press, 2008.

Rainey, Lawrence. *Revisiting "The Waste Land."* New Haven, CT: Yale University Press, 2007.

Rajchman, John. *The Deleuze Connections*. Cambridge, MA: MIT Press, 2000.

Rampersad, Arnold. *The Art and Imagination of W. E. B. Du Bois*. Cambridge, MA: Harvard University Press, 1976.

Ransby, Barbara. *Eslanda: The Large and Unconventional Life of Mrs. Paul Robeson*. New Haven, CT: Yale University Press, 2013.

Rée, Jonathan. *I See a Voice: A Philosophical History of Language, Deafness and the Senses*. London: HarperCollins, 1999.

Rendell, Jane, Barbara Penner, and Iain Borden, eds. *Gender, Space, Architecture: An Interdisciplinary Introduction*. London: Routledge, 2000.

Robeson, Eslanda Goode. *Paul Robeson: Negro*. London: Victor Gollancz, 1930.

Robeson, Paul. *Here I Stand*. London: Dennis Dobson, 1958.

Robeson, Paul, Jr. *The Undiscovered Paul Robeson: An Artist's Journey, 1898–1939*. New York: Wiley, 2001.

———. *The Undiscovered Paul Robeson: Quest for Freedom, 1939–1976*. New York: Wiley, 2010.

Rodowick, D. N. *Reading the Figural, or, Philosophy after the New Media*. Durham, NC: Duke University Press, 2001.

Rogin, Michael. *Blackface, White Noise: Jewish Immigrants in the Hollywood Melting Pot*. Berkeley: University of California Press, 1996.

Rohdie, Sam. *Promised Lands: Cinema, Geography, Modernism*. London: BFI, 2001.

Rose, Phyllis. *Jazz Cleopatra: Josephine Baker in Her Time*. New York: Vintage, 1989.

Rubin, William, ed., *"Primitivism" in 20th Century Art: Affinity of the Tribal and the Modern*, vol. 1. New York: Museum of Modern Art, 1984.

Rushdie, Salman. *Imaginary Homelands: Essays and Criticism, 1981–1991*. London: Granta, 1992.

Sartre, Jean-Paul. *Being and Nothingness*. Translated by Hazel Barnes. New York: Washington Square, 1993.

———. *Nausea*. Translated by Lloyd Alexander, introduction by Richard Howard. New York: New Directions, 2007.

———. "New York: Colonial City." In *Modern Times: Selected Non-Fiction*. Edited by Geoffrey Wall, translated by Robin Buss. London: Penguin, 2000.

———. *We Have Only This Life to Live: The Selected Essays of Jean-Paul Sartre, 1939–1975*. Edited by Ronald Aronson and Adrian van den Hoven. New York: New York Review Books, 2013.

Savran, David. *Highbrow/Lowdown: Theater, Jazz, and the Making of the New Middle Class*. Ann Arbor: University of Michigan Press, 2009.

Saxena, Jennie, Ken Weissman, and James Cozart. "Preserving African-American Cinema: The Case of *Emperor Jones* (1933)." *The Moving Image* 3, no. 1 (2003), 42–58.

Schwarz, Bill. "Black Metropolis, White England." In *Modern Times: Reflections on a Century of English Modernity*, edited by Mica Nava and Alan O'Shea, 176–207. London: Routledge, 1996.

Scott, David. *Conscripts of Modernity: The Tragedy of Colonial Enlightenment*. Durham, NC: Duke University Press, 2004.

Seshadri-Crooks, Kalpana. *Desiring Whiteness: A Lacanian Analysis of Race*. London: Routledge, 2000.

Seton, Marie. *Paul Robeson*. London: Dennis Dobson, 1958.

Shack, William A. *Harlem in Montmartre: A Paris Jazz Story between the Great Wars*. Berkeley: University of California Press, 2001.

Sheaffer, Louis. *O'Neill: Son and Artist*. London: Paul Elek, 1974.

Shelton, Marie-Denise. "Primitive Self: Colonial Impulses in Michel Leiris's *L'Afrique fantôme*." In *Prehistories of the Future: The Primitivist Project and the Culture of Modernism*, edited by Elazar Barkan and Ronald Bush, 326–338. Stanford, CA: Stanford University Press, 1995.

Simmel, Georg. "The Metropolis and Mental Life" [1903]. In *Simmel on Culture*, edited by David Frisby and Mike Featherstone, 174–186. London: Sage, 1997.

Skipwith, Joanna, ed. *Rhapsodies in Black: Art of the Harlem Renaissance*. London: Hayward Gallery, 1997.

Škvorecký, Josef. *The Bass Saxophone*. New York: Alfred A. Knopf, 1977.

Sollors, Werner. *Ethnic Modernism*. Cambridge, MA: Harvard University Press, 2008.

Sparshott, Francis. *A Measured Pace: Towards a Philosophical Understanding of the Arts of Dance*. Toronto: University of Toronto Press, 1995.

Staiger, Janet *Perverse Spectators: The Practices of Film Reception*. New York: New York University Press, 2000.

Steen, Shannon. "Melancholy Bodies: Racial Subjectivity and Whiteness in O'Neill's *The Emperor Jones*." *Theatre Journal* 52, no. 3 (2000), 339–359.

Stein, Gertrude. *Useful Knowledge*. London: John Lane, Bodley Head, 1928.

———. *The Autobiography of Alice B. Toklas*. New York: Harcourt, Brace, 1933.

Stern, Ludmila. *Western Intellectuals and the Soviet Union, 1920–40: From Red Square to the Left Bank*. London: Routledge, 2007.

Stewart, Janet. *Fashioning Vienna: Adolf Loos's Cultural Criticism*. London: Routledge, 2000.

Stewart, Jeffrey C., ed. *The Critical Temper of Alain Locke*. New York: Garland, 1983.

——, ed. *Paul Robeson: Artist and Citizen*. New Brunswick, NJ: Rutgers University Press, 1998.

Tanzer, Kim. "Baker's Loos and Loos's Loss: Architecting the Body." In *Center 9: Regarding the Proper*, edited by Kevin Alter and Elizabeth Danze, 76–89. Austin: University of Texas Center for American Architecture and Design, 1995.

Thompson, Emily. *The Soundscape of Modernity: Architectural Acoustics and the Culture of Listening in America, 1900–1933*. Cambridge, MA: MIT Press, 2004.

Tournikiotis, Panayotis. *Adolf Loos*. New York: Princeton Architectural Press, 1994.

Trotter, David. *Cinema and Modernism*. Oxford: Blackwell, 2007.

Tuck, Stephen. *We Ain't What We Ought to Be: The Black Freedom Struggle from Emancipation to Obama*. Cambridge, MA: Belknap Press of Harvard University Press, 2010.

Turvey, Malcolm. "The Avant-Garde and the 'New Spirit': The Case of *Ballet mécanique*." *October* 102 (2002), 35–58.

Van Vechten, Carl. *"Keep A-Inchin' Along": Selected Writings of Carl van Vechten about Black Art and Letters*. Edited by Bruce Kellner. Westport, CT: Greenwood, 1979.

Vattimo, Gianni. *The Transparent Society*. Cambridge: Polity, 1992.

Vernant, Jean-Pierre, and Pierre Vidal-Naquet. *Myth and Tragedy in Ancient Greece*. Translated by Janet Lloyd. New York: Zone, 1990.

Vernon, Doremy. *Tiller's Girls*. London: Robson, 1988.

Vertovec, Steven, and Robin Cohen, eds. *Conceiving Cosmopolitanism: Theory, Context, and Practice*. Oxford: Oxford University Press, 2003.

Vincendeau, Ginette. "The *Mise-en-scene* of Suffering: French Realist Women Singers." *New Formations* 3 (Winter 1987), 107–128.

——. *Pépé le Moko*. London: BFI, 1998.

Vogel, Shane. *The Scene of Harlem Cabaret: Race, Sexuality, Performance*. Chicago: University of Chicago Press, 2009.

Walton, Jean. "'Nightmare of the Uncoordinated White-Folk': Race, Psychoanalysis, and H.D.'s *Borderline*." In *The Psychoanalysis of Race*, edited by Christopher Lane, 395–416. New York: Columbia University Press, 1998.

Waugh, Evelyn. *Decline and Fall: An Illustrated Novelette* [1927]. Boston: Little, Brown, 1956.

——. *The Diaries of Evelyn Waugh* [1976]. Edited by Michael Davie. London: Phoenix, 1995.

Weber, Samuel. *Return to Freud: Jacques Lacan's Dislocation of Psychoanalysis*. Cambridge: Cambridge University Press, 1991.

White, Hayden. *Metahistory: The Historical Imagination in Nineteenth-Century Europe*. Baltimore, ND: Johns Hopkins University Press, 1973.

Wigley, Mark. *White Walls, Designer Dresses: The Fashioning of Modern Architecture*. Cambridge, MA: MIT Press, 2001.

Williams, Linda. *Playing the Race Card: Melodramas of Black and White from Uncle Tom to O. J. Simpson*. Princeton, NJ: Princeton University Press, 2002.

Wood, Ean. *The Josephine Baker Story*. London: Sanctuary, 2000.

{ INDEX }